Hello Charlie

Hello

LETTERS FROM

Charlie

A SERIAL KILLER

Charlie Hess
and Davin Seay

ATRIA BOOKS

NEW YORK   LONDON   TORONTO   SYDNEY

ATRIA BOOKS

A Division of Simon & Schuster
1230 Avenue of the Americas
New York, NY 10020

First Atria Books hardcover edition February 2008

ATRIA BOOKS is a trademark of Simon & Schuster, Inc.

For information about special discounts for bulk purchases,
please contact Simon & Schuster Special Sales at 1-800-456-6798
or business@simonandschuster.com.

Designed by Paul Dippolito

Manufactured in the United States of America

1   3   5   7   9   10   8   6   4   2

Library of Congress Cataloging-in-Publication Data
Hess, Charlie.
Hello Charlie : letters from a serial killer / Charlie Hess and
Davin Seay.—1st Atria Books hardcover ed.
p.   cm.
Includes index.
1. Hess, Charlie. 2. Police—United States—Biography. 3. United
States. Federal Bureau of Investigation—Biography. 4. Browne,
Robert Charles, 1952–   5. Serial murderers—United States—
Biography. 6. Murderers—United States. 8. Murder—United States.
I. Seay, Davin. II. Title.
HV7911.H44A3 2008
364.152'3092—dc22
[B]   2007034143

ISBN-13: 978-1-4165-4485-2
ISBN-10:   1-4165-4485-2

In Loving Memory

Of Josephine "Jo" Hess

Beloved Wife

Closest Companion

Best Friend

Trusted Adviser

And Constant Compannion

September 16, 1934 – October 25, 2007

This book is dedicated to my dad and mom, Charles and Beatrice Hess, who are the most honest and industrious people I have ever known. Also to my daughter Candy, who has the heart of a lion and would have been a great investigator or agent. Further, to my daughter Chris, who does not care for the work I do or the people I associate with but loves me just the same. And for Steve Vought.

To my dearest wife, Jo, who supported me in every way, even when I was wrong (which was not rare), and lived with me several years on an island, twenty miles from the nearest human being.

And, most important, to the friends and families of all of Robert Browne's victims.

—Charlie Hess

CONTENTS

Author's Note — ix

PART ONE

1 Black Forest — 3
2 Dead Man's Shoes — 17
3 The Culvert — 33
4 One Too Many — 43
5 Coffee and Cigarettes — 59

PART TWO

6 The Lie Detector — 75
7 The Traces — 87
8 The Intruder Theory — 97
9 The Apple Dumpling Gang — 111

PART THREE

10 "He Did It" — 123
11 Miank — 135
12 "Call Me When You Pull the Switch" — 147
13 Closure — 161

CONTENTS

PART FOUR

14 86504   *171*

15 "What's Important to You Isn't Important to Me"   *183*

16 The White Grand Am   *193*

17 Derkesthai   *201*

PART FIVE

18 Flatonia   *215*

19 The Trip   *225*

20 "I Don't Do Names"   *235*

21 Rocio   *245*

PART SIX

22 Snakes and Snails   *257*

23 Sugar Land   *267*

24 The Cowboy Lady   *277*

25 The Plea   *287*

26 The Way He Done Her   *295*

Epilogue   *303*

Acknowledgments   *307*

Index   *309*

AUTHOR'S NOTE

Cops don't like to talk about themselves.

I wouldn't call it a code of professional conduct, or an unwritten rule, or anything like that. It's just a habit we get into, a way of acknowledging that the work that each of us does is part of a greater effort. We're part of a team, and being a member in good standing means you don't take credit for doing the whole job.

I thought about that when I was first approached to write this book. After a lifetime in law enforcement, I'd learned the value of humility. There was no way I could have cracked the case of Robert Charles Browne by myself, and to say that I could have would have done a serious disservice to my colleagues. The last thing I wanted to do was to shine a spotlight on myself, to call myself a hero.

Don't get me wrong. I believe that I was the right person in the right place at the right time. But that's all because of the opportunities I've been afforded over the course of my career, the chance I've been given to develop my skills and hone my craft. I just got lucky. It comes with the territory. That's something every cop knows, and it's what keeps us humble.

There was something else that made me uncomfortable when I thought about writing this book. I wanted to make sure this wasn't going to be just a whodunit. I wanted it to be about the real people whose lives were cut short in senseless and violent ways. They aren't just characters playing parts in my story. In fact, it's the other way around. I was the one who stepped into their lives—and their deaths. I had a responsibility to them, not just to bring their killer to justice but to do honor to their memory. If I was going to write this book, it wasn't going to be about me. It was going to be about them.

When I first sat down with my collaborator, Davin Seay, these concerns were uppermost in my mind. And as we kept talking, not just to each other but to all those who were involved in the investigation, I began to realize that the further we dug into the details of the case, the less I could understand or explain my own part in it. I knew the facts—the when and where and how—but at the middle of it was a big question mark. It wasn't Robert Browne. It was me.

That's really not so surprising when you think about it. None of us are really sure what makes us tick. Others see us differently from how we see ourselves, and in that difference is where you can sometimes find out the truth about yourself. I come from a generation that never put much stock in self-examination. You did what you did, what you were told to do, no questions asked. I've always been comfortable that way, particularly as a cop.

The further we got into this book, the more I realized that the questions I'd never asked myself were the same ones that would make sense of what had happened and why. Let me give you an example: the one thing most people want to know about this story is how I could have befriended a guy like Robert. He's a vicious killer, and I'm pretty sure he wouldn't hesitate to add me to his list of victims if he had the chance. But I still considered him my friend: we shared some common interests; we enjoyed talking to each other; we remembered each other on birthdays and holidays.

It doesn't keep me up at night, wondering how I could call

Robert a friend. But I can see that that part of me was a factor in how this case was solved. Without my becoming his friend, he would never have told me his secrets during the course of our official investigation. And this story would have never made sense without my knowing how that happened.

It was my collaborator who suggested that this book didn't have to be just about me telling my story from my point of view. It could be about stepping *into* the story, becoming a participant; one of the many whose life was changed—and cut short—by Robert Browne. I could stand back, watch the story unfold, add my two cents to those of many others, and together we could tell the whole story as completely as it could be told.

Along the way, I might get the chance to learn something about myself. What I don't understand about what makes me tick, maybe others do. It could be a way to take the focus off me and put it where it belongs—on the victims of Robert Browne.

Davin and I worked hard to bring as many voices to this book as possible. Those voices knew things I didn't. They were witness to things I wasn't. They could make the judgments—about me and Robert and what brought us together—that I can't. And in the end I could be just another character in a story with a lot of heroes. I could find my rightful place among them.

At least it was worth a shot.

—*Charlie Hess*

PART ONE

CHAPTER ONE

BLACK FOREST

In the brisk Indian summer of 1991, Black Forest, Colorado, was a high-end suburban enclave waiting to happen. With its spectacular mountain vistas and free-ranging alpine meadows, the wedge of land between I-25 and Highway 24, just north of the rapidly expanding reach of Colorado Springs, was a prime piece of real estate, a developer's dream. Directly across the interstate from the United States Air Force Academy, Black Forest was poised to become the latest in a long string of upscale bedroom communities encroaching from Greater Denver, two hours to the north.

In the meantime, however, the 200,000 acres of unincorporated El Paso County clung stubbornly to their bucolic charms. Named by an early German immigrant for the similarity of its dark ponderosa pines to the forests of his native Bavaria, the land, teaming with wildlife, was ideal for camping, hiking, and horseback riding. Nearly 8,000 feet at its highest elevations, Black Forest was in fact largely given over to grasslands so spacious that most of the subsequent housing sites would be lopped off in sprawling five-acre parcels.

But there was at the same time something austere and desolate about this all-but-virgin land, especially now, as summer's heat gave way to the first chill of impending autumn sweeping down off the towering reaches of Pike's Peak and the Rampart range. Bisected midway by the crosshair intersection of Black Forest Road and Shoup Road, most of the region ran out along unpaved arteries, dead-ending at the horizon. Its high-end residential future notwithstanding, Black Forest seemed remote from the heartland bustle of nearby Colorado Springs, one of the most prosperous communities on the western edge of Middle America. It's a region that literally embodies the nation's faith and fighting power in a plethora of local military bases and an intense concentration of evangelical outreach organizations.

A pioneering spirit lingered across this windswept expanse of meadow and primeval forest, with homesteaders clearing space for double-wides down dusty roads from which, one day, McMansions and spacious residential streets would spring. Before it became one of Colorado Springs' better suburbs, Black Forest was home to more than a few who cling to the outskirts of society.

Not that the Church family were outsiders. Far from it. Michael and Diane Church may have had few neighbors along their sparsely populated stretch of Eastonville Road, bounding the northern quadrant of Black Forest, but they were still citizens in good standing in the newly minted community. Their thirteen-year-old daughter Heather attended nearby Falcon Middle School, while two of her three younger brothers—Gunner, seven, and Kristoff, ten—were active in the local Boy Scout troop. The whole family regularly attended the area's Mormon church, and they were an integral part of a tight circle of fellow Latter Day Saints and its built-in social and spiritual network. Black Forest was a good place to put down roots, and that's just what the Churches had worked so hard to accomplish.

But the roots had withered. That summer Diane filed for divorce, marking the end of a thirteen-year union that the one-time college sweethearts both acknowledged had long since been over. For a time Diane had attended group counseling sessions for women. Michael, meanwhile, maintained his job as a metrologist at Atmel, a Honeywell offshoot, calibrating tolerances for semiconductors in the region's fledgling high-tech sector. He had moved into town pending the dissolution of their troubled marriage, set to be finalized before the holidays.

4

He left behind a forlorn aura that hung over the Churches' home that September, a lonely, quietly bereft aspect that well suited its remoteness and seclusion. The couple had recently put the property up for sale.

Situated on a 5.8-acre lot a quarter-mile down a badly maintained track from the Eastonville Road and all but hidden from view by wooded bluffs, the Church residence was a small single-family home with four bedrooms, one of which served as a family den. Decked out in a lackluster southwestern motif with a flat roof and tacked-on exterior beams, its windows, trimmed bright blue against the peach-colored stucco walls, overlooked a vista of desiccated grasslands spiderwebbed by narrow roads. A low cinder-block wall sheltered a half-finished patio, and a small garden of mountain flowers was strewn with boulders and a de rigueur rustic wagon wheel. There were other houses scattered across the sward, but the inescapable impression was of a place well off the beaten track, a homestead stubbornly clinging to a bare patch of land and the fading dreams of the family inside.

It was 8:30 PM on the evening of September 17, 1991—the moist air presaging a damp night to come—when Diane Church put in a call to home. A petite, vivacious forty-one-year-old with auburn-tinged hair, Diane still had traces of a southern accent from the Ashland, Kentucky, upbringing she shared with her identical twin sister Denise. She had earlier driven Kris and Gunner to a Scout meeting at their local Mormon church some fifteen miles down the Black Forest Road and had stayed on to attend a women's homemaking class, leaving her daughter Heather to watch over her five-year-old brother Sage, the youngest of the four Church children. Heather had been especially anxious to please her mother, volunteering to babysit and straightening her room without being asked, all because she had been granted permission to attend a school dance scheduled for that Friday.

After an hour of housekeeping dos and don'ts, the class was

over. Diane stayed on to talk with friends. She took time out to check on Heather, concerned, she later recalled, because Sage had just gotten his multipurpose DPT vaccination shot earlier that same day, and she wanted her daughter to keep an eye out for any adverse reactions.

At thirteen, Heather Dawn Church still seemed a safe distance from the perilous shoals of adolescence. Measuring only five feet tall and weighing a slight seventy-eight pounds, her sharp oval face was dominated by the oversized front teeth she had yet to grow into and huge pair of brown-framed, thick-lensed glasses, magnifying her hazel eyes even as they seemed to diminish the rest of her already elfin features. She wore her light-brown hair shoulder length in the tight-permed fashion of the day, acknowledging her impending maturity only with the gaudy pairs of plastic earrings she often wore in her triple-pierced lobes. It was the unfinished countenance of a child, still waiting for all the pieces to fit together.

In some way similar, Heather was also assembling the first tentative elements of her own identity. Earnestly studying the violin, she was nonetheless concerned about her participation in a class talent contest and finally decided on handing out caramels to her schoolmates, announcing, "I don't dance. I don't sing. I don't play a musical instrument. I don't do cartwheels. But I sure do love candy." An A and B student who had recently tested for Falcon's eighth-grade gifted program, she had so far evaded drugs and alcohol and the other pressures of her peer group, thanks largely to her parents' decision to avoid suburban snares by locating to this secluded area. It was a measure of the Mormon Church's centrality to the family's life that on a Sunday-school questionnaire asking where she wanted to be in ten years' time, Heather had answered, "I'd like to be on my mission," referring to the mandatory evangelizing work required from every member of the Church of Latter Day Saints. Australia was her choice of mission field, while Brigham Young, her parents' alma mater, was the university she most hoped to attend. Yet even as she held closely to the family's avowed articles of faith, she was also beginning, however hesitantly, to find herself. "Tall, blue-eyed, blond hair," may have been the typical response to the question "What do you want your husband to look like?" but there were imaginative hints of individuality elsewhere in Heather's responses, as when she was asked the name and number of children she would want to have. "One," she replied: a girl, to be named, beguilingly, Persephone.

When Diane called in the mid-evening, Heather and Sage were settled in the family room watching the end of an episode of *Home Improvement*. It was past the boy's bedtime, but as Heather explained to her mother, she had allowed him to stay up especially to watch the popular sitcom with its idealized family dynamics. Cautioning her daughter to keep an eye out for signs of a fever and reassured of her children's well-being, Diane hung up. "I love you," she would later remember telling Heather, promising to be home by ten.

It was only natural that Diane would have felt an extra measure of concern, especially where it touched Heather. Her oldest child had been born shortly after her marriage to Michael, who, more than a decade later, still had the fit and well-maintained physique that had initially attracted her. Heather had had the longest stretch of all her children to form a strong bond with her father and stood to suffer the most from the disintegrating marriage, since her siblings were still too young to understand fully what was happening to the family. Diane's faith helped sustain her through this difficult transition, but she also suspected that prayer could go only so far in helping her daughter come to terms with the insecurity and guilt that were all too often the outcome of divorce for a sensitive child.

Yet, in the seven months since Diane's husband had moved out, Heather hadn't displayed any outward signs of trauma, thanks in part to the open visitation agreement she had arranged with Michael. To all appearances Heather had taken her parents' separation in stride, and any overt reaction, from inappropriate anger to delinquent behavior, hadn't manifested itself. Against the odds, Heather seemed to be a happy, well-adjusted young girl on the cusp of puberty. If the family crisis had wounded her, she was either hiding the hurt or had yet to face its reality.

Thanks to solicitous friends lending their ears and offering sympathetic advice on her troubles, Diane was fifteen minutes late arriving home that evening, at 10:15. In the back seat of the car, still in their Scout uniforms, Kris and Gunner were already drifting off to sleep as the headlights cut through the thick darkness of the high, empty vista that opened from the Churches' front yard, already partially obscured by a gathering fog. Pulling into the driveway, the first thing she noticed was that most of the house lights were off: Either Heather and Sage were already in bed or, more likely, her daughter was watching television in the dark, as was her inclination. Trailed by the sleepy boys, she crossed the driveway to a pair of sliding glass doors at one side of the home, her house keys at the ready. But she didn't need them: the patio door was unlocked, a fact that momentarily puzzled her, since on leaving at 5:30, she had made sure that all the doors on the property were secured. Still, the family had two cats, and it seemed likely that Heather had let them out for the night and forgot to lock the door behind her.

Inside, the house was in its usual lived-in condition yet still orderly enough for Diane to register that one of the dining-room chairs was tilted against the table. Not the way she'd left things, but kids would certainly be kids.

She first tended to Kris and Gunner, sending them off to the bedroom the two boys shared with their younger brother. Depositing her handbag and taking off her coat, she was heading down the hall to tuck them in and check on Sage when the pair returned to report that the youngster was not in his bed. Diane quickly investigated, only to find the boy hidden in a tangle of blankets and sheets. The mystery resolved, she next headed down the hall toward Heather's bedroom in the northwest corner of the house. She was guided on her way by the brightness from the open door—as much as Heather liked watching television in the dark, she liked falling asleep with the lights on, particularly after reading *Communion*, Whitley Strieber's frightening account of alien abduction.

But Heather wasn't asleep in her bed. It was a fact Diane quickly determined after rummaging through the blankets as she had done in her search for Sage. A quick flash of concern escalated over the next hour as she turned the house upside down searching for her daughter. "I looked everywhere," she later recounted. "The clothes hamper, the kitchen cabinets. I tore them up. I just thought that maybe she had seen something frightening and was afraid to come out." After the brief scare with Sage, it was hard at first to credit that Heather was actually missing. It seemed she would just turn up at any minute, as her young son had done, appearing from the folds of a quilt with a sleepy smile on her face.

"When I couldn't find her," she continues, "I called some people whom I thought she might try to reach if there was a problem. They hadn't heard from her." One of her calls was to a friend, Jan Schalk; another was to a neighbor, Diane Pietras, who advised her to search around the perimeter of the house. "I went outside to look for her," she recalls. "I walked around the property and took a look in the toolshed and the little play-house we had for the kids." Forcing herself not to give voice to her worst fears, she called back the Pietras residence, and her friend immediately volunteered to come over and help in the search.

While waiting for assistance, she put in another call, this time to the home of Amber White, one of her daughter's closest friends. Amber had in fact received a phone call from Heather earlier in the evening but had not seen or heard from her since. The White family also immediately offered to come over and help locate the absent girl. After a brief moment of lingering uncertainty—What if she suddenly turned up? What if there was a simple, silly explanation for all this?—she dialed 911.

It was 11:30 that night when El Paso County Sheriff's Deputy Les Milligan, responding to a missing person's report, arrived at the Church home. By that time Michael Church had also been summoned, and the house was crowded with concerned friends and neighbors, including Claudia Gatti, the secretary at Falcon Middle School and another close acquaintance of the family. In the midst of the spiraling confusion, Milligan began methodically assessing the situation. Over the next few hours he painstakingly assembled as complete a description of Heather Dawn Church as her distraught mother could provide. Dubbed in the dry police terminology of the subsequent sheriff's office narrative "the reporting party/victim," Diane detailed everything from the small mole on the left side of her daughter's mouth, to the scar above her right breast where she had once picked at a scab, to a patch of light skin on the small of her back. It was a heartbreaking inventory of physical characteristics suddenly seeming all the more poignant and precious in her absence.

It was also determined that Heather's thick glasses, without which she would have had trouble navigating at night, had yet to be located and further that she had accessorized her small silver chain necklace with pairs of black, turquoise, and pink earrings. The last time her mother had seen her, she had been wearing black flower-print pants and a black blouse, which she subsequently found on her daughter's bedroom floor near the clothes hamper in the course of her increasingly frantic search. The pair of black, ballet-like slippers—size eight to accommodate Heather's gangly feet—which she had been wearing earlier in the evening had also been found by her mother, laid alongside a school outfit, including a training bra, which had been selected by the girl for the following day. It was a skirt-and-blouse ensemble that had been purchased earlier that afternoon and which Heather had been excited about wearing for the first time. With remarkable clarity under the circumstances, Diane Church had been able to ascertain that all of Heather's shoes as well as all her coats and jackets were still in the house, but her daughter had too much underwear for her to make a full accounting. In fact, all that seemed to be missing from the child's wardrobe was the white Mickey Mouse T-shirt she often wore to bed.

It was a little before noon on September 18, a late morning still heavy with thick, low-lying mountain mist, when an exhausted and overwrought Diane Church answered a knock at the front door to find Sheriff's Detective Mark Finley, who had been assigned by Lieutenant William Mistretta to take charge of the case. By now the property, taped off at its perimeter, was buzzing with activity, mostly revolving around a search-and-rescue team that had arrived at sunup that morning with Dixie, a bloodhound, in tow. As Finley was introducing himself, Elinor McGarry, a sheriff's laboratory technician, arrived and began photographing the premises and the outlying property.

The probing, circumspect, but relentless questioning continued over the next few hours. No, Heather had never run away from home before. Yes, she was a good student, well liked by her classmates and teachers. No, she did not seem unduly troubled by her parents' impending divorce. Yes, she got along well with her father. No, Diane had noticed no unusual activity, unless you counted the real estate looky-loos who drove by the for-sale house on occasion. Yes, Heather had been instructed not to open the door to strangers without hearing a special pre-arranged code word. No, to her knowledge Heather did not have a boyfriend.

As the interview continued, Finley was, however, able to elicit the earliest intimations of what might, to his trained ears, eventually develop into leads. A bully who rode with Heather on the school bus had cursed and kicked her on occasion. A few months earlier, a skinny white man with long brown hair had responded to a service call for their broken well and, using a mirror, had shown the children the reflection of water from the bottom. A pair of young neighbor boys reported having seen a "long white car" following the school bus over the past two weeks. Still another car, metallic blue with rust spots, had been reported prowling near two other county schools, as well as a third in Colorado Springs.

Yet there was one aspect of the inquiry to which Finley paid particular attention: the abusive behavior of Michael Church. Acknowledging that it was the "basic reason" for their impending divorce, Diane nevertheless insisted that Heather and her father had a good relationship, despite the fact that she claimed he had, on occasion, "slapped Heather around." As if to underscore his basically good intentions, she went on to reveal that her husband was attending a divorce recovery workshop at the nearby Presbyterian church.

Other intriguing fragments of the unfolding case continued to present themselves as the afternoon wore on. Finley's questions were interrupted by the arrival of search-and-rescue supervisor Mike Collins, reporting that his team had discovered a small, rusted watch in the driveway to the west of the property. Shortly afterwards, near an old barn a half-mile from the house, another team had found two new dollar bills. Sergeant David Bartels, who was overseeing Dixie the search dog, debriefed Finley on their progress. Taking a scent from Heather's pants and blouse, the canine alerted only in the immediate vicinity of the house, showing frustration when he was led beyond the driveway. Based on Dixie's behavior, it was Bartels's opinion that the girl had left the property in a vehicle, although when they subsequently searched around a small pond southeast of the home, Dixie once again alerted, despite the fact that there were no footprints in evidence.

By now it had been decided that the missing persons case was in all likelihood either an abduction or a kidnapping, and the phone company was contacted to put a trap-and-trace on the line. Finley also requested that a tape recorder be sent to the home to capture all incoming calls. At the same time, Detective Stan Presley was dispatched to the Colorado Springs apartment of Michael Church, who had returned with his three sons to await a possible call from Heather.

Lab tech McGarry also had her work cut out for her. A red stain directly inside Heather's bedroom door aroused suspicion until her field test confirmed it to be a spill of Kool-Aid. Both the girl's and her parents' bedroom were dusted for prints, and scattered bits of anomalous evidence—a single gold hoop earring; the sheets and pillows from Heather's bed—were gathered and tagged. The white Mickey Mouse T-shirt was at length discovered in Heather's clothes hamper, and the conundrum of a pile of wet clothes in the laundry alcove was solved when Diane Church explained that the toilet had backed up that afternoon and the clothing had been thrown quickly on the spill to sop it up.

Detective Presley was, meanwhile, conducting a preliminary interview with Michael Church, who, he later reported, "appeared emotionally upset, spoke in a broken tone and began to cry several times." Through his tears, Michael would relate the unexceptional circumstances of the proverbial "evening in question" up to the point when he received the fateful call from his estranged wife, shortly after 10:30 PM. It was a story that would effectively determine his whereabouts on the seventeenth, establishing what, to all intents and purposes, was an ironclad alibi. Leaving work at 5 PM, he had stopped for a workout at the nearby Heath Matrix Gym, where he was seen by the sports center operator as well as by a young woman named Heidi Johnson with whom he had struck up a conversation. From there he drove to the First Presbyterian church, where he attended a divorce recovery workshop, the large gathering eventually breaking up into smaller groups, one of which he joined. The session was overseen by a staffer who would also attest to his attendance. The meeting ended at 9:30, and half an hour later he was back in his apartment, where he received a call from Heidi Johnson, continuing their conversation from earlier that evening at the gym. A half-hour later they were interrupted by an incoming call from Diane Church.

Back at the Eastonville Road home the press had assembled, assiduously digging for newsworthy facts in an unfolding case that, less than twenty-four hours after the initial missing person report, already seemed on the verge of stalling. "A million things could have happened," Diane told reporters, reaching beyond the grim implications to lay hold of a fierce hope. "But I think she's safe. It's just a 'mother' feeling. She may be hurt, but I think she's safe."

Authorities had considerably less cause for optimism. "We're going on seventy-two hours now," Lieutenant Mistretta would remark on September 20, "and I don't like it." With the crucial three-day time frame for finding and following fresh leads rapidly expiring, the search for Heather had taken on a frenetic urgency. The FBI had joined the case on the nineteenth, eventually assigning almost thirty agents to the investigation, and there were persistent suggestions that the bureau was attempting to make good on its lackadaisical response to a pair of earlier missing children cases dating from the late eighties; in one, the disappearance of seven-month-old Christopher Abeyta, the FBI did not mobilize for several weeks, and the infant was never found. It was not a mistake agents intended to repeat, and they commandeered a helicopter from nearby Fort Carson to scour the Black Forest environs on the fourth day of the ever-widening search.

The Colorado Springs community had likewise rallied. Volunteers circulated more than ten thousand flyers all across the region known as the Front Range, from Denver south to Pueblo, as well as in several states where the Church family had relatives. The Center for Missing and Exploited Children announced plans to distribute posters in more than four hundred outlets throughout the region, while a local Boy Scout troop passed out photos and descriptions of Heather at an air show staged at Peterson Air Force Base over the weekend. As a second phone line was installed at the Church home to accommodate investigators and keep the main line open for an expected ransom demand, prayer vigils were being held in churches and sanctuaries around the county. "One of our young daughters—almost as if into thin air—has disappeared," Bishop Willy Scott reported from the pulpit of Black Forest Mormon church. "There has been almost a void in information concerning where she might be," he added before breaking down in tears. By early the following week, John Condren, a family friend and founder of a successful regional marketing company, had posted a $10,000 reward for information leading to Heather's whereabouts, while a group calling itself the Friends of Heather Dawn Church continued to scour the arroyos of the Black Forest backcountry in the increasingly chill autumn air.

On September 26, a little more than a week after the disappearance, a rumor spread that Heather had been found. Several businesses took down the missing posters they had prominently displayed before the wildfire word of mouth was finally extinguished. Two days later, news came that bloodhounds had picked up her scent along a stretch of abandoned railroad tracks, but an extensive search of the area revealed no new clues. Before the month was out, the sheriff's department found itself running down phone tips that hinted darkly at the involvement of satanic cults in the disappearance. One after another, the initial flurry of leads, tips, and sightings were dead-ending.

"There's got to be a lead," said El Paso County Sheriff's Captain Willie Alexander, with a palpable air of desperation on the eve of a rally for Heather in Colorado Springs' Memorial Park. "Anything. We just haven't found it."

In point of fact they had. Amidst the growing mountain of evidence, reports, and police narratives that comprised the files of the increasingly frustrating case was a brief reference by Detective Finley to a set of three elongated rectangular windows in the master bedroom. During a follow-up interview on the morning of September 18, Diane Church mentioned in passing her recollection of having left one of these windows cranked open four to five inches before leaving the house the previous evening. It was during her frenzied search of the home that she noticed the same window, now closed, with its attached indoor screen askew and its curtain hanging out of place. Further examination established that the screen had been placed backward in its track. Diane asked those who had assembled that night to help look for Heather but could find no one who remembered closing the window, much less removing the screen.

Lab technician McGarry was duly summoned to dust the metal frame of the wood-trimmed windows and was able to lift a remarkably clear set of three fingerprints. Finley's next move was to submit the prints to the Automated Fingerprint Identification System on the assumption that a match might be found in the nationwide database. The result was negative. The searchers moved on.

CHAPTER TWO

DEAD MAN'S SHOES

"I've been told I have a reputation for never being wrong."

Offering up the précis of a career approaching the half-century mark, Lou Smit seems comfortable indulging in a bit of hyperbole. He is, after all, on familiar ground, among kindred spirits.

Sitting opposite him in the Old Heidelberg, a fusty German pastry shop in a down-on-its-heels Colorado Springs neighborhood, are two of his oldest friends, Charlie Hess and Scott Fischer. The pair have heard Smit's ruminations many times before, just as, over the years, he has heard theirs, sharing innumerable cups of coffee and sticky, sweet Bavarian pastries beneath the alpine vista of the café's contact-paper decor.

The trio is something of a fixture at the Old Heidelberg; their regular spot in the back is a virtual round table of law-enforcement lore. In the long shadows of this cool afternoon they settle into an easy routine, talking and listening, nodding assent and murmuring asides. They are three seasoned cops, each with a lifetime of stories to tell and retell, yet among these equals it is Smit who is most often afforded pride of place.

It's not surprising. At the age of seventy-one, Lou Smit has dedicated better than half his years to bringing killers to justice and in the process has racked up a record of success remarkable by any measure. Since joining the Colorado Springs Police Department in 1966, he has investigated over two hundred homicides, the vast majority of which he has solved with the characteristic combination of dogged determination and unerr-

17

ing instinct. It has made him a legend in the annals of Colorado law enforcement.

But Smit isn't given to embellishment. Nor for a moment would he allow himself to claim credit unearned. A spruce, tidy, bald man with a warm smile, watery blue eyes, and a voice so soft that it seems to carry no further than the friends who sit listening, the veteran detective exudes a self-effacement bordering on invisibility. It's what gives his assertions the unassailable ring of truth.

"Look," he continues, as the day draws on, "I'm not saying I solved every case I've ever gone after." His thin lips purse, and the parchment-thin skin of his face furrows as if making a mental inventory of the ones that got away. "But when it comes to sniffing out the bad guys, I get this gut feeling that I've learned to trust implicitly. I can't tell you the number of times I've interviewed a suspect and walked away knowing for certain that I'd just talked to the murderer. I can't always prove it, but I've never been proved wrong."

As an exemplar of a dying breed of quintessential shoe-leather and pencil-stub police sleuths, Lou Smit has dealt daily with proof and the procedures by which it is ascertained. Yet he also evinces a paradoxical ambivalence toward anything that smacks of the hard and fast in his line of work. If experience has taught him anything, he insists again and again, it is that as much as the art of investigation employs the science of forensics, catching criminals is all about vague feelings, hunches, and vibes. It's a certain tingling of the skin and the erecting of short hairs that he has come to depend on and that, he asserts, has never let him down. With a respect for the law that seems all but genetically encoded, Smit is a by-the-book cop who has been around long enough to know how to read between its lines.

And like his comrades in arms in the Old Heidelberg, Smit has more than a few illuminating stories to illustrate his tried and true methodologies, stories he loves to tell, relishing each rendition and returning time and again to a leitmotif of cops and robbers who speak the same language, share the same code of honor, and dispense the same version of rough justice. "You're always dancing right up to the edge of the cliff that divides good from bad," is the way he describes it. "The trick is not to stray too far over, to become one of them. In order to do your job, you've got to learn to think and reason like a criminal—which, if you're not careful, will bring you to that short step when you're actually behaving like one yourself."

For Lou Smit, the down-and-dirty business of making the world safe for solid citizens has been tempered over the years by the necessary knack of suspending judgment. "I've sat in a jail cell with my arms around a murderer, weeping with him just because, despite what he did, he was such a pathetic specimen," he recounts. "You're constantly face to face with the horrific things human beings do to each other and yet you can never forget that when it comes down to it, that's just what they are, no more and no less: human beings."

"He's a straight shooter," is the estimation of a reformed pimp whom Smit once sent to jail and who was later interviewed by the local newspaper in one of its periodic paeans to the detective. "If you get on the bad side of the law, he gets you no matter how good an outlaw you are, and I was good. But he'll also use his own time to set you straight. I can't tell you everything he did for me. I've turned into a pretty good person because of him."

Known for spending his vacations driving around the country visiting victims' families and inmates he helped put away, who often send Christmas cards, Smit's intrinsic empathy—part of the attitude and outlook necessary for him to do his job—does not come without a cost. In his yellow-painted home on a leafy suburban street in Colorado Springs' modest westside neighborhood, the retired police captain keeps an extensive database comprising decades' worth of homicide cases: opened, closed, active, and moribund. They are files replete with the evidence of every conceivable variety of murder and mayhem. The light in Smit's placid eyes seems to dim as he reviews the ghastly gallery of dismemberments and decapitations, stabbings and shootings, battery and bludgeonings. What replaces it is a kind of stubborn pride—in his lifelong role as society's shield, in his ability to contemplate calmly the depravity of his fellow man, and in his disquieting disdain for the timorous qualms of clueless civilians. He peruses the coroner's reports and crime-scene photos with a knowing squint, born of prolonged exposure that has inoculated this gentle and unassuming man, taking on a bit of the disease in order the better to eradicate it. If Lou Smit has never been wrong, it's because he knows exactly what he's dealing with, from the inside.

It's a balancing act, he admits frankly, that would be impossible without a deep and abiding faith in God. In point of fact, Smit unwaveringly attributes divine guidance to the fact that he went into this line of work in the first place. "I start every case by saying a prayer at the crime scene," he explains. "God has given me this job, and I need constantly to ask for the wisdom and guidance to accomplish His will. Then, at the end of every case, I say another prayer, one of thanksgiving, if possible at the graveside of the victim. It's what keeps me centered and sane. I like to say that I'm an ordinary detective with an extraordinary partner."

Smit's dependence on supernatural agencies, whether divine intervention or his own sharply honed sixth sense, is all the more remarkable considering his affiliation with the Reformed tradition of Christianity. An offshoot of the austere Dutch Reform Church, it espouses the stern Calvinist formulation of the elect and the preterite, foreordained to salvation and damnation respectively, a stark division of good and evil that accords well with Smit's chosen profession. Yet there is a subtle contradiction to his belief as well: as he pursues the damned and brings them to justice, he still sees in them that stubborn spark of humanity lighting the possibility, however dim, of redemption. As a servant of an implacable God, Smit indeed walks a fine line between doing His inexorible will and leaving room for the human agencies of grace.

It is that same God, he will tell you with utter certainty, who led him to his true calling in a moment when, on his knees and at the end of his tether, he experienced a moment of utter surrender and found a clear path forward. The God he petitioned was the same one he had first learned of in the church-run private schools, initially in Denver, where he was born into the home of second-generation Dutch immigrants, then in Chicago, where he moved with his family as a child.

He would bounce between the Midwest and the Rockies throughout his childhood as his father tried to support the family in the depths of the Depression. Yet the regular migrations of the Smit family never extended beyond the protective embrace of the mother faith. "Growing up," he recalls, "I felt isolated from the world. Our life was very church-centered, very much influenced by my grandparents, who still spoke the native tongue."

For a time Smit's father, a failed Wisconsin farmer, earned a living as a harmonica teacher in local schools across Illinois and Indiana. "He was a virtuoso," Lou recounts. "He'd put together these enormous harmonica bands using his students and put on concerts." He pauses before answering the question left unasked by his companions. "I picked it up from him," he admits. "I can play, but I'm not nearly as good as he was."

As a teenager, Smit found himself back in Denver and at age seventeen joined the Navy. "I was stationed in Hawaii for four years," he continues fondly. "They were some of the best years of my life. It was during that time that that I started corresponding with my childhood sweetheart Barbara, and in 1958 we got married."

After his discharge and after earning a degree in electronics, Smit would go on to take a variety of less-than-fulfilling jobs, beginning at a Southside Chicago supply company working in a prototype lab on the initial Atlas space program. "I knew after a week what I *didn't* want to do," he recalls. "I just wasn't cut out to go in one door at the beginning of the day and then out the same door at the end of the same day." He would try his hand at selling bottled gas before rejoining his father, who had meanwhile started a Midwest tree business. "Two weeks after we got started, he had a heart attack," Lou remembers. "I tried to keep the business going but I didn't know a thing about trees." With a family to support that would eventually include three children, he scraped together a backbreaking living running a stump machine for the next several years until coming back, this time for good, to Colorado.

"I had no prospects. Everything I'd tried up to that point had failed. But there was still a lot of pride in me. I was determined to do it my way, which was the example my brother John had set. We were very close, born four years apart to the day and married to sisters. He was a successful businessman, and when he died of a heart attack at forty-one, that changed the way I looked at life. Suddenly I wasn't so cocky and confident anymore."

Whatever it was that drove Smit to his knees, his prayers were quickly answered. "I'd been drifting for a long time," he reveals. "The moment had come to ask for help, for a purpose to my life."

It was a cousin, a Colorado Springs cop, who suggested a few months later that he apply to the force. Lou: "I had nothing to suggest law enforcement in my background, but I was drawn almost immediately to the prospect. I think it really did feel that my prayers had been heard. At least it seems that way in retrospect."

Looking back, Lou attributes his decision to join the Colorado Springs Police Department in 1966 as the turning point in his life. "I've loved every day since," he says. "I've loved it with all my heart." Passing the entrance examination proved less of a challenge for the thirty-year-old than meeting the force's height requirement. "The examiner said that I was a half-inch shy of five feet nine inches," he recounts. "My cousin arranged to have me retested, and we thought up a bunch of ideas from elevator shoes to newspaper in my socks. I was sure they'd be up on all those tricks so I told him to knock me on the head with his nightstick. After a couple of tries we managed to raise a half-inch bump. I measured five feet nine and a half."

It's one of those stories he loves to tell, especially now, in the midst of a restless retirement, alone since the death in 2003 of his wife of forty-six years. The memories are a repository, evoking even more than the accumulated wisdom of a consummate professional, but a life lived doing God's will.

"The academy lasted eleven weeks," he continues. "Then they put you on the street as a beat cop for six months. I really learned the ropes, but it wasn't until I made detective in 1972 that I really felt I was doing what I was meant to. I also knew it was something I could do, that I was naturally good at. At the same time, I was blessed to be able to learn from the best: experienced detectives who knew how to develop a lead and cultivate an informant."

These two simple skills are, Lou insists, "the lifeblood of a detective." He recounts a time when a two-thousand-dollar slush fund was available exclusively to facilitate "chumming." "That's what we called it," he explains. "You knew these people because you'd see them out on the street every day. You'd even put some of them in jail. As unlikely as it may seem, that can create a bond, a place where your lives intersect. So you'd invite them out to lunch and give them twenty bucks if they were down and out. It was like making friends. Hell, they *are* your friends. You're listening and they're talking, and you want to keep them talking for as long as possible, about anything— their life story, their loves and hates, what makes them tick. You have to develop a light touch. For instance, I prefer, whenever I can, to do my interviews in a car. There's something nonconfrontational about it, sitting side by side, next to each other, just looking out the window."

He continues. "I've learned how to eliminate the chaff from a case and look at every situation in its simplest terms. Murder isn't really all that complicated. The motives are simple. People get carried away. Nine times out of ten, it's a spur-of-the-moment thing, which means they haven't thought through anything as premeditated as how to cover their tracks. Very rarely do you deal with a 'whodunit.' It's usually pretty obvious who killed who and why. The trick is gathering enough information to make a case. That's what a detective does: puts together bits and pieces until he's got the whole thing. Knowing how to preserve a crime scene is a big part of it, but most of the job is organizing and accessing information."

It's a talent at which Smit excels. "I've got a mind for details," he avers, "and I've learned how to keep a lot of data in my head at the same time." He laughs. "I like to maintain my files and I can always tell the state of any case another cop might be working on. At first the file is front and center on the desk. As the case drags on, it's moved to the side. Later still, it's in a box on the floor and finally on a shelf in the archives. But almost any of those cases could be solved by simply going through that file, constructing time lines and networks of names and numbers. That's where you find the leads, where, nine times out of ten, crimes are solved. It's all in the details. As much as anything, it's about patience."

A description by an officer under whom he once worked aptly sums up Smit's approach to police work. "He just grinds away," retired Captain Gene Stokes would be quoted as saying in yet another newspaper profile of Smit. "He stays at it until he uproots the evidence," he adds, purposely evoking the detective's early career in stump removal.

As is the prerogative of any old-timer, Smit is critical, in his characteristically understated way, of many modern methodologies, especially when it comes to policies of manpower allocation. "These days, there's so much rotation in and out of police jobs, it becomes very difficult to develop the skills you need to break cases. The best approach I ever saw for getting the job done was to assign three cases at a time to three-man teams. They each knew what the other was up to and they had the benefit of three perspectives on each case they had in common. By staggering the work hours, you've got someone on the job seven days a week. And it's never about who gets the credit."

Yet despite his nostalgia for the selfless camaraderie of a simpler time, it's clear that Smit has earned his reputation single-handedly, the kind of individual prowess that lends even more authority to his unassuming demeanor. After eighteen years as a detective with the Colorado Springs Police Department, Smit was promoted to sergeant. "I lasted about two weeks," he confesses. "I just couldn't sit still behind a desk, regardless of how much more they were paying me. I asked to be bumped back to detective, the first time that had ever happened in the department."

As a man who well knew his own capacities—his limitations as much as his talents—Smit's surprising career move was a simple admission that he had long since found his niche. It was as far back as 1975, three years after first earning his detective shield, that Smit was handed his breakthrough case, bringing into play a flair for details and the slow, steady persistence he had painstakingly nurtured over his early years in the force. It all came together in solving the savage murder of Karen Alicia Grammer, doing much in the process to establish his near-legendary reputation as a natural-born investigator.

A lively, vivacious eighteen-year-old, the body of the Florida native was found that summer in Colorado Springs, where she had relocated after taking a year off from college. She had been stabbed in the throat behind the Red Lobster on South Academy Avenue. She broke away from her assailant and, running and crawling the length of a city block, had made her way to a nearby mobile home park before collapsing outside the manager's front door, her bloody handprint a few inches from the doorbell.

Smit's initial challenge was simply to identify the body. "She had nothing on her," he recounts. "No purse, no wallet. Just a house key. We must have tried that key in a hundred doors around the area, but it didn't fit any of them." It wasn't until a friend of the victim reported her missing a few days later that the detective tried the lock at Grammer's apartment, opening the door and finally putting a name to the body. He would follow up by notifying her next of kin, in this case a twenty-year-old aspiring actor named Kelsey Grammer, who would, of course, go on to find fame as one of the regulars in the long-running television comedy *Cheers* and as the star of his own series, *Frasier.*

"There was a lot of tragedy in that family," Smit mused. "Their estranged father had been gunned down outside his home in Bermuda, and their grandfather, the man who'd raised them, had also recently passed away. Karen's death just underscored for me what a terrible crime murder really is. It takes away something precious and has an effect on the victim's family that in some cases can last for generations."

For the next several days, Smit would regularly begin his morning in the alley where the young woman had been killed, sitting in his car with a cup of coffee, studying the crime scene for any stray detail or overlooked clue—anything, however tenuous, that might turn into a lead. "After a while I noticed something that in retrospect seemed pretty obvious," he continues. "The alley was a dead-end. It kind of begged the question of why anyone would pick it as a place to commit murder. There was only one way out. It was too easy to get boxed in."

It was a speculation that next led Smit to an apartment complex opening on the back end of the cul-de-sac. "I figured that if it was too risky to make a getaway from the entrance of the alley, maybe the murderer had gone out through the back way, into one of those apartments. So I went to talk to the manager."

As part of his investigation, the detective had familiarized himself with other crimes that had occurred at or around the time of the Karen Grammer murder. Among them was a botched robbery at a nearby Red Lobster restaurant by a trio of African Americans whose bearing suggested the radicalized militancy of the Black Power movement roiling the country at the time. What had immediately caught Smit's attention was the fact that Grammer's boyfriend worked at the same eatery. It was a tantalizing coincidence with as yet no thread to connect it to the homicide.

With nothing more than a vague description of the would-be robbers, Smit played a hunch and asked if any of the residents in the apartment units might fit the profile. The manager didn't hesitate: three black soldiers from nearby Fort Carson had rented an apartment together before moving out a few days before Lou's arrival. Searching the empty premises, Smit turned up a document bearing a name that set another bell ringing: a second recent murder victim, who had been shot twice in the face. It was a similar MO to yet a third homicide, this time of a hotel kitchen worker, killed execution style a few weeks before Karen Grammer's death:

"I never would have put this all together if I hadn't done my homework," Smit asserts. "I had to read a lot of files and study the police reports on cases that didn't seem in any way related to what I was working on in order to connect the dots. Hollywood stereotypes aside, there's not a whole lot of glamour in police work. Gathering information, sifting through it all to find bits and pieces of data that may or may not fit together—it's tedious, thankless work. But that's how it's done."

Eventually joining forces with a team of prosecutors that included Robert Russell, who would subsequently help to bring Ted Bundy to justice, Smit began assembling evidence against a vicious gang led by Michael Corbett, an army officer whom the detective would later call "one of the most dangerous men I've ever met."

A textbook psychopath, Corbett had served a stint at Fort Carson, where he began his crime spree while still in the army, running over a fellow soldier with a tank to settle a grudge. "He was completely without a conscience," Smit asserts, "and he could turn on and off like a switch. There was no telling what might trigger him. He was a very gung ho military type, who took his training very seriously and prided himself on his martial arts skills. That might be why the army brass accepted his story that the tank episode was an accident."

Once discharged, Corbett began gathering a coterie of devoted followers, most notably his roommates Freddie Glenn and Larry Dunn, drawn as much by his cold-blooded charisma as by his addled rants of black empowerment. Also part of the gang was Winslow Watson—like the others, a former GI—who had ended up in the morgue after crossing Corbett by stealing a loaf of bread from some next-door neighbors. It was Watson's name that Smit had found in the deserted apartment; one in a string of capricious killings carried out by Corbett and his crew. That growing list of victims also included Daniel Van Lone, the hotel cook, who, after being robbed, was summarily dispatched when the infuriated killer found only fifty cents in his pocket.

Smit and his colleague, a young prosecutor named Chuck Heim, had taken the first steps down a bloody trail left by the ruthless killers. "We had a couple of other cases—a cab driver killed at Fort Carson and another soldier gunned down at a rest stop ten miles from the base—but we were never able to make those stick," he recalls. "As it was, we had plenty to keep us busy anyway."

The investigation broke wide open in short order when Smit was able to elicit a confession from Larry Dunn, the gang's junior partner, after persuading New Orleans authorities to arrest him on an unrelated crime. "We had seven murders we were looking at by that time," Smit recalls, "and Chuck Heim offered Dunn immunity in exchange for his testimony. He told us the whole thing, sitting there in the New Orleans House of

Detention, beginning with Van Lone, who had begged for his life as Corbett forced him to lie on the ground and then put a .38 to his right temple and pulled the trigger." "Did you see that motherfucker jump when I shot him?" was Dunn's recollection of Corbett's exultant comment as they drove away.

A week later, according to Dunn, Corbett met a young soldier named Winfred Profitt on the secluded shoreline of nearby Prospect Lake, where Corbett had arranged to sell him some marijuana. Instead, Corbett stabbed Profitt in the chest with an army-issue bayonet. "He wanted to see what it felt like to stick one into somebody," Dunn would later tell the cops, adding that Corbett had always seemed anxious to put his military training to use.

On July 1, Corbett was absent from the apartment he rented with Glenn, Dunn, and the doomed Winslow Watson, spending the night back at Fort Carson. But the cold-blooded example he had set for the others continued to assert its baleful influence. Freddie Glenn, especially, was eager to emulate his murderous mentor. According to the loquacious Dunn, Glenn had self-consciously adopted Corbett's swaggering manner and was eager to prove himself committed to the savage racial recompense the gang leader espoused. Michael Corbett may have been absent that evening, but it was clear to the investigators that his malign spirit guided the evening's ensuing mayhem.

On their own, Dunn, Glenn, and Watson decided to rob the nearby Red Lobster where Karen Grammer's boyfriend worked, planning to raid the place just at closing time, when the day's receipts would presumably be easy pickings from the walk-up window. It was perhaps an indication of the trio's wannabe status that their plan went quickly awry when the restaurant's employees told them the money was locked in the safe, neatly foiling the robbery before it began. As the night crew put in a call to the cops, the would-be robbers sullenly retreated. Karen Grammer had been sitting in the parking lot waiting for her boyfriend to finish his shift. Thinking she could identify them, the hapless gang kidnapped her, although Smit would assert another motive entirely to the horrific event that ensued.

"It was more basic than that," he insists, "more primal. They were trying to prove they were as ruthless and vicious as Corbett. They had seen what he could do and wanted to believe they were capable of the same thing, particularly Glenn, who worshipped the guy. They wanted to have someone at their mercy, dominating them completely while they pleaded for their life. That someone was Karen Grammer, who just happened to be in the wrong place at the wrong time."

While Grammer was still in the car, the trio robbed two convenience stores before returning to the apartment, where they took turns raping her over the next four hours before eventually telling her that they were going to let her go. It was, according to Dunn, their standard procedure for keeping victims cooperative and compliant; Corbett assured Van Lone, for instance, that no harm would come to him if he lay down on the ground and did what he was told.

"They took her blindfolded into a car and told her they were going to turn her loose," Prosecutor Chuck Heim would subsequently reveal in his report. Driving around the block, they entered the blind alley, where Glenn dragged Grammer from the car and, standing behind her, stabbed her in the throat. "He just did it once," Smit explains. "He got her real bad. Cut her carotid artery."

Left for dead, Grammer broke away and staggered into the mobile home park. Her blood was later found on the screen-door frame of the trailer where she had gone for help. With nobody at home and her life quickly ebbing away, she made her way to the manager's office, where she died as she tried to reach for the doorbell.

Based on Dunn's immunized testimony and additional evidence gathered by the detective and the prosecutor, Corbett and Glenn were arrested, tried, and eventually convicted in separate trials on three first-degree murder counts apiece. Their death sentences were subsequently commuted to consecutive life terms following the Supreme Court decision overturning capital punishment.

While the Karen Grammer murder case did much to establish Lou Smit's reputation for inspired police work—an instructive example of what he calls "keeping it simple" —it did little to resolve the basic quandaries of human nature that arise from his line of work: not simply the only-too-natural need to comprehend what motivates men to the furthest extremes of malice and cruelty, but the necessary expedient of seeing such individuals as still recognizably human. Throughout Smit's life and career, that suspension of judgment, predicated on religious sensibilities that acknowledge both our utter depravity and our innate need for God's grace, has remained a razor's edge on which he would balance his whole moral and ethical foundation.

Facing Corbett in court, Smit recalled how the cop and the criminal got into a staring contest. "He was cold," he says. "His eyes were really cold." Yet over the years he has also seen Corbett come to terms, however haltingly, with his crimes. Converting to Islam after decades in prison, the multiple murderer would later tell a newspaper reporter, "I had no value or compassion for human life. I'm not the person I was twenty years ago today."

"He has softened quite a bit," allows Smit. "I will say that." He is nevertheless assiduous in his efforts to keep Corbett behind bars, working diligently with DA Robert Russell to deny parole annually to "the most dangerous man I've ever met."

During forty years in law enforcement, Smit, for all his practiced ability to understand and even extend compassion to those he hunts down, seems never to have lost sight of his essential role, assigned to him in a moment of intense spiritual surrender. Scattered about the same unassuming suburban home where he keeps his ghastly gallery of crime is a curious collection of knickknacks: porcelain and plastic and wooden shoes in all shapes and sizes, mounted on plaques and pediments. They are all gifts from his friends and colleagues, variations on the theme of the quiet detective's personal motto, a bit of vintage police doggerel by which he has chosen to live his life.

"Shoes, shoes, dead man's shoes," the poem reads in part. "Who will stand in the dead man's shoes?" From the evidence of a dedicated life, it is clear that Lou Smit knows where he stands. It's a responsibility he takes as a virtually sacred trust, as evidenced in an essay he wrote on the theme for a law-enforcement journal in 1983, evincing in the process a flair for a vivid turn of phrase in sharp contrast to his innate diffidence.

"It's 3:00 in the morning," Smit wrote in his punchy noir style, "and we're looking down at a lifeless corpse. Many things are racing through our minds: Who is he? How was he killed? Who did it? I don't know why, but in almost every case my eyes are drawn to the victim's shoes. When he put them on for the last time, did he suspect it would be the last? I remember something I read long ago, about how it's the detective who stands in the dead man's shoes, to protect his interests. It's an awesome responsibility. It means becoming personally involved in the case, and with the victim; consoling relatives and friends; respecting that person's integrity, regardless of past faults or reputation, always remembering that something has been taken from him which is priceless and irreplaceable—his life.

"It also means putting into the case a part of yourself, going that extra distance and striving for everything that the courts and the law will allow. It means never forgetting that you work for the victim and that someday, as you travel through eternity, you may meet him and, when you do, he will hopefully say, 'Well done, friend.' "

CHAPTER THREE

THE CULVERT

By September 18, 1993, two years and a day since Heather Dawn Church had vanished, the case that once galvanized the entire Colorado Springs community had steadily faded from public awareness.

In the weeks immediately following the disappearance, there had been a frenzy of activity by concerned citizens. A rally in Memorial Park had been organized under the auspices of ChildSafe, a national organization championing the cause of abducted and abused children. Informational flyers had been distributed throughout the region and eventually the state, and the local press supplied a steady stream of stories to maintain awareness. Private planes and government helicopters relentlessly crisscrossed the lonesome hills of Black Forest for any sign of the missing girl.

In the interim, a raft of rumors had come and gone. It had been speculated that Heather was simply a runaway troubled by her parent's impending divorce. The adolescent had subsequently been spotted at various locales around the state, including hitchhiking along the Peyton Highway, in a phone booth on the Austin Bluffs Parkway, and at a bus stop in Aurora. Others had seen her hanging around the vicinity of a nearby elementary school or blindfolded in the back of a van. A man swore he had had a conversation with her at a local Loaf 'N Jug convenience store and that she had moved to Emerald, Texas, to get married and start a family. A claim was made that her grave could be found near the north entrance of the Air Force Academy. Frantic hunts through the four-hundred-acre Fox Run Regional Park were spurred by anonymous phone calls to the police department and the *Colorado Springs Gazette*. In both cases the callers sounded like teenage girls. In neither case did the tips amount to anything more than a cruel prank.

The sightings went nationwide, then worldwide, thanks in part to an *America's Most Wanted* posting on the widely watched program's Web site in 1994. She was seen boarding a cross-country Greyhound in Salt Lake City, where a hastily erected roadblock turned up nothing. She was working as a prostitute in Florida, attending a Pentecostal church in Oregon, receiving treatment in a California hospital. In the course of a single day, sightings would be reported in four separate states and eventually as far away as Israel.

As Halloween approached, the Sheriff's Office was inundated with claims of involvement by a satanic cult. "Yes," admitted Captain Willie Alexander, "it's something we've checked out." Assorted supernatural allegations would in fact take up an inordinate amount of police manpower. A mental patient whose doctor insisted that one of her multiple personalities was a legitimate psychic told detectives that a witch's coven had stolen the child. A fruitless afternoon was spent driving around a Briargate Boulevard subdivision until the deranged spiritualist revealed that every resident of the subdivision was a member of the coven, an assertion duly noted in the police report with the dry aside that it seemed "unrealistic and slightly out of touch with reality."

"There are some things that some people don't take seriously," Captain Alexander sighed. "We have to take it seriously. We've run down leads in all areas you can imagine. It's really bad for a family to go through."

It was the kind of understatement made all the more poignant by the prospect of the impending holidays with the aching absence of a missing child. Just before Christmas that year, Jim and Gloria Matthews—whose twelve-year-old daughter Jonelle had vanished without a trace from their Greeley, Colorado, home seven years earlier—offered their comfort and support to the Church family. Heather's mother, Diane, was becoming aware of a de facto network of parents who were suffering the same anguish, including Eileen and Michael Miller of the Denver suburb of Idaho Springs, whose daughter Beth, fourteen, had been abducted in 1983. "It's scary to think that something like this has gone on for so long," Diane Church stated pensively, while beneath her words the horrific prospect of unending years of unresolved heartache resonated. "I keep thinking it will be over soon, but then I can't imagine what they have gone through."

As time dragged on, she would slowly come to that imagining, even as Heather's classmates at Falcon Middle School composed poems in her honor and memory to mark the one-year anniversary of her disappearance. As the days turned to weeks and then to months, the phone bank at the Friends of Heather Dawn Church Foundation grew silent and the volunteers slowly went on with their lives, their numbers shrinking from over a hundred to less than fifteen before they disbanded completely. The pink ribbons that had been tied to trees in Black Forest as a sign of solidarity with the family were fast fading in the cold winter light and with them, the memory of the gawky girl with the oversized glasses.

It would be another long year before Diane and Michael Church ultimately gained a grim and mocking version of closure, and even then, it is beyond comprehension whether clinging to hope by not knowing was in any way a crueler or kinder fate than being deprived of hope by knowing, at last, the worst.

The worst came that September morning in 1993 when a hiker along a rugged stretch of road skirting the Rampart Range near the town of Cascade—not more than thirty miles from the Churches' Black Forest home—discovered the battered skull of a child at the bottom of a culvert piled with the detritus of the nearby city. There, near the rusting hulk of an abandoned car, the tragedy of Heather Dawn Church had come to its awful conclusion.

"I told them I didn't want to know any details," Michael Church would later recount of the moment the police broke the news. "I just wanted to remember her as the little girl that I knew." There was instinctive wisdom in his wish to be spared the particulars of his child's murder. Initial reports from the El Paso County Coroner's Office, identifying the skull from dental records, indicated that a blow to the head had killed Heather. Three days later, after an extensive search, the girl's jawbone was discovered eight miles further up the Rampart Range Road. Sheriff's Department personnel, meanwhile, continued to rummage through the ditchside dumpsite trying to find the rest of her body; bloodhounds eventually led them to half a dozen bone fragments scattered in the waste. The dogs also sniffed out the tattered remnants of a pair of girl's large-sized pajamas, which Diane Church told police did not belong to her daughter. All in all, in the shadows of that desolate gulch, it was impossible for anyone to tell whether the carnage had been wrought by the killer or by some other kind of wild animal.

Maybe it was better that way. Not knowing the particulars, it seemed, was a way to handle the crushing realization that there would no longer be, as Michael Church had put it a year earlier, "a ray of hope." "I pictured that phone call," he had said. "Daddy: This is Heather. Or that knock on the door." Now, instead, was the unfathomable fact that his daughter had been simply discarded like so much trash, in an act of evil utterly mystifying in its meaninglessness. "Why would someone want to hurt a child?" was the question begged by Del Stiewart, a former Drug Enforcement Agency official and director of the Friends of Heather Dawn Church Foundation, a group that reunited to share their grief at the news. "There was almost relief to know that Diane is going to be able to resolve in her mind where her daughter is," remarked volunteer and fellow church member Judy Scott. "She doesn't have to worry about her being frightened and all the other things that mothers worry about their kids."

Such wan sentiments were cold comfort for everyone who had been touched by the death. There was vague talk of starting a fund for the three surviving Church children, but those who had given so much of themselves in the first frantic days of Heather's disappearance now seemed drained of purpose and direction. Just the day before, the foundation had quietly observed the second anniversary of the event by passing out flyers. There was not much else to do; over the past three months not a single tip had come into the offices, a far cry from the days when a direct-mail card featuring Heather's face had been sent to over fifty-two million homes nationwide. Now, suddenly, with the grim discovery, those closest to the case instead found themselves preoccupied with other, imponderable realities. "We felt safe and secure in our world," mused Don Burgess, a bishop at the Black Forest Morman church, "and all of a sudden, maybe we're not as safe as we thought we were."

Four days later, Michael and Diane Church met with reporters for the first time. Amidst their sincere thanks for the support and comfort the community had provided—"Like this was their daughter," as Michael put it, "their little girl, their sister"—were other, darker intimations of resentment and rage. With the lack of any viable suspect, suspicion quickly fell on Heather's parents. Probing questions were asked about their financial difficulties and marital problems. The two would eventually submit to lie detector tests, which they both passed. "Diane and me," Heather's father continued, "I feel were prime suspects," adding, "There was a lot of feeling that I had something to do with it because I wasn't there. As a father, your role is to provide for your children and protect your children and when you're not there you feel you've let them down. All I want now is the memory of my daughter as a beautiful young child, sweet and naïve and not of this brutal world."

But the brutal world had intruded, and for Diane Church,

who had taken back her maiden name of Wilson following the divorce, its perimeters stretched in all directions, despite her best efforts to hold it at bay. "My favorite pet theory," she would later reveal, "was that someone who had lost a grandchild that looked like Heather had kidnapped her thinking they could have their family back, that she was off in a cabin someplace with some old grandma or grandpa type of person, being taken care of."

Yet, increasingly and inevitably, suspicion and doubt intruded. "I can't look at people I knew before without any type of suspicion," she confessed, recounting that from the beginning authorities had told her that whoever was responsible for the abduction was in all likelihood well known to the family. "I continue to come up with names, real friends, friends of the family. I just don't want any stone unturned."

"Am I skeptical of the people that I meet?" she would later speculate. "There's a couple of instances where I said to myself, 'I wonder if this person could have done that.' But I don't dwell on it. I try to separate myself from it. People always ask me: Who do I think it was? I wish I had some kind of idea, some kind of inspiration. But I don't."

Nor, for that matter, did the police. Even as two hundred well-wishers gathered at the Falcon Middle School Auditorium for a memorial service nine days later, it was clear that the bones unearthed at the Rampart Range dump site were not going to be the break that detectives had been hoping for. A flurry of activity had kicked into gear immediately following the find, as authorities shifted from a search for a missing child to a full-blown homicide investigation. Witnesses were reinterviewed, old leads retraced, old theories reexamined, all in light of the new evidence. But by year's end the case had once again decisively dead-ended.

Speculation rushed in to fill the void created by the lack of any real suspect or motive, creating theories that for Heather's mother amounted to no more than desperate wishful thinking.

"Right now, my favorite idea would be that it was something like an accident," she remarked in the summer of 1994. "Maybe someone stopped by, they were just horsing around, and she slipped and fell and hit her head. Maybe they panicked. Maybe they got too scared to tell the truth. It's easier than thinking that somebody had deliberately gone there to get her."

Investigators, meanwhile, were keeping the scant information they had gathered close to the chest as promising leads came and went. When questioned by detectives, a Black Forest teenager with an arrest record maintained that he had appropriated his father's truck to go four-wheeling on the night of Heather's disappearance. On further interrogation his story changed, and his friend failed a polygraph, and in the end authorities had to cross him off their list. So, too, with an acquaintance of the Church family, an old man whom Heather had claimed to a friend had fondled her and who was under investigation for a similar incident. Once again, the trail led nowhere, leaving the bereaved family and friends to weigh as best they could the rumors and gossip that continued to surface and swirl. "It was a relief to hear that the law-enforcement people believe that she died the day she disappeared, in that she didn't suffer very much," Diane Wilson would venture, inadvertently revealing a prevailing police conjecture of the chain of events.

"We have our suspicions," was the cryptic comment of District Attorney John Suthers, "but it has not narrowed down to the point we would have liked it to."

In truth, the dearth of progress on the case was becoming something of a lingering embarrassment to the local authorities. "I'm sure it's not a number-one priority any more," was the way Michael Church diplomatically put it. "I don't want to go out on a limb and say the department isn't doing what they should. Of course, as a father I want them to do more."

"I think they pretty much chased whatever leads they had," agreed his ex-wife. "I think they're kind of waiting for someone to get religion or feel guilty or something. But whoever did this got away with it and is getting away with it. That all by itself is wrong."

Wrong or not, by the summer of 1994, Heather Dawn Church had become just another name in a backlog of unsolved child murders that together stood for some unknowable darkness in the depths of the human heart. "Wondering now about the person still out there," Michael Church would observe, "they could do this again to some other dad's daughter. This person is very sick. People that do this know they're sick. I can't understand why they would want to live this way."

It would be tempting to assert that the agonizing lack of resolution hanging over the case was a factor in the ensuing shakeup of the El Paso County Sheriff's Department, which was scheduled to elect a new chief in the upcoming November elections. And while the unsolved murder never became a campaign issue, in the subsequent reforms enacted by a colorful and controversial cop named John Anderson, there was a clear recognition that Heather Dawn Church still haunted the community whose well-being Anderson had been chosen by its citizens to protect.

The election proved to be a highly charged affair, even by the rough-and-ready standards of Colorado politics, which still seemed to cherish its Wild West ethos. Anderson was a twenty-two-year veteran of the Colorado Springs Police Department, where he had served stints as a patrolman, an administrator, and an investigator with expertise in violent crime. For the previous three years he had also moonlighted as a trainer of detectives with his own business, the Criminal Investigations Institute, and was working as a sergeant on the community relations desk when he decided to throw his hat in the ring. He was prompted in part by the memory of his uncle, Red Davis, a tough-as-nails former marine who had held the post in the mid-eighties and was a personal hero of the fledgling cop.

Running against Anderson in the Republican primary was a challenger who encounter problems early on in the campaign for padding his resume, most notably claiming that he had served eight years on the Vineland, New Jersey, police department, rising to the rank of sergeant, when city records showed that he had worked only part-time for three years without a supervisory rank.

It was hardly clear sailing for Anderson, either. In July, a city councilwoman and supporter of his opponent accused him of conducting a campaign strategy session while on duty with a dozen fellow officers at the Old Heidelberg, a favorite cop haunt not far from sheriff headquarters. It was in fact the fourth complaint of misconduct filed against him since the rowdy contest had gotten underway, a point made by his Democratic challenger, who himself had a bit of an image problem, having been dismissed from the police department four years earlier for discipline problems. Meanwhile, the incumbent sheriff, on the job for a dozen years, had abruptly announced his retirement after coming under fire for making racial slurs to his employees.

With such a checkered field, Anderson, running for elective office for the first time, had the distinct advantage of being a fresh face, combined with a sterling service record highlighted by over fifty commendations from commanders, citizens, and other police departments. It also didn't hurt him with the fiercely independent electorate that his platform advocated radically easing requirements on concealed weapons permits. He sailed to victory with a two-to-one margin, thanks also in part to the endorsement of the outgoing sheriff.

The echoing tragedy of Heather Dawn Church was never mentioned in the campaign, but virtually from his first days in office Anderson, at least implicitly, seemed to acknowledge the dark specter of the unsolved crime in his announced goal to "professionalize" the department and at the same time remove some of the long-entrenched bureaucratic deadwood. The implications was clear: the sheriff's department was in dire need of some fresh investigative talent. Accused by the Democratic candidate of being part of the county's good-ole-boy law-enforcement establishment, Anderson quickly proved the contrary by dismissing his heads of Internal Affairs, Special Operations, and Support Services, eliminating in the process a pair of captain's positions. He spent the night in the county jail to observe firsthand the chronic overcrowding of the underbudgeted facility, eliciting the amused disbelief of the inmates. "If you're the sheriff," one of them crowed, "then I'm the fucking mayor!" He also garnered international attention for his concealed weapons policy, delighting journalists with his middle name, Wesley, which seemed to underscore the cowboy tradition of citizens carrying peacemakers, à la John Wesley Harding. Within weeks, the citizens of El Paso County had voiced their enthusiastic approval for the new ordinance by flocking in the thousands to obtain the quick and easy applications to tote their firearms.

"It kind of evens out the odds a little bit," Anderson observed laconically. "Sooner or later, you're running up against a victim who's armed."

But for all his swagger and studied disregard for protocol, Anderson did indeed seem to have unfinished business on his mind. Even before taking office he announced his intention to make two key changes in his executive staff. The first would be to appoint a new undersheriff, the second, a new head of investigations. It was for that position that he had already narrowed the field to one: Lou Smit.

"I remember meeting with Lou at the Old Heidelberg even before the primary got underway," Anderson recounts. "I told him that I thought I might actually have a chance of winning and if I did, I wanted him to come aboard with all the authority he needed to get things done. He told me to win the primary first and then we'd talk about it."

CHAPTER FOUR

ONE TO MANY

"I've always done basically the same job," Lou Smit avers in a 2006 interview with the authors on the subject of his involvement in the Heather Dawn Church case: "But I've done it for a lot of different bosses: the police and the sheriff's department; as a lead investigator for the district attorney; for the coroner's office; even as a sort of a designated hitter for other jurisdictions at times. They all want results, but there's a slightly different wrinkle to each approach. It's given me a lot of insight into how separate branches of the system work together . . . and don't work together."

A good part of the enormous respect Smit commands in law-enforcement circles is directly attributable to this extraordinary breadth of experience, graphically illustrated by the display in his home office, its walls festooned with framed badges collected over the course of his career from an encyclopedic array of agencies and departments. While hardly a political creature, he has nevertheless learned to navigate the often labyrinthine corridors of power and influence across a broad swath of the Colorado justice system, making influential allies along the way.

One of them was newly elected El Paso County Sheriff John Anderson. In early 1995, when he was tapped to become part of Anderson's new administration, Smit was working as a detective for the Fourth Judicial District DA, covering El Paso and nearby Teller County. "John and I were partnered together back in homicide in the Colorado Springs PD," he explains. "You could say we earned each other's respect."

Respect certainly played a part—after all, Smit had served as a de facto mentor for Anderson, who was a neophyte homicide detective when they first met—but the new sheriff had a more immediate and pragmatic purpose in mind for hiring his old colleague to the key post. "One of the first things he asked me to do," recounts Smit, "was to take another look at the Church case." It was a revealing decision, one that plainly pointed up Anderson's own well-honed populist instincts. If, as he was wagering, Smit could actually crack the case, it would go far toward delivering on the brash sheriff's campaign promises and help to quiet the rumblings in the ranks over his swift and sweeping reforms.

But public relations and departmental harmony were hardly the only reasons. "I felt I had an opportunity, sure," Anderson told the authors in the comfort of his spacious home in Colorado Springs, where, after an aborted run for Congress in 2005, he currently works for the aerospace industry as a security consultant. "I was very much aware of the impact a first impression can make. But I also had a responsibility. The Church case, even though it had been going on for four years and counting, was still very much in the public mind. There was a snippet of videotape that Heather's father had shot up at the house in happier times, and the image of that happy thirteen-year-old just being a kid must have been played hundreds of times on the local TV station, especially during the anniversaries of the disappearance. It personalized the case, brought it to life for the community, and what I wanted very much was to bring some kind of resolution and closure to the public."

It was a motivation contrary in many respects to the standard procedure of any new administration. "Usually you want to move forward," Anderson continues. "It's a new day. Whatever happened on the other guy's watch was his responsibility. But the Heather Dawn Church case was different, primarily because there had been no arrest, which meant that in all likelihood the killer was still out there among us somewhere. I was also convinced that we still had a very strong lead in that latent print on the window screen."

That conviction was based on the tried and true forensic principle Anderson describes as "comparing the known to the unknown." "As long as the owner of that print remained unknown, and as long as we couldn't satisfactorily resolve his identity, it remained to my mind a viable avenue of investigation. Of course, those prints could have belonged to anyone: a real estate agent, a family friend, a meter reader. But until we established who put them there, they could also have just as easily been Heather's murderer. It was up to us to finally make that determination.

"It was all the more compelling," Anderson continues, "since the latent prints were found at what many of us close to the case considered the point of entry. The backward screen, the out-of-place curtains—until we could establish a plausible reason for the altered condition of that window, we couldn't rule out the fact that it was how the killer had gotten in."

As certain as he may have been that the key to the case lay in these unresolved anomalies, Anderson kept his views largely to himself. "I certainly didn't make solving the Church case an issue in my campaign," he asserts. "In the first place, I would have considered it highly unethical to use such a highly charged emotional issue in any way to my advantage. Heather's parents and to a lesser degree the whole community had already suffered enough. But I'm also no fool. I wasn't about to make promises I couldn't keep. What if it was another dead-end? People were going to remember if I claimed that I could solve one of the most notorious homicides in the county's history."

At the same time, given their close and long-standing relationship, Anderson was quick to inform Lou Smit of his theories on the case and his intentions going forward. For his part, Smit wasted no time in initiating the deliberate and painstaking

process of reopening the stalled probe. "We had my inaugura-
tion ceremony," Anderson recounts, "and then I turned around
and swore in Lou. He went back home, changed into his uni-
form and was on the job that afternoon, putting together a lead
sheet on the case, taking it from the top."

Whatever urgency Anderson might have felt to break the
case, his new head of investigations would proceed with all
characteristic deliberation. "I did what I always do," the detective avows. "I studied the files, put together an index of evidence and witnesses, and started sniffing down the same trails
everyone else had been on, but maybe with a little more attention to the details and the way things might fit together this
time. I had no problem with the way the case had been handled
up to that point. I just wanted to take a crack at it myself."

It's a fine point, but one that touches directly on any cop's
reluctance to criticize the means and methods of a brother officer. "Forensics is a science that must consistently be adjusted
for new advances," is the way John Anderson puts it. "The
tools available now may not have been in existence a year ago,
much less four years ago. DNA is a perfect example. And when
these techniques do come on line, a good cop needs to go back
and reexamine his evidence from the new perspectives these
technologies afford."

At the same time, Smit's initial evaluation of the Church
murder also confirmed his patented keep-it-simple approach.
"There were all kinds of theories floating around, like that
Heather's killer had been her father. I knew as soon as I talked
to him that he was innocent. I just didn't get the vibe, and that's
a feeling I've learned to trust. As for all the rest—the satanic
cults and that kind of thing—it just obscured the basic fact that
was staring me in the face from the very beginning. This had
not started out as an abduction. No one, to my mind, travels
way out into the wilderness to kidnap a child. It was obvious to
me that what was going on here was a burglary that had turned
into something else: a crime of opportunity. The thief got into a

house that he thought was empty and found a little girl instead. What happened next was on the spur of the moment. And the best way to proceed from that premise was to treat it as a breaking and entering and see where that got us."

Applying this fundamental new approach to the mounds of evidence at hand proved to be a daunting task. There were at once too many and not enough potential clues collected on the case since its inception to discover a clear way forward: lockers full of Heather's personal possessions taken from the Black Forest home; reams of police and FBI reports; the considered opinions of dozens of cops who together had run leads on over forty suspects. All told, documents on the case filled fifteen leatherbound volumes. On the other hand, as Anderson succinctly stated, "We didn't even have the body for two years after the crime. It's difficult to solve a murder when you don't have a body."

None of this seemed to daunt Smit, who plowed through the piles of paperwork and physical evidence looking for anything that might trip that hypersensitive alarm to which, it seemed, only he was attuned.

The break, when it came, was, as expected, from far left field. "I was actually lending a hand on another case," he recounts, "involving some neighborhood kids who had gotten into minor trouble. I put in a routine request for a fingerprint check and was surprised when it came back around to me, asking what jurisdiction I wanted the query to be run in."

It's an indication of the often baffling complexity of the sprawling, multifaceted American law-enforcement enterprise that even by the late nineties there was no centralized data bank to which any cop anywhere could submit a fingerprint query for a match. What was generally known as the Automated Fingerprint Identification System (AFIS) was in fact a patchwork of regional, state, and even local law-enforcement agencies, each maintaining their own files of manually inked fingerprints, called "tenprints."

This bewildering array of overlapping AFIS services severely hobbled the effectiveness of fingerprint searches, with databases operated by everyone from the Delaware State Police to the Utah Bureau of Investigation to the Texas Department of Public Safety. Similarly, competing technologies had sprung up to meet the needs of the burgeoning science of biometrics, sophisticated systems each requiring their own technical training and expertise.

This confusing welter of conflicting networks, further hobbled by underdeveloped collection, storage, and retrieval protocols, undermined the ability of law enforcement to match an unknown print to all known prints. Critical delays regularly occurred because of the need physically to transport tenprint cards to the data collection centers. A lag time of three months between submitting a request and receiving a result was not unusual.

The situation was all the more frustrating considering the relatively straightforward methodology involved in matching prints. In most cases, a submitted print is subjected to what is called a "one-to-many" search, taking into consideration a range of arcane features from "image rotation invariance" to "independence from a reference point." Results are measured on a probability scale, the ideal being a single match, although it is not unusual to produce fifty or more matches for any given print.

Obviously, the success of any fingerprint identification search depends on the completeness of the database. In the early spring of 1994, that information was scattered far and wide. "I have to admit I was taken by surprise," confesses Smit. "I just assumed that when you send a fingerprint to get matched, it goes to some big computer in an underground bunker somewhere to be processed against every other print of every other bad guy in the world. When I was asked what jurisdiction I was interested in getting a match from, I realized how hit-and-miss the whole process actually was."

It didn't take long for Smit's thoughts to turn back to the Black Forest crime scene of the Heather Church kidnapping and murder. "I was still thinking through my burglary scenario," he continues. "What had helped to clinch it for me was the fact that the screen in the window had been dislodged from its track and that the draperies were askew. It was plain as mud that whoever did this had come up to the house for one reason, to rob it, and since there was no car in the driveway, he naturally assumed that no one was home and that the coast was clear. What he didn't bargain on was Heather. If it was about her seeing him and being a possible witness, why didn't he just kill her there? Why abduct her? I felt as if this guy's MO was slowly becoming clearer to me, that this wasn't the first time he'd broken into a house and maybe not the first time he'd killed someone. And, if he'd done it before, there was a chance at the very least that he had gotten caught at it someplace at some time. Clearly, he had gained access through the window, which was also the only place the earlier investigation had found those three unidentified prints, on that frame. I couldn't figure that out. Why hadn't there been a match? Now maybe I had an answer, or at least a chance at an answer."

Bolstering the detective's conjecture was the all-but-forgotten pair of large-sized girl's pajamas found by the bloodhounds at the Rampart Range dump site where Heather's skull had been discovered. Diane Church had said they hadn't belonged to Heather, and they had ended up in the evidence locker with the other piles of fruitless evidence. Sold and distributed by Mervyn's department store during a four-month period in 1991, the lace-trimmed sleepwear now seemed to offer an intriguing new possibility: Had the perpetrator stolen them from another home and used them to dress his victim? Had another burglary been reported in the Black Forest area in or around that time period, a theft that included a pair of girl's pajamas?

But in keeping with Smit's methodical approach, first things were first. He buttonholed Colorado Springs Police Department Laboratory Technician Tom Carney, who had originally alerted him to the plethora of AFIS databases nationwide. "I asked him how much he thought it would cost to run checks on the windowsill print through all of them. At the time there was a real budget crunch going on in the department, and I'd been instructed to watch every nickel. He estimated six to eight hundred dollars. I didn't think twice about it. I had a feeling. I gave him the go-ahead."

Carney did indeed go ahead, not stopping until he had made a hundred photocopies of the latent windowsill prints, which had always been considered remarkably distinct under the circumstances, and sent them to over ninety law-enforcement agencies nationwide as well as bureaus in Canada and Mexico for good measure. In a newspaper interview after the case broke, Carney recounted saying to himself, "If this doesn't work, that's it. We're done."

But they were in fact at the beginning of the end. On the morning of March 24, 1995, Detective Captain Lou Smit summoned three members of his staff into his office, including Mark Finley, the first officer to arrive at the Church house that fog-shrouded morning nearly three and a half years before and whom Smit had specifically requested be put back on the case. "I told them we'd gotten a match on the prints lifted from the window screen," Smit recalls. "It had come from Louisiana, a place called Coushatta in the north of the state, which had just recently gotten an AFIS link up. I told them the name that had come up on the match: Robert Charles Browne, his date of birth, October 31, 1952, Halloween, and the number under which he was listed on the FBI criminal identification files. I told them to get to work."

The next ranking officer on the team, Detective Sergeant Richard Hatch, immediately sat down at his computer terminal and ran a search on the name he'd been given through the FBI's National Criminal Information Center, as well as the Colorado

Crime Information Center. Moments later, he got a hit: Robert Charles Browne was described as a white male, 6 feet 2 inches, 180 pounds, with brown hair and hazel eyes. A native of Louisiana, he had served an eighteen-month sentence in 1986 at the state's Hunt Corrections Center for, among other things, resisting arrest.

Hatch dug further, spending long hours hunched over his computer terminal following the faint trail of Browne's criminal exploits. His next big break came when he found a California charge, also lodged in 1986, for vehicle theft. But that wasn't all. California had also issued a Fugitive From Justice warrant that had subsequently been dismissed.

With a growing sense of excitement, Hatch's next move was to log onto the Colorado Department of Revenue Web site. There he discovered that Browne had been issued a driver's license in the state, a document that included an address, listed as a 1991 homemade trailer berthed on the Eastonville Road in the Colorado Springs suburb of Elbert, adjacent to Black Forest. It was less than a mile south of the Church home. Next, connecting to the El Paso County Assessor's site, Hatch discovered that Browne and his wife, Diane, had owned the property since 1990.

As the eventful day unfolded, the feverish desktop pursuit continued apace. The Sheriff's Office Records Section revealed that Browne had been issued a speeding ticket and was listed as an "arrested party in a littering case" in which garbage illegally dumped on a Black Forest backwoods property contained a metal plate stamped "Barclay," Diane Browne's maiden name. Meanwhile, Detective Mark Finley was on the phone to the Bureau of Investigation at Louisiana State Police headquarters in Baton Rouge, where he confirmed that the photo of the prints sent to them by Tom Carney indeed matched those of Browne. Gwen Brashear, a latent fingerprint analyst in the department, assured him of that fact and that the identification had come from a tenprint made at the time of Browne's auto theft arrest, lining up precisely with his right and left index finger. To confirm her findings, she had consulted with two other analysts in the office, who promptly verified the match.

Within hours of Smit's receiving his orders, Finley and the others had gathered a wealth of information about a man who had suddenly become the prime suspect in the murder of Heather Dawn Church. From his speeding citation they found his phone number and confirmed that it was still in service when they called it and heard Browne's soft-spoken answering machine message on the other end. The next step was to gather details on a pair of vehicles registered to the couple—a 1987 Ford pickup and a 1988 two-door sedan, also a Ford.

Just before lunch, in response to an earlier telephone request, Finley received a call from the Sheriff's Office of Red River Parish, Louisiana, where Browne's hometown of Coushatta lay, half hidden in swamp water and generational poverty. On the line was Chief Deputy Warren Perkins with an impromptu background briefing on Browne.

"Everyone 'round here knows the family," he explained with a deep Dixie twang. "Lived out there at the crossroads, just where Highway 1 and 71 meet. Have for some time. Big family. Nine kids in all, I think. Got kin spread out all over the parish. Everybody knows the Brownes."

An hour and a half later, Finley got another phone call from Louisiana, this time from the parish's chief investigator, Larry Rhodes, who, like his colleague, seemed only too happy to pass a lazy afternoon on the phone with a brother officer. He knew Robert well. "He likes to smoke dope and steal," he drawled. "One time he bought himself a pickup truck, put down a fifty-dollar deposit, and took off for a test drive. Never did come back. Made it all the way to California, and they sent me out there to fetch him back. One time or another, we'd have him in here on burglary, assault, resisting arrest, you name it. Once I recall he was dating the district attorney's secretary. Women seem to go for him; don't ask me why. He'd hang around the office all day, making a nuisance of himself until the DA called me over to throw him out." He chuckled. "Son of a bitch tried to bite me that time."

Before the day's end, the newly formed task force had grown to include Detective Michele Hodges, recruited to assist with the rapidly expanding investigation. She was set to work detailing Browne's employment and residential history. A job application at a Kwik Stop on North Murray Avenue showed that he had attended high school in Coushatta and subsequently enlisted in the army, which mustered him out with a ranking of E-6. "Strange and somewhat transient in nature," was the convenience store owner's estimation of his former employee, who lived at the time in Fountain, another Colorado Springs bedroom community just south along the I-25. A Kwik Stop clerk for five months in the winter of '87, he had been fired for closing the shop fifteen minutes early.

Browne's work history bore out the transient description. From 1985 through 1987 he was self-employed in the catchall category of "general home repair." He briefly held down a route sales job at a Sibley, Louisiana, wholesale supply company distributing artificial flowers and served a stint as a night manager at a truck stop. His references listed a woman named Marcia Miank, a local resident whom he claimed to have known for a dozen years, and in the forwarding address blank on his job separation form he listed a Colorado Springs apartment, then told the store owner an entirely different address on his way out. Following up on yet a third address, this time for Diane Barclay, the building superintendent showed Hodges a postcard with a request that mail be forwarded to Glendale, Arizona.

The momentous day concluded when the entire team, including Smit, drove out to Browne's Eastonville Road digs in a requisitioned surveillance van. Hodges took photographs of the property, detailing a ramshackle mobile unit, a freestanding garage, and assorted outbuildings, all painted shades of dun and green. There was no one home.

The surveillance resumed on March 25, a Saturday, after Mark Finley had spent the morning at his desk preparing a request for a search warrant to the Eastonville Road property as well as an arrest warrant for Browne when and if the time came. The task force then returned to the forlorn trailer—perched on the west side of the road with two of its outlying sheds visible to passersby—to make a follow-up reconnaissance, cruising slowly by as Hatch videotaped its approaches and Hodges snapped more still photographs, documenting the single-wide trailer's yellow exterior and dark-brown roof, its north-to-south site and its front entry opening east. The property, according to county records, extended a considerable distance west of the road, and from the van the detectives could see dozens of pine saplings planted in neat rows around the perimeter.

On Sunday, Smit spent his day of rest mulling over what had transpired during the past two days and considering his next move. "This was shaping up to be one of the easiest cases I'd ever worked on," he recalled in his interview with the authors. "Things were happening fast, and circumstantial evidence was really starting to pile up, but in a situation where all the pieces seem to be falling into place like that, you have to be extra careful. Do the legwork, don't jump to conclusions. This case already had more than enough false leads and supposedly prime suspects, each one of which had turned out just to bring more heartache for the family. I'd met with these folks, Michael and Diane. I made it my business to get to know them. They were good people. If I was going to tell them I'd found the killer of their little girl, I wanted to be one hundred percent sure I was right. I owed it to them. We all did."

He pauses for a moment, "Of course," he finally concedes, "I had a feeling, a strong feeling, that we had our man. I wasn't going to let him slip away. We had to act soon, to get this guy off the street and bring some long overdue closure to Heather's murder. I had to weigh it all out, but by the end of that day I knew we were ready to move."

District Judge Gilbert Martinez agreed and, without hesitation, signed off on Finley's search and arrest warrants when they were put before him the following Monday. Browne was charged with first-degree murder, first-degree kidnapping, and first-degree burglary, and permission to search the mobile home, the garage and outbuildings, and both vehicles belonging to the suspect and his wife was likewise granted. The judge then ordered the documents to be sealed. The rest of the day was spent with the team reviewing the evidence, briefing additional detectives, and prepping for the search, scheduled for the next day.

On that Tuesday, a typically pristine Rocky Mountain morning, Detective Sergeant Hatch, accompanied by Detectives Ric McMorran, Tom Davis, William Claspell, and John Jones as well as a pair of evidence technicians, a photographer, and a staffer specifically designated to draw diagrams of the entire area, entered the empty premises of 16660 Eastonville Road in an unincorporated area of El Paso County to execute a search warrant pursuant to case number 91-008818. As part of search team number 1, charged with covering the south end of the property, McMorran and Davis entered the bedroom at that end of the trailer. The investigators first came upon a cardboard box on a bookshelf containing a jumble of papers, including an inspection form for the property made out to Robert and Diane Browne, confirming to the officers that they had come to the right place. The document, along with a gas station receipt made out to the same names, was seized as "indicia."

On a lower shelf of the same bookcase, Detective McMorran noted a number of videotapes, both commercially produced and homemade. He carefully noted their titles, an all-too-typical agglomeration of hit movies, self-help programs, and grainy, handheld mementos of forgotten parties and social events. Among the inventory McMorran listed were *Bambi*, *Lady and the Tramp*, *101 Dalmatians*, *Emotions Impacted by Job Change*, *Diane and Robert Browne Wedding*, and *HPS 1992*

President Club Commemorative. Hidden behind this innocuous hodgepodge were three additional videos: *Playmate Exercise, S World*, and one titled simply *Girls*, all of which were duly seized as evidence.

Next, on the bedroom floor at the north end of the house, McMorran discovered a pillowcase stuffed with clothing of a size, he later reported, "that appeared to be that of a child," as well as "a large amount of women's jewelry."

In the bedroom closet, the detective took note of two rifles, a Ruger M77 and a Zbrojovka Brno, both loaded. More videos came to light on an upper shelf: *Caddyshack, Dead Poets Society, Thornbirds, Saturday Night Fever* . . . a mundane menu of entertainment fare. There were power and hand tools scattered anomalously around the bedroom floor along with assorted audio gear, a 19-inch Sony television, and a miscellany of boxes and loose papers. "I later assisted in a cursory check of the outbuildings located on the property," McMorran noted in his subsequent written report. In what the search team had dubbed "Shed B" he found "several bundles of newspapers in the northeast corner . . . these newspapers were found to contain several articles pertaining to the disappearance of Heather Dawn Church."

In the south bedroom, Detective Tom Davis was also busy ferreting out potentially incriminating evidence, thumbing through volumes on the shelf for any hidden documents and coming across a topographic map of three surrounding counties and a book titled *Child Development I, A Systematic Empirical Theory.* "In the book," Davis would report in his narrative of the search, "were sections that were underlined indicating child development and stimulation of children."

In hindsight it is tempting, of course, to fault the detectives for zealously seeking to fit the evidence to a predetermination of Browne's guilt. It is not, after all, against the law to underline a passage in a book on child development, even if they might refer to the topic of "stimulation of children." But it is also undeniable that, as the search continued, the circumstantial discoveries became considerably more interesting. After uncovering a large cache of ammunition—boxes of 12-gauge shotgun shells, boat tail hollow points, and high-velocity rifle rounds, Davis moved on to the bedroom's bureau. "In the bottom drawer," he wrote, "were located two flesh-toned dildos, appearing to be rubber in texture, one with scrotum attached and another without scrotum attached. The items," he added without apparent irony, "were not measured and were turned over to the evidence technician."

In the back of the same drawer, Davis came across Browne's stash of video porn. "The first movie was titled *Star Cuts: Angel Kelly No. 17*, with a cover showing a black female with what appeared to be a white male behind her inserting his penis into her vaginal area." It was more of the same on a second tape, titled *Last Video: Foreign Slut,* "a full two hours long," Davis noted. Moving on to the bathroom, the detective thought enough of a framed plaque hanging on the wall to copy down its inscription: "In the Mountains We Forget to Count the Days."

In the north end of the trailer, search team number 2, comprised of Detectives Claspell and Jones, were also keeping the evidence technicians busy. The mobile's master bedroom turned up a small hatchet with a broken handle—a possible instrument of blunt force—and in a jewelry box atop a chest of drawers, two Polaroid pictures of a nude man sprawled on a bed.

Both teams would eventually converge on what was termed "Building C," described by Davis as "some form of a well or subterranean water control mechanism." There, in that shadowed and claustrophobic space, they concluded the search and departed the ransacked property, pondering the mixed results of their work.

The discoveries at the Browne residence—newspaper accounts of a notorious child disappearance, sex toys and cheap pornography—together seemed to comprise the detritus of an aimless and unremarkable life. If such mundane memorabilia could convict a man, then half of America would be behind bars. Whatever the search of 16660 Eastonville Road had achieved, it was hardly the slam dunk or the smoking gun for which the detectives had been hoping. While it was initially intended that the search would take several days, it seemed as if most of the work had already been done. Nevertheless, Detective Hatch took the precaution of posting a uniformed deputy to keep watch over the now-sealed property.

In the end, nearly a hundred items were taken from the Browne home, everything from a pair of handcuffs to a gold loop earring to computer floppy discs to *Star Cut: Angel Kelly No. 17*. What it all added up to no one except Robert Charles Browne could exactly say.

But Robert Charles Browne wasn't saying anything, least of all to sheriff's department interrogators who at that very moment were asking him all sorts of potentially compromising questions.

CHAPTER FIVE

COFFEE AND CIGARETTES

There is a mercurial quality to the firm-jawed face of Robert Charles Browne: a changeling's ability to assume an array of attributes from one moment to the next, a shape-shifting imprecision that stays stubbornly unfocused in the sum of his features.

It's a chameleon's craft magnified by his own restless alterations—serially bearded or clean-shaven, long-haired or closely cut, tousled or tidy. He looks to be, singularly and in kaleidoscopic combination, a good ole party animal and an acetic mountain man, a misanthropic loner and a gregarious next-door neighbor. He is everybody and nobody all at the same time, a guy you might like to meet or cross the street to avoid. It is part of his power, the way he gets next to people or keeps them at arm's length, projecting an image, assuming a role.

In time these powers will fade, his chiseled features growing gaunt, his wide, expressive mouth sinking into a permanent scowl, his instant charisma evaporating into the hard glint of his coffee-brown eyes. His beard will straggle and grow grey, his skin turn sallow, hanging loosely on the bones beneath. He will in short come to embody who he had been from the beginning, his nature revealed in long, lonely years of imprisonment, wrought by bad food and neon light and the constant scrape of locks and keys. It will be in some small measure a fitting punishment, this stripping away of veneers and facades, the slow ebbing of good looks and persuasive charm and palpable menace—the way he held sway. It will be as if the real Robert Charles Browne, the one who had been hiding behind all those disguises, has at last leeched to the surface, freezing into the mask of a dead-eyed killer.

Of course, hindsight is famously twenty-twenty. Whatever was reflected in the face of Robert Charles Browne may have been there, for those with eyes to see, from the very beginning. What is impossible now to separate from the imprint of his crimes is the very ubiquity of his face, passing unnoticed on the street or caught in a glint of recognition. Something about the murderer is just like the rest of us . . . only more so.

For Deputy Daniel Dilts, of the Colorado Springs Police Department, the only thing that really mattered about the face of Robert Charles Browne was that it matched the description on an arrest warrant broadcast from headquarters in an all points bulletin. On the morning of Tuesday, March 28, four days after Browne's fingerprints had first been matched to those on the window screen of the Church home, Dilts spotted the suspect during a routine patrol in the city's dilapidated downtown district. Emerging from an arts supply store at the intersection of Cucharras and Weber streets, Browne headed toward the 1988 Ford Bronco also listed in the warrant. Pulling to the curb behind the truck, Dilts detained Browne until Detectives Finley and Hodges arrived and, along with Sheriff's Captain Donald Kessler, took custody of the suspect. The matter-of-fact police report, filled out by Deputy Dilts later that afternoon, made no mention of a sociopathic gleam in Browne's eye nor any of the popularly conceived affects or intonations of a child killer, but it was difficult for the detectives, as they drove back to the sheriff's office with their handcuffed suspect in the backseat, to suppress the excited conviction that, after all this time, the Heather Dawn Church case was about to blow wide open. Dilts stayed behind to wait for the tow truck to haul away the impounded evidence and whatever new clues the Bronco might divulge.

Within an hour of his arrest, Browne faced Finley, Hodges, and a video camera in an interview room of the Sheriff's Department's Investigations Division. Finley had handed him a copy of the warrant and in a low, modulated voice advised him that he was under arrest for first-degree murder, first-degree kidnapping, and first-degree burglary, all in connection with the disappearance and death of Heather Dawn Church. His Miranda rights were duly cited, and Browne, who seemed decidedly calm, even a bit underwhelmed at the turn of events, equitably agreed to answer, "what he could," his voice softly pitched and slightly reedy with the faint tracings of a southern drawl in his elongated vowels.

Yes, he lived on the Eastonville Road and had for nearly the last five years. Of course, he knew about the Church case—who didn't? Naturally, he had often passed by the family's house on his way back to the trailer where he lived with his wife, Diane. Well, lived with her most of the time, anyway. She worked during the week in Denver at U.S. West Airlines, training flight attendants, and came back down mostly on the weekends. Browne himself owned and operated a tree nursery on the property. It was one of the reasons they'd bought the land in the first place, back in September of '90 when it was just an uncleared vacant lot. He had wanted room, he said, to grow things and was proud of the four thousand saplings he was nurturing on his nine acres.

If not exactly relaxed, Browne showed no immediate signs of realizing that life as he had lived it up to that morning had just come to an abrupt end. He was forthcoming and cooperative, to all appearances a person of interest, in the common parlance, helping the police with their inquiries. After all, he lived less than a mile from the crime scene. It was only natural that, sooner or later, they'd get around to talking to him. They'd certainly taken their time, in his opinion. Not that he could be much help. To the best of his recollection, he'd never been on the Church property. Sure, he'd been in construction once, home repair, too, but had never done anything at that particular location. He was sure of that much.

Which made it hard to explain how his fingerprints had

ended up on that windowsill, inside the house on a screen sitting backward in its sill. At that news, revealed by Finley, Browne seemed genuinely surprised. It wasn't possible. There'd been a mistake. He demanded that the cops take his prints again, right here and now, to prove the truth of what he insisted was a case of mistaken identity.

The detectives ignored the request as Finley zeroed in on the morning of Heather's disappearance. Like the suspect had said, who could forget that day? It had been cold and foggy, a socked-in mountain morning, and Browne had known right away, before he even got out of bed, that something was up, from the heavier-than-usual traffic on the Eastonville Road and the choppers circling in low over the tree line. Through the window he had seen a big orange Chevy Suburban with a Search and Rescue shield pull into his turnoff, and a moment later, he heard the doorbell ring. That was a little surprising, considering all the dogs he had around the place. Visitors mostly stayed in their cars until he came out and called off his pack. But that morning, the dogs hadn't even barked. It was chilly, and most of the lazy animals were still sleeping inside the warm trailer. The rest were probably distracted by all the excitement up the road. But he would make sure, anyway, to warn the search team, a man and a woman, about going back up into the property. Those dogs were mean. He'd trained them that way, on purpose, to protect what was his.

Browne seemed to remember the morning in question pretty well, Finley observed. What about the night before? That wasn't so clear. But if he had to guess, he'd probably just watched TV and gone to bed. "A night's a night," was how he put it, not like any particular time you would especially remember. Not like when a little girl turns up missing in the neighborhood. Maybe if he'd been asked earlier about his whereabouts on that evening, when it was fresher in his mind. . . . The detectives duly made note of the sly dig.

Browne asked for a cup of coffee and a cigarette, and Finley left the room to get them, turning over the interrogation to his partner, Michele Hodges. "So the Search and Rescue team arrived," she continued. "What happened then?" Browne shrugged. They told him a girl was missing and they wanted to see if she was hiding out somewhere on his place. He volunteered to show them around, and together they checked under the trailer and had a quick look in the outbuildings. "Kids," he remembered thinking ruefully at the time.

"You like kids, Robert?" Hodges interjected. "You relate to them?"

Brown shrugged. "I never had much experience with kids," he revealed. "I've never been around them very much. Once in a while it's nice, I guess, to talk to them, but to tell you the truth, they make me nervous. They're so hyper."

When the detectives prompted him to continue his account of the morning's events, Browne recalled that when the searchers got to the fenced-in area that led to the back acreage they stopped, a little nervous, it seemed to him, about the dogs. There was nothing out there, anyway, Browne assured them, no place to hide. And that was that. They left. He shook his head: the one and only time anyone had come over to look for the girl. It was kind of strange when he thought about it, considering all the publicity. Within days, there had been posters everywhere and her face was on TV all the time. He naturally assumed they'd come back to follow up sometime. It was becoming something of a theme for the interview—the lack of follow-though by the authorities—and Hodges couldn't help but wonder if it wasn't a ploy by the suspect to deflect their attention from him.

After about twenty minutes, Finley returned with coffee and a pack of cigarettes. "I've been smoking since I was eighteen," Browne volunteered. "Never did care for menthols." But the detectives were less interested in his tobacco preferences than in how he might explain the fingerprint match that tied him directly to the scene of the abduction and murder. Browne was adamant: he'd never been to the house; never met the Churches. What was the closest he'd gotten? Finley persisted. Browne thought a moment. There was that time a florist truck had gotten stuck in the snow, just off the main-road turnoff to the Church place. He'd come by in his Ranger pickup, a four-wheeler, and helped to tow the guy out. That was the nearest he'd ever been in proximity to the scene of the crime.

Browne paused. "I guess I'm not a very good neighbor," he continued after a moment, his voice softer now. "I didn't go out looking for the girl because I don't like getting involved in other people's stuff. I had no idea who she even was. I hardly ever saw kids around that neighborhood. The only people I had contact with was the guy living up the road whose father had sold me the place and a woman named Sandy just south of me." He smiled, a broad, open grin. "I could be a hermit," he admitted. "Easy." As quickly as it had appeared, the smile vanished. "Most of the time, it's an effort for me to deal with people at all. I've been a loner most of my life. I don't join in. That's why I love the mountains, being alone up there. If it wasn't for the cold, I could be happy all by myself."

When Finley pressed harder for an explanation of the fingerprint match, Browne bristled. He again demanded to be re-fingerprinted, this time by "someone who knows what they're doing." There was no way he could have left his prints in a place he'd never had a reason to be. "You'll have to check them again." In response, Finley reminded the forty-three-year-old that he had more than once been in places he had no reason to be.

"You mean back in Red River?" Browne retorted with a wave of his hand. He'd cleared out of the parish way back in '87, because there was "too much crap in Louisiana. It's all about small-town politics and they'll stick it to you any chance they get." They'd certainly stuck it to Browne, convicting him of burglary and what was called "unauthorized use of a movable," which was nothing more than joyriding, he insisted, "except if they catch you at it back there, it's a felony." He'd pled guilty to the burglary and had been given a suspended sentence, even though, to begin with, he never stole anything, like they'd claimed, from the International Paper Company's office where he'd worked at the time. But it was for the movable that he had served ten months on a year-and-a-half sentence, first in the county lockup and later at a state facility in Shreveport.

"Pleading guilty doesn't mean a thing," he maintained to Finley and Hodges. "If you can't fight, you plead guilty. Everyone knows that's how the system works. Normally they would have let me walk. It had been a long time since the burglary, but it was an election year and they wanted to make an example of me."

But that was all a long time ago. He had moved to Colorado Springs right after he got out of jail, back in 1987, and hadn't been in trouble since. The last time he'd even set foot in Louisiana was in early 1993 to attend his mother's funeral. "I live a very secure life now," he told them. "I'm peaceful and content. I've got hobbies, growing trees and raising dogs and ducks and reading the old classics. I like Hemingway," he offered. "Weeks go by and I never leave the property. If I get restless, I roam around in the backwoods. Sometimes I even go camping, out by Phantom Creek. I found a little spot up there." How about the Rampart Range Road? Finley asked, bringing the sometimes-rambling suspect back to the particulars, in this case the dump site where Heather Church's battered skull had been found. Had Browne ever been out that way?

Not that he could recall. They'd been going at the interview for a few hours now, without much progress to show for the effort. After Browne declined an offer of lunch, the detectives kept pushing, revisiting events on the morning of the disappearance again and listening for any discrepancy between the first and second accounts. Alternating with the relentless repetition of the same set of questions, Finley and Hodges also threw in a variety of seemingly unrelated queries, looking for a way to get behind Browne's tautly controlled demeanor and crack his stubborn insistence on his innocence.

"Says here you've been married five times, Robert," Finley remarked, looking over his Louisiana rap sheet. "Why didn't any of those wives work out for you?"

"Hot sex," Browne replied with a shrug, "and no follow-through."

"But you're happy now, right?" interjected Hodges. "Peace and contentment, like you said."

"Sure," replied Robert, suddenly cautious of this new approach. "You know, there's the regular stuff. Like anyone else. I got back problems, for instance."

"Take any medication for that?" Finley probed.

Browne shook his head. "Used to. Painkillers, but they didn't do much good."

"Anything else?" It was Hodges's turn now.

There was a barely perceptible beat before the answer, a split second of hesitation that spoke volumes to the detectives. The suspect had no idea how much they knew about who he was and how he lived, which made it imperative to tell the truth whenever he could while still avoiding the possibility of incrimination. "I have moods," he admitted at last. "And depression once in a while. Over the years I've tried different things. I talked to a psychiatrist two or three times, down on Cascade Avenue, but he just wanted to drug me up until I was mummified. I only stuck with it a few days. About a year ago I tried Prozac, but it just made me nervous. Then they gave me Ritalin for what they said was attention deficit disorder. Just made me jumpy. Of course, I can get pretty jittery and irritable even if I don't eat regularly. They call that hyperglycemia. But nothing does much good."

"Nothing at all?" Hodges wanted to know.

"I smoked weed back when I was a kid, if that's what you mean," Browne shot back. "But I don't drink, except for a beer once in a while. Other than that, I'm clean."

"Did you ever have dreams about Heather Church?" Finley's loaded question hung heavily in the stale air of the interrogation room for a long moment.

"I never really have any dreams that I can recall," Browne replied at length, but the suggestion seemed to have rattled him. "I'm the youngest kid in my family," he added, apropos of some tangential connection only he had made. "There were three sets of twins, nine of us in all."

The detectives glanced at each other, agreeing silently to let the suspect continue down any route he wanted, in hope that something unexpected might turn up. "All those twins," Hodges prompted. "They must have stuck together."

Browne nodded. "Yeah," he agreed. "There was Ronald and Donald, Ruby and Raymond, and Will and Wera."

While the advent of so many sets of twins in a single brood might lead to speculation of backwoods inbreeding and a tainted gene pool, there turned out to be no hard evidence of intermarriage or incest within the extended Browne clan. Nor, for that matter, was there a previous history of double births in the family. It was simply a remarkable fluke and one that terminated with Robert, the youngest of the siblings.

"I was an accident," he told the detectives. "That used to bother me a lot, thinking about how my parents hadn't planned for me. But I've got a different perspective on things now."

"What's that?" asked Finley. But Browne didn't seem to be listening, cast back now instead to the mixed memories of his origin and a hardscrabble life on the humid margins of Northwest Louisiana.

Named after a Native American tribe, Coushatta, his hometown in Louisiana, is the county seat of Red River Parish, a little less than four hundred square miles of heavily forested pinewoods that provide a well-dispersed population of under ten thousand with its primary means of support. The region's most important employers include Almond Brothers Lumber, B&C Wood, and Leibhardt Mills, while the parish's economic diversity, such as it is, includes the local Natchitoches Meat Pie factory, cattle ranching, and the cultivation of row crops, specifically soybeans and cotton. Small sports-fishing and duck-hunting enterprises have sprung up along the Red River and around the shores of nearby Toledo Bend, Black Lake, and Bistineau, while bass and white perch inhabit the Grand Bayou, a 2,700-acre swamp east of Highway 71 that advertises itself as "stump free."

But like the rest of the region, Red River's struggle for economic stability has never been easy. Hundreds were thrown out of work when a Sunbeam appliance plant closed, and a small company making pillows for Martha Stewart shut its doors after the good-living doyenne went to jail on insider-trading charges.

Hugging a bend in the Red River at the west end of town, Coushatta sits inside a bisecting triangle of two-lane interstates, rumbling with logging trucks and strung with dollar stores, swayback motels, clapboard Baptist and moldering Catholic churches, and a plethora of drive-in eateries serving catfish and hushpuppies along with the ubiquitous "meat-and-three"— shredded pork or chicken and a trio of steam-table veggies. Just down from the Cream Cup, a favorite hangout for students from Red River High School, Robert Browne's alma mater, an archetypal southern courthouse occupies the sun-baked town square. A little further along is the Coushatta Depot, the town's haphazardly restored railroad station, where senior citizens supplement their social security checks by selling homemade quilts for the gift shop.

Two-thirds black, with a 12 percent unemployment rate and a per capita income of less than $12,000, the surrounding Red River Parish holds proudly to its past, once a hotbed of support for celebrated demagogue Huey Long and a bastion of virulent Jim Crow segregation. As late as 2006, in fact, a parish school bus driver gained notoriety for forcing black students to take seats in the back of her bus. Coushatta itself is home to the

Louisiana National Guard's A Troop 2 of the 108th Cavalry Squadron, a unit dating back to the Civil War, when it first adopted the sobriquet "The Wild Bunch."

The colorfully corrupt chronicle of Red River politics also has a long history, bolstering Browne's contention that power in the parish was in the hands of the privileged few. "They make money by putting people in jail," he would avow, "and get paid by the state for keeping them there." It would have been a charge difficult to prove, unlike those regularly leveled at such local grandees as the Fowler family. For nearly half a century the dynasty had held the reins of the Louisiana electoral process by turning the office of Custodian of Voting Machines into a virtually hereditary post passed from father to son. Hendrix "Mutt" Fowler, the one time mayor of Coushatta, served a brief jail term for bid-rigging, while in 2000 his nephew Jerry pleaded guilty to state and federal charges of laundering kickbacks from state voting-machine vendors.

The Browne family could hardly be counted among the Red River elite, but neither were they at the bottom of the parish's steep social ladder. Robert's father, Ronald Sr., had served a stint as a deputy sheriff and had even landed a short-lived job for his youngest son as a dispatcher for the department, although Robert would admit to "not really knowing him very well."

Donald, one of the Brownes' two eldest sons, had been a Louisiana State Police officer before being shot in an off-duty incident. Confined to a wheelchair, he subsequently took a supervisory job for a regional community service program. "I didn't get along with him," Robert would assert. "In fact, I think it's because of my brother that I've never liked cops to begin with. You know, they have problems at home so they take it out on you whenever they get the chance."

The law-enforcement link may have helped to connect the Browne clan, however tenuously, to the local power brokers, as well as offsetting the familial stigma when a close relative, a nephew of Robert's named Alex, committed suicide at the age of twenty-one. But Ronald and Beulah Browne hardly had an easy time providing for their sprawling brood. They ran a dairy farm in the sixties on land originally owned by Ronald's father and subsequently foreclosed on when the family could no longer support the burden of the taxes and mortgage. After the business failed they kept food on the table with a wide range of part-time and seasonal jobs that often required the entire family to pull in harness to make ends meet. To all appearances hard-working, tightly knit, and public-spirited, the Browne family was well respected in the Coushatta community, an outward image of rectitude all too befitting the Southern Gothic contours of their private lives, especially that of Robert, the youngest and most vulnerable member of the tribe.

"Not sexual," Robert would adamantly insist when he was later asked to describe the varieties of abuse to which, he claimed, his siblings subjected him. "Never sexual," and while it is difficult to know whether his obdurate assertion was based on fact or reflexive homophobia, he was nothing if not graphically, even obsessively, candid in describing the casual cruelties that defined his childhood.

"I was physically and verbally abused by all my brothers and sisters," he would later contend, recounting an episode in which his siblings conspired to take him into the woods, strip him naked, and tie him to a tree. "They all did it," he said. "They all took their turns on me, even the ones closest to my age."

As the interview wound down in the lengthening shadows of that spring afternoon, the accumulation of Robert Browne's grievances became an oppressive fog obscuring the man and his motivations in the maudlin litany of wrongs, real and imagined. Whether guilty or innocent of crimes great or small, he had, it seemed, already exonerated himself of everything as a victim of circumstances beyond his control. The torment of his back-woods upbringing, described in vivid detail, was sufficiently dire to elicit sympathy from even the jaded detectives. But it was the use to which he put his horrific history that robbed him of the victim's status to which he stubbornly laid claim. Robert Browne nursed his grudges with elaborate care, with nothing forgotten or forgiven, no matter how far faded in time.

Years later Browne put down his earliest memories on paper in attempt to justify his vicious criminal propensity. . . . *"How old am I?"* he began. *"Three, maybe? What am I feeling? Safe, secure, warm, loved, and with a sense of belonging."* Those feelings would come to an abrupt end when his mother moved him out of his nursery room crib into his brother's bedroom. He continues, *"One of my brothers runs in and says, 'They're coming to take your bed. Hahaha!' I run and climb into my crib. I'm thinking, 'They can't take my bed. This is my place. They can't take it."*

It was an event from which seemed to stem Robert's enduring impression of the world as a cruel, cold place. *"Where am I going to sleep?"* he remembers asking himself. *"My mother takes me into a strange room. She puts me in one of the beds between two boys. As soon as she leaves the room the boys start hitting on me and telling me to get out of their bed. I start crying. This nightly ritual goes on and on. What a wonderful childhood I have. This was just the beginning of the endless joys of my childhood."*

PART TWO

CHAPTER SIX

THE LIE DETECTOR

Charlie Hess knows what murder means. Worlds removed from police blotter recaps in the Metro section, the contrived plot devices of mystery writers, or the amped-up melodramas of a thousand movies and cop shows, Hess knows that murder—real murder—has horrific and enduring consequences. The taking of a life takes something else with it: the assumption of a shared humanity, the fundamental compact of a civil society, and the essential security and stability that allow us to coexist free from fear. Whatever you want to call it, it is destroyed by murder. And Charlie Hess had learned that lesson the hard way.

Hess had, of course, often seen murder's outworkings over a law enforcement career that had spanned fifty years. Yet it wasn't merely his professional perspective, as extensive as that might have been, that had revealed so clearly the devastating ripple effects of one life taken by the hand of another. He had personal experience, a face-to-face encounter with the deep evil of homicide, all the more inexplicable for its utter randomness.

Hess's son-in-law, Steven Vought, an affable, burly, self-made family man with a streak of rugged independence, was forty years old in December 1991. After a stint in the air force, where he'd climbed to the rank of staff sergeant, the San Diego native had worked his way up in the Colorado Springs building trade from carpenter to construction superintendent for a major builder, eventually buying a home in the suburb of Peaceful Valley, just south of town. Like Black Forest, Peaceful Valley was a semirural outpost of unincorporated El Paso County, an area slated for major development as the burgeoning city continued its relentless expansion in all directions.

Vought was a skilled tradesman in a fast-growing region, and his professional prospects were accordingly bright. As a devoted husband to his high school sweetheart, Hess's youngest daughter Candice, and a conscientious father to their seventeen-year-old son, Steven Jr., so, too, were his personal prospects.

Prior to the holidays, Vought's brother Don, who lived less than a half-mile to the south along Pleasant Valley Road, had left on a vacation trip to South Dakota to visit his wife's family. He had asked Steven to keep an eye on their place for the duration, a request Vought's son, Steve Jr., had in mind when he and a pair of schoolmates cruised by his uncle's house late on Christmas Eve, a cold, crisp night beneath a bright mountain moon. As they drove past, the teenager noticed the automatic garage door closing and on arriving at his friend's house, he immediately put in a call back home. "Is Donnie back already?" he asked his father, going on to relate the suspicious activity.

Alerted to a possible break-in, Vought, instead of calling the police, jumped in his car with his wife for the five-minute trip down Sandtrap Drive to his brother's home. Pulling into the driveway, he punched in the code on the security terminal at the side of the house to open the garage door. It rolled up to reveal a strange car backed in, with its trunk wide open and full of purloined household items. As Candice watched, her husband entered the ransacked residence where he confronted a trio of seventeen-year-olds, two African-Americans—Adam Cooper and Thomas DeGraffe—and a Caucasian—William Mangham—on a spur-of-the-moment burglary run down from their turf in Widefield, a few miles further north along the I-25.

Mangham was armed and, surprised by Vought, shot him point-blank in the chest. Staggering through the front door onto the lawn, Vought held his hands over his heart and gasped, "I'm dying" before falling into his wife's arms. Two of the panicked intruders, Mangham and DeGraffe, jumped into their vehicle and peeled out of the garage, very nearly running over Candice, cradling her fatally wounded husband, and their son, who had in the meantime arrived at the scene. Left in the lurch, the third accomplice, Cooper, took off across the open fields while Steve Jr. put in a frantic 911 call.

Moments later a sheriff's patrol car came speeding down Marksheffel Road, where the deputy noticed a figure in tattered clothes hurrying down the street. It was a breathless Adam Cooper, who had just disentangled himself from a barbwire fence at the far end of a patch of stubbled pasture. He told the officer he had been in an auto accident and was out looking for help. Coaxed into the back of the black-and-white, he was driven back to the murder scene. There, Candice Vought, covered in the blood of her dying husband, promptly identified him. Just as quickly, Cooper named his accessories and was taken to the Zebulon Pike Detention Center, even as a Flight For Life helicopter arrived to airlift Vought to nearby St. Francis Hospital. He was pronounced dead in the emergency room just after midnight on Christmas morning.

The Sheriff's Department moved quickly to round up Mangham and DeGraffe, informing their respective parents of the first-degree murder charges that had been filed against the pair and warning them that if the adolescents did not turn themselves in, the necessity of apprehending them on the run carried with it a palpable risk, especially considering the aggravated circumstances of the crime. By the end of the day, the two had made phone contact from Albuquerque and the next morning arrived, escorted by their parents, at the sheriff's office to surrender.

The senseless murder of Steven Vought had coincided with an alarming spike in juvenile arrests for violent crimes in the Colorado Springs area at the time, with nineteen local youths in jail on homicide charges since the spring of 1991. The problem had attracted the attention of Widefield Superintendent Gene Cosby, who had, ironically, scheduled a meeting to discuss the crisis in the auditorium of the local high school, from which all three of Vought's killers had recently dropped out. "We have a plan," Cosby plaintively insisted. "We have a proactive plan. But I think the problem stems from society."

Such hackneyed speculation was cold comfort for the Vought family. With the cheer and goodwill of the season turned to sudden and overwhelming grief, Candice, who had been Steve Vought's wife for eighteen years, could not even find the strength to contact her father with the tragic news. It was left up to sheriff's patrolman Brad Shannon to make the call on her behalf.

As the lives of those dearest to Charlie Hess were forever changed on that star-crossed Christmas Eve in 1991, so, too, was the self-contained world the retired FBI and CIA officer had painstakingly created for himself from the ruins of drinking and divorce. The time he would later call "the best years of my life" was over. What was about to begin would call up all the courage and conviction, the experience and expertise he had accumulated over the course of a remarkable life.

Charlie Hess is short and stocky, with a full head of silver hair and a close-cropped goatee, and his fine-grained features convey with great accuracy the guarded range of emotions he chooses to present to the world: a taciturnity that downplays his innate sympathies; a reticence at odds with his natural volubility; a proud self-sufficiency muted by intense loyalties and profound gratitude for unearned blessings. A squint-eyed skepticism gives the unmistakable spark of authenticity to those flashes of compassion that occasionally light his gray-green eyes. Hardheaded and softhearted, he portrays himself, in open-ended monologues that circle back on themselves or randomly branch into the rich reserves of his memory, as a no-bullshit old-timer with little patience for pomp and pretension. But he also takes a childlike pleasure in the tall tales of his extraordinary exploits: the things he's done, the people he's met, the places he's been.

Charles James Hess was born on April 21, 1927, in Cicero, Illinois, and was raised on the mean Czech, Polish, and Italian Catholic streets of Al Capone's celebrated stomping grounds. He was an only child, and it was his father who set an unwavering moral plumb line in his son's life. "My dad was straight as an arrow," Charlie avows. "Everything was either black or white. You knew what the rules were and you stayed inside them." Coming of age in the depths of the Depression also instilled in Charlie a flinty resolve: life was indeed a cut-and-dried proposition, its ambiguities best left to someone else to parse.

The Hesses eventually relocated, first to Fort Wayne, Indiana, and then to a ramshackle fishing camp his father had bought in northern Wisconsin. For the next two years Charlie would thrive in the isolated splendor of the Lake District, working as a guide for visiting fishermen up for blue gill and walleyed pike and muskellunge. When winter set in, his father taught him how to trap and skin beavers, selling the pelts to Sears and Roebuck.

Yet by his late teenage years, the defining regard for his father's authority had come up short. "He wanted me to be an electrical engineer," Hess remembers. "I wasn't interested. To tell you the truth, aside from football, I wasn't interested in much." It was the war that rescued him from his father's unbending will. Enlisting in the navy, he shipped out to the Philippines in the waning months of the conflict and returned stateside to attend Wisconsin State at Superior on the GI Bill. Earning a teaching degree, he eventually landed a job at a high school in Grand Marias, on Michigan's Upper Peninsula, teaching science and coaching football. It was in college he married a local girl named Joanne, sired two daughters, Christine and Candice, and began to feel the financial pressures of a growing family. "The fishing industry up there had been wrecked by lampreys," he remembers. "People were so hard up, they lived on a barter system, trading chickens and cabbage for goods and services."

It was in 1951 that Hess made a sudden and surprising career change. "A friend of mine joined the FBI," he continues. "He told me the Bureau was paying twice as much as I made teaching. I can't say I saw myself as a lawman. It just seemed like it might be interesting work—work I needed." A year later he became an FBI special agent, government pay grade GS10.

Hess's first posting was in San Antonio, Texas, where he moved with his family in the summer of 1952. "I enjoyed the work," he says, "even though I was pretty much confined to minor federal beefs: selective service violations, deserters, interstate car theft . . . stuff like that." More significant for Hess's future than catching draft dodgers were the scores of interviews he conducted as part of the government's effort to recruit a wave of new security personnel at the height of the Cold War.

"They sent me all over the jurisdiction," he remembers, "talking to people's maiden aunts, looking for communists in the woodpile. I learned how to establish a rapport, to get people to talk about themselves. At the same time, word had come down from Hoover that every agent was expected to cultivate as many criminal informants as possible. The old guys weren't happy about it. Informants were more trouble than they were worth. But I took to it right away. It was by far the most rewarding part of the job. I'd figured out early that these rural sheriffs who kept law and order out in the wilds of west Texas were masters of human psychology. Those good old boys knew how to deal with a person's pride and fear and foolishness. I learned more from them than I ever learned at the academy."

He would apply those lessons to his own coterie of informants—hookers and junkies and thieves from the wrong side of the San Antonio tracks. "I learned how they like to be treated," he continues, "with courtesy and without judgment, acknowledging up front that you're no better than they are. Let's face it: you're on one side of the street, they're on the other, but it's the same street."

Hess would prove extraordinarily adept at finding and developing informants, first in San Antonio, then later in Houston, El Paso and San Diego. "These people became my friends," he says. "You can't help it. You'd just kind of bleed into each other's lives. I worked with a one-armed shoplifter who used to steal Christmas presents for me, which I couldn't accept, and a hooker with a habit who helped me to bring in a couple of fugitives. There were times when I'd even help get her drugs. Not because she might give me a tip but because I was trying to help her however I could, and that included easing the pain of withdrawal. You did what it took because you got to care about these people.

"There's a lot of things I can't do," Hess continues, "but I can deal with criminals. I never tell a guy he's a liar or a murderer. No one wants to be called that. At the same time, I'm willing to depreciate myself a little. It's not about who's the toughest hombre. Believe me, some people are just wired wrong. You'd just as soon not be in the same room with them. But you can't let that get in the way. You have to make a human connection."

Over the course of his FBI career, Hess would receive numerous letters of commendation, all from Hoover himself praising his "outstanding service in the developing of confidential sources of information." He was eventually assigned as a resident agent covering nine west Texas counties. It was an idyllic interlude with a bit of cowboy color, chasing down cattle rustlers and pursuing fugitives on the run to Mexico. "One old lawman out there wouldn't even talk to me until I broke a wild mustang," he laughs. "I'd never been on a horse in my life."

Behind the scenes, however, Hess's marriage was crumbling. "It was mostly my fault," he admits. "I was doing a lot of drinking at the time. I thought I was in control because it never interfered with my work and I made sure the kids never saw me with a bottle. But my wife knew what was up." He paused before concluding, "I don't blame her for what happened. Our marriage was dead. We were both just going through the motions."

Nevertheless, by the mid-fifties Hess was very much an agent on the fast track, repeatedly, if euphemistically, singled out for his "effective liaison work." It was a skill that would garner him postings in Puerto Rico, monitoring the island's restive independence movement, and San Diego, where he became the Bureau's chief contact with the Mexican police.

Then, in 1962, his career at the Bureau came to an abrupt end when he was reassigned to New York City. "That was the last place I wanted to go," he recounts. "I liked San Diego. It was a good place to raise kids, and the weather was perfect. I was twenty miles from the border, which represented a kind of escape for me. I pleaded my case directly to Hoover, but it was New York or nothing."

Hess agonized over the decision. "I was proud of my ten years with the Bureau," he reflects, "but with all the drinking and the secrets that went along with it, I'm not sure how clear my judgment was. I was desperate and depressed in my personal life and I figured a change, any change, might help."

It didn't. After a brief and stultifying stint in city government, Hess returned, after a fashion, to law enforcement, opening his own detective agency in downtown San Diego. Slogging through four years working for defense attorneys on all types of cases, from shoplifting to murder, escape became a powerful preoccupation, and in 1966 he was offered the ultimate exit from the assorted cul-de-sacs into which he had backed himself.

"An old friend from the Bureau got in touch," he remembers. "He was working for the Agency for International Development, training new cops in Saigon as part of the ramp-up for the Vietnam War. He was pretty sure I could have a job for the asking. So I asked."

Hired in 1967 by the State Department to oversee infrastructure development in the provinces surrounding Saigon, Hess quickly came in contact with the legendary John Paul Vann, a civilian advisor to U.S. forces in Vietnam. The brilliant, bantamweight war hero's role as the first civilian ever to command U.S. combat troops would win him a posthumous Medal of Freedom. He took to Hess immediately, naming him his executive officer.

"Vann taught me some very practical lessons," Hess reflects. "We were all strangers in a strange land, trying to figure out which of these people were friends or enemies. But Vann didn't let that stop him from seeing a kind of common humanity. I think a lot of Americans in that war, out of necessity, reduced the Vietnamese to the lowest common denominator. We had a term back then: 'Doubtfuls.' That kind of summed it up. But Vann never thought that way. He saw it as part of his job to reach past all the stereotypes and make a human connection, even though the person he was trying to understand may want nothing more than to blow his head off."

It was in that influential post that Hess next came to the attention of the CIA, which recruited him for the Phoenix Program, perhaps the most infamous clandestine operation of the war.

Created to identify, isolate, and "neutralize" Viet Cong organizers operating in the south, Phoenix initially used assassination as its preferred method of persuasion. "The problem was," Hess recalls, "it didn't work very well. Killing these guys was getting us nowhere. Another would just step up to take his place, and we'd have to start all over again. What we needed instead was a way to recruit informants, which was right up my alley." Directly utilizing Hess's experience in the FBI, Phoenix took a new tack, enlisting Vietnamese draft dodgers, deserters, and petty criminals to blend in with the local population in an effort to elicit information.

"Some guy might need money to pay his gambling debts," Hess recounts, "or send his kid to school in Canada, or get himself a little farm in Thailand. Our operatives would set up a rendezvous, and I'd come out and try to close the deal. It wasn't all that different from some of the work I'd done at the Bureau." Phoenix was ultimately undermined, according to Hess, by its very counterintuitive nature. "There was nothing second-rate about the men we had working the program," he insists. "The staff of Phoenix was smart and dedicated. But most of them came from military backgrounds. They caught on to the concept that our goal was not just to kill the enemy but to turn him to our advantage. But I can't say they weren't frustrated by the reality of finding them only to let them go. Especially since we never heard from most of our potential informants again."

Not surprisingly, Hess excelled at his job. "What I loved was to get below the surface, where the down-and-dirty stuff was happening. I was a long way from home with a bunch of guys I really liked. The country was beautiful. The women were beautiful. I could have kept it up indefinitely."

But Hess's excellent adventure in Vietnam came to abrupt end just short of a year after his arrival. Contracting an exotic and debilitating tropical malaise, he was shipped home with a raging fever, his clothes soaked in sweat during the long return flight to San Diego.

After a lengthy convalescence and a tortured effort to return to family life and civilian routines, he was once more faced with the necessity of making a living. Hess eventually found work as an investigator for Federal Defenders, a large Southern California semi-government agency with a reputation for digging up mitigating, if not always reputable, evidence in cases endemic to the border region. "Pot busts," Hess remembers, "run-ins with the Border Patrol, immigration beefs—we did it all. For me, it was a way to make a living, nothing more."

After he had been treading water with Federal Defenders for two years, the company offered him the opportunity to go to polygraph school and become a licensed examiner. "I jumped at it," Hess continues. "It seemed like something I'd have a natural affinity for." It was an attraction grounded in Hess's abiding fascination with human nature. "The first thing I learned was that lie detection is as much an art as a science," he asserts, "and the results you get are only as good as the guy who administers the test. You've got to be able to read people, to get past their defenses, to make them accept the fact that you're completely impartial. And to a very real degree, you have to maintain that impartiality in your own mind. You're part of the process, and that makes you part of the result, which in turn makes all the difference in determining truth or deception."

Hess would prove to be an extraordinarily skilled polygraph examiner with an intuitive grasp of its complex blend of technology and psychology. "It's not enough to just hook someone up and start asking questions," he explains. "You have to understand human responses and how to evoke them, to bring them to a point where the truth and a lie can be traced out in black and white with a needle on graph paper. To do that, you've got to learn how to talk to people, how to establish a connection in a relatively short time. It's like making friends, ingratiating yourself, putting the subject at ease as much as possible. Yet at the same time you're collecting and processing information. The goal is to reach one of two conclusions: truth or deception. Sometimes, of course, you get an unavoidable third result: inconclusive."

Truth and falsehood and the subtle shades of conclusiveness between them quickly became Hess's stock-in-trade. Within two years of obtaining his polygraph examiner's license, he was lured away from Federal Defenders to become an instructor and partner in a lie-detection school founded by the legendary Cleve Backster, another ex-CIA operative, who recognized a natural when he saw one and made Hess a partner in his thriving San Diego–based polygraph company in 1974.

Yet as adept as Hess might have been in detecting the veracity of others, the truth of his own situation continued to evade him. As his drinking continued unabated, his marriage entered the final throes of its protracted eclipse. It all finally collapsed on an early summer morning in 1977 in a downtown San Diego saloon.

Just hours before, Hess had been released from a local hospital after the most recent and serious in a string of heart attacks that had begun in his late forties, this time requiring a quadruple bypass to keep him alive. Handing him several bottles of pills, his doctor had warned him not to mix the medication with alcohol. Taking the instructions as a multiple-choice option, Hess discarded the pills and headed to one of the seedy waterfront dives that had long made San Diego a favorite liberty port for sailors.

Hess had already had a fractious run-in with his wife, who, after nearly thirty-two years of marriage punctuated by her husband's increasingly frequent bouts of binge drinking, had finally come to the end of her rope. Alternately cajoling, weeping, and threatening, she finally underscored her demand that Charlie check himself into a detox facility by spraying him with mace.

Finding himself alone in the saloon at the ungodly hour of 6 AM, Hess stared perplexedly at the double shot of bourbon set before him on the bar. He had a problem: he knew that the drink would steady his frazzled nerves and numb the ache in his chest where the surgeon had reached deep to re-plumb his leaky valves. But his hands were shaking too violently to risk picking up the glass. The last thing he wanted was to spill a single drop of the elixir, which left him with a single expedient: to lean over and slurp the liquor up out of its glass. As he leaned forward, he happened to glance up at the mirror behind the bar. "I saw myself," he recounts. "Lapping up booze like a dog. 'What the fuck are you doing?' I asked myself, and I knew right then that I was finished with drinking. It wasn't like seeing a burning bush or anything, but just the certainty that it was finally over. I was finished. I'd hit bottom."

CHAPTER SEVEN

THE TRACES

When the call came from El Paso County Sheriff's Deputy Brad Sherman informing Charlie Hess of his son-in-law's death, the phone that rang was some six hundred miles away in the office of a rustic motel off the I-15 in Cedar City, Utah. For several years in the early nineties, Hess and his second wife, Jo—a petite, vivacious woman whose sunny disposition balanced her husband's innate reserve—had worked as an advance team for a real estate consortium investing in undervalued motel property. The job had taken them across the country half a dozen times, including a stay in Cedar City, where they had set to work reconditioning a dilapidated motor court.

"As soon as we heard, we packed up and left for Colorado Springs," Charlie remembers. "Whatever we had been doing up to that point; whatever we thought we might do next—none of it mattered anymore. We had to be there for my daughter and grandson."

It was a resolve that Hess arrived at after a decade of painstakingly rebuilding his own life, assembling the elements of serenity and selflessness with a characteristically unorthodox approach. His determination to stop drinking might have been the first step, but the path it led him down could hardly have been less conventional, taking him in time to the shores of a literal desert island.

After seeing his reflection in the barroom mirror, Hess fought off his addiction over the course of what he would call "his lost years." His fractured family life finally fell completely apart, and he moved in with his mother, resisting the solace of the bottle to ease his loneliness. Freshly sober, Hess would continue his polygraph career for the next several years and by the early eighties had set up his own shop, with clients that included the U.S. Attorney, the Border Patrol, and the IRS.

It was in 1978, after taking a job with the San Diego Police Department, that he met Jo Marino, feisty and high-spirited daughter of Sicilian immigrants, on a blind date. Hess fell hard, and with someone he cared about and who cared for him, warts and all, suddenly anything seemed possible. "In the FBI I used to go down to Mexico a lot," he remembers, "especially the Baja Peninsula, where I was a liaison with local officials. The desert was right next to the ocean and both of them were miles away from anything else. For years I'd had this crazy dream of living down there. When I met Jo, it suddenly didn't seem so crazy. It made sense . . . just pack up and head south."

For the next several years the couple pooled their resources and in 1985 piled all their strictly necessary possessions in the back of a truck and headed south for the remote village of Bahia de los Angeles on the Sea of Cortez. "I'd been close enough to dying," Charlie reveals, "to realize that I didn't want to be on my deathbed regretting all the things I'd never done. It was amazing that Jo went along with me. After all, I was playing Robinson Crusoe."

For the next seven and a half years, Charlie and Jo lived an idyllic existence in a wild desert landscape of glancing blue skies, arid scrubland, and a vivid cobalt sea. Building a rustic hideaway on the shores of a placid bay that opened onto the Canal de Ballenas—the Channel of the Whales—they started to build a fishing camp for visiting Americans, in a distinct echo of Hess's best childhood memories.

"It was the isolation I really liked the most," Hess recounts. "There was a contentment to it. We had everything we needed, and we didn't need much. Our plan was to make our bankroll last until we were old enough to get social security, then live off that. We figured we'd be down there forever."

But the money ran out before the plan came together. In early 1990, they accepted a friend's offer to become the point team for a real estate group, scouting and renovating motel property around the country. The plan this time was to make enough to return to Bahia de los Angeles for good. It was a year later, on Christmas Day, 1991, that they received word of the murder of Steven Vought and by the next day were in Colorado Springs.

It was clear from the beginning that putting back together the shards of the shattered family would be difficult, demanding, and open-ended. "I needed people around me," Candice Vought recalls in an interview with the authors. "Initially I had a lot of friends and family staying by my side day and night. But eventually people had to get on with their lives. After a while, it was down to Dad and Jo. And I still had a terrible fear of being by myself."

"We put up a steel fence around the yard," Charlie continues. "And I bought a hundred-and-fifty-pound Rottweiler named Zeppelin." He smiles. "I know that Candice was not afraid of intruders anymore. But I do know that she needed to see lights on and familiar people at the window when she came home at night. So we built a mother-in-law apartment at her place and moved in with her."

"They were really there for me," Candice says with palpable affection. "They were at every trial date, every lawyer's meeting. As much as they could, they were walking through it with me, although they also knew how to leave me alone when the time came to sort out my feelings and try to find a way forward."

"I think she did all the right things," her father asserts. "She went to classes and meetings. She talked to people and tried to deal with her emotions."

Not surprisingly, Candice remembers it differently. "One of

my biggest regrets is that I didn't get more professional counseling early enough. A Victim's Assistance staffer from the DA's office paid me a visit, but it was too quick and too soon. I had no idea what I really felt, except for this huge void. Eventually that turned into anger. I went to a half-dozen meetings of Parents of Murdered Children, just to try and find out how to deal with what Steven Jr. was going through, and they tried to help me deal with my grief. But mostly, I just stayed mad and afraid."

In the early months of 1992, it was announced that the three seventeen-year-olds charged in the death of Steven Vought would be tried as adults for first-degree murder. Their appearance before District Court Judge Richard Toth was attended by a dozen sheriff's deputies stationed in and around the courthouse as a security precaution in the high-profile case. But it wasn't until late that summer that sentencing was finally handed down: after pleading guilty to the reduced charge of burglary with aggravating circumstances, Cooper and DeGraffe each received twenty years while Mangham was handed a forty-year sentence. All would be eligible for parole.

The law had been served, but it was harder for Candice and her loved ones to put the terrible event behind them, and the consequences of the senseless crime continued to echo ominously in their lives. "I was beginning to feel a little more together," Candice says of the time shortly after the pleas had been entered. "I wasn't so afraid, or at least I knew that my fear wasn't entirely reasonable. Then one day I was shopping at a supermarket where the brother of one of my husband's murderers accosted me, shouting and swearing and threatening to get back at me for putting his brother in prison. I was terrified, and the downward spiral started all over again. After that, I had to have someone with me constantly, accompanying me everywhere."

It's hardly surprising that Candice, struggling with her own overwhelming sorrow, did not have the wherewithal to appreciate fully what her son was going through. She nevertheless feels guilty to this day that she made what she calls the "major mistake" of not getting Steven Jr. more help. "I thought he was doing OK," she explains. "What I had no way of realizing was the depth of guilt that he felt about being the one who had, however inadvertently, put his father in harm's way. No matter how much we assured him that he was in no way to blame, no matter how much my dad told him that it had been Steven's choice alone to go over to the house that night, I don't think he ever really fully accepted it."

The teenager would in fact make a complete break from his family. "He got involved with a girl who had some problems," Charlie picks up. "I think he was trying to fix her to compensate for what had happened to his family, but whatever it was, it drove him far away from all of us for a long time. Which didn't make things any easier."

Eventually, however, Candice slowly began to emerge from the protective cocoon she had wrapped around herself. "I got to the point where I needed to do something more positive to change the dynamic," she says. "That's when I started volunteering to work with kids at a detention center." She pauses. "Maybe it was also a reaction to the alienation I was experiencing with my own son, but at the time it felt like the right thing to do: healing for me and a way to stop maybe just one young person from doing something stupid to ruin their lives."

By the same token, the widow was determined that the ones who *had* been stupid enough to throw away their own lives, along with the lives of others, would serve as an object lesson. "We went to every parole hearing of Steven's killers," she reveals. "Even while I was doing what I could with other troubled kids, I was testifying at every opportunity, explaining why I didn't want the murderers of my husband back on the street. I was no bleeding heart. I wanted justice to be done, as far as it could be. At the same time I knew I had to do everything I could to personally prevent this from happening to someone else's family."

For Candice, another step in restoration came with the 1994 election for El Paso County Sheriff. "I have no complaints about the way Steven's murder investigation was handled," Candice allows. "It's was just that, as I moved through the system, I made a lot of friends in law enforcement." One of them was Michele Hodges, who had been on the team of detectives assigned to the Vought case and who would later take the lead, along with Lou Smit and Mark Finley, in bringing Robert Browne to court, where he made a plea. "She became a good friend of mine," says Candice. "And when she said that it was time for a major change in the Sheriff's Department, I listened."

As a result of her determination to make a difference and at the same time somehow make sense of Steven's death, Candice would assume the role of campaign manager for dark-horse candidate John Anderson. "I'd never run a political campaign before," she admits. "Maybe it was another distraction from what I was feeling, of what was happening between me and my son, but I also had the satisfaction of knowing I'd helped to elect a good man."

Candice would eventually get remarried, moving out of state and leaving Charlie and Jo to resume a life together that up to that point had been largely put on hold. "I played racquetball to stay in shape," Hess recounts, "and did a few polygraph exams to keep my hand in. It seemed like what retirement might feel like, only I didn't feel retired. In the back of my mind, I was waiting for what would happen next. I didn't feel used up yet."

Hess was in fact struggling with a growing restlessness. "I needed to get back in the traces," he admits. "I felt like my skills were atrophying and that if I didn't start using them again, I was going to lose them. I started looking around for some way to be useful. After everything I'd been through, I figured there must be a reason that I was still hanging around."

It was in late 1998 that Charlie approached the volunteer coordinator for the El Paso County Sheriff's Department. A vital but often underappreciated mainstay of most local law-enforcement organizations, volunteers have long performed a surprising array of services for overworked and underfunded departments across the country, taking up such posts as clerical workers, jail chaplains, posse deputies, firing-range assistants, search-and-rescue workers, and wildland firefighters. Volunteers escort kids to prisons on "scared straight" visits and even work as reserve officers, taking academy training and buying their own uniforms and equipment, all without compensation. In El Paso County alone, volunteers would log almost fifty thousand hours, in the process saving a total of nearly a million dollars for the Sheriff's Department, in the year 2000 alone.

"I knew I could be useful," Hess asserts. "But I wanted them to take me on because I could pull my weight, not because they were doing me a favor. I knew a lot of people in law enforcement." He chuckles dryly. "Hell, some of my best friends are cops. My daughter had run John Anderson's election campaign. But none of that mattered unless I had something to offer."

As it turned out, Charlie didn't get the chance to prove himself, at least not right away. "Shortly after I went to see the volunteer coordinator, I had another heart attack, followed by another round of open-heart surgery," he relates. "I wasn't much good to anyone for a while and didn't really follow up after that first visit. It wasn't until 2001 that I was finally back on my feet and ready to pick up where I had left off. My itch hadn't really gone away. In fact, it came back stronger than ever."

Early that same year, Hess returned to the sheriff's office with another offer to volunteer. "The lady there was very nice and suggested all sorts of different options," Hess recounts. "I told her I was only really interested in one thing: investigations. I think that stumped her a little bit. She gave me a blank look, and I figured, well, that's that. I went home and a few hours later, got a call from Brad Shannon."

It was the same Brad Shannon who, almost ten years previously, had made the telephone call to tell Charlie that his daughter's husband had been murdered. Since then the affable officer had become a personal friend of the family, particularly after Candice helped put his boss John Anderson in the sheriff's seat. Now the department's investigations division sergeant, Shannon was back on the phone to Hess again. "He said he'd heard I'd come in to volunteer," Charlie continues. "He asked me what I had in mind. So I told him I'd like to have a chance to look over his cold-case files to see if I couldn't come up with some fresh angles on cases that had been set aside and forgotten.

"I knew that one of the most precious commodities to a cop was time," Hess continues. "That was the one thing I had a lot of. If it took me a couple of months to read through a case, so what? It wasn't getting solved just sitting on a shelf waiting to get shipped to the archives."

For his part, Shannon immediately understood the resource Charlie was making available with his experience and expertise. "He asked me when I could start," Hess recalls. "I showed up bright and early the next morning."

As investigations commander, Shannon wasn't, however, quite prepared to give Hess full rein over the department's cold-case repository, which turned out to be a windowless, closet-sized office in the bowels of the department's downtown headquarters. "He suggested we go slow," Charlie recounts, "maybe put me on a cold case that was already being worked by a couple of detectives in their spare time. But it pretty quickly became apparent to me that nothing was going to get accomplished without being able to access what was already there. The place was in complete disarray." Hess's first task was to make some sense of the daunting piles of cardboard boxes, three-ring binders, and sheaves of unfiled paperwork that littered the tiny room. "So I started with the first file that was lying in front of me," he recalls. "I just opened it up and started reading."

As overwhelming as the task might have seemed, he quickly

developed an approach that served his purposes well. "Anyone could have come in there to alphabetize that stuff in a filing cabinet," he asserts. "But I wanted to familiarize myself with what was there." He laughs, almost proudly admitting to being utterly computer-illiterate. "This wasn't about data input," he adds. "I took notes by hand on a pad of yellow legal paper. There wasn't anything particularly scientific about my approach. When I came across information or evidence that caught my attention, I'd write it down; any scrap of information that might point to another scrap of information. I took special note of leads that didn't seem to have been followed through on. I was rebuilding these cases, one fact at a time."

With his methodology established, Hess settled down to a routine, treating his volunteer time as a real job, arriving promptly at the cramped cold-case room several mornings a week and leaving at the same time in the evening. He would take files home to study and notate over the weekend. "There was something very satisfying about it," he confides. "I wasn't out to prove anything, but at the same time these were cases that the system had more or less given up on. Justice hadn't been served. Maybe it wasn't too late."

It was at that point, in the early summer of 2001, that help arrived.

CHAPTER EIGHT

THE INTRUDER THEORY

Preceding Lou Smit through the door of the El Paso County Sheriff's Department cold-case file room was an unmatched reputation both in the public eye and among the professional elite of Colorado's law-enforcement community.

As much as for the all-but-unbroken string of cases he had solved, Smit was renowned for his incredible determination, fueled by the genuine compassion he felt for the loved ones of the victims on whose behalf he sought justice, no matter how long it might take or how much dreary police work might be involved.

He had in short taken up the mantra of the "dead man's shoes" and made it his life's credo, turning each case into an all-but-personal crusade. His vacations were often spent on road trips around the country, visiting grieving families on his own dime, praying at the graves of murder victims, or stopping off at prisons to talk to inmates who might still provide clues to the homicides he was single-mindedly seeking to solve. "He's a top-notch investigator," his former boss, Colorado Springs Police Chief James Munger, told the authors. "It's not just that he never gives up but that he really cares. I used to get letter after letter from the families of victims about his sensitivity."

Lou's spare time was often spent reading police reports or cruising time and again past the homes of the slain, hoping that at some point, some random scraps of information might come together. And with surprising frequency, they would. While perusing old files, for example, he had come across the unsolved

1982 murder of Cynthia McLuen, who had been abducted from a Colorado Springs shopping center, taken to a cemetery, and killed. Buried in the yellowing sheaves of police narratives and crime-scene reports on the case was a letter from a Florida cop seeking information on James Rhodes, a onetime Colorado resident who had killed a young woman at a mall in his jurisdiction. Alerted to the passing similarity of the two cases, Smit ran the name and, after nothing came up, took the additional step of checking traffic violation records. He got a hit—a ticket issued to Rhodes three days before McLuen's death and in the same general locale. A further probe disclosed that Rhodes and the victim had worked at the same shopping center during the period in question. With nothing else to go on, Smit flew to Florida, where he convinced the killer he had been caught and elicited a full confession.

In another case that had sat stubbornly unsolved since the early seventies, Smit had assisted in putting Park Estep, the murderer of a massage-parlor owner, behind bars, coaxing testimony from a witness who was initially so frightened of talking to him that she literally wouldn't come out of her closet. Ten years later, however, Ottis Toole, a suspect in a string of murders nationwide, also confessed to killing the same victim. Once again, Smit went to Florida, where Toole had moved, this time to examine literally thousands of job-service and blood-bank records in an attempt to place Toole in Florida instead of Colorado at the time of the murder. His search yielded a police report of a tire-slashing incident filed by Toole's mother on the day of the slaying. Without revealing the time frame, Smit asked the suspect if he recalled the episode. "Sure," Toole replied. "I was there." It was information that helped to keep Estep behind bars.

Tales were told of the intrepid detective sifting through literally hundreds of bags of garbage until he found the spent shell cases that proved yet another case, this time against a woman who had murdered her husband. According to Dave Spencer, one of his former partners, "It wasn't uncommon for Lou to interview the same witness twenty or thirty times." One of them, who finally agreed to testify after being inveigled by the indefatigable investigator, told his attorney, "Every time I turned around, I saw Lou Smit. I saw him in my sleep." A murder suspect who had fled Colorado Springs fourteen years earlier turned around on a crowded Hong Kong street to see Smit following close behind, immediately recognizable in his trademark three-piece suit with a toothpick stuck in the corner of his mouth.

Yet Smit's life consisted of more than memorable feats of inspired investigation. In 1990, five years before he rejoined his old partner John Anderson as lead investigator for the new sheriff, Smit had actually retired from law enforcement. He had resigned his job at the Colorado Springs Police Department to care for his cancer-stricken wife, Barbara, a deeply religious woman with whom he had had three daughters and a son. It was work that was more demanding in many ways than his police career. Barbara, who had played church organ since childhood, was in an agonizingly slow decline, and while he was grateful for every day he had left with her, there was a sense in which Lou's loving care of his wife was little more than a prolonged death watch. It was a measure of their mutual regard, nurtured in a marriage that had begun in 1958, that Barbara did not stand in the way when her restless and underutilized husband was given a chance to return to the work he loved. For his part, Smit's acceptance of Anderson's offer was contingent on his being able to provide Barbara with the continuing care and attention she required.

Happily back in the fray, Smit immediately confirmed the faith the reform-minded sheriff had placed in him as his right-hand man. "I think we have a couple of things going for us," Anderson would tell one reporter, shortly after taking office. "One is new technology; the other is the bulldog tenacity of Lou Smit." For his part, the veteran investigator immediately declared his intention to dust off every unsolved case lingering on the department's shelves. "I have never, never read a case where I couldn't find new leads," he avowed. He was also determined to upend the misguided policy of shifting personnel from post to post in the interest of creating multitasking career officers. Aiming to "turn out some of the best detectives in the country," he proposed keeping investigators working at the same job, polishing the same set of skills, throughout their tenures.

It was a change intended not simply to create experienced professionals but to encourage the dissemination of vital knowledge and investigative techniques from generation to generation. He cited his own early mentor, legendary Colorado Springs Deputy Police Chief Carl Petry as a prime example of an "old-school" detective who had passed on the tricks of the trade to younger officers such as Smit. Employing the same tried-and-true methods he had learned from Petry, Lou would indeed take a fresh look at the county's backlog of unsolved cases. Foremost on that list was, of course, the horrific events at Black Forest in 1991. "I'd love to see if there is anything more we can do with Heather Church," he said at the time.

But it wasn't the Church case that would earn Lou Smit a national reputation or catapult him to the forefront of one of the most controversial and protracted murder investigations in the annals of American crime. That would come with an unexpected phone call from baffled authorities anxious to solve a case that had riveted the attention of the whole country, a case that to this day remains one of the few unsolved murders in Smit's dossier and one of the most painfully emotional experiences of his professional life.

Lou had been at his post as the sheriff's captain of detectives a little more than a year when his wife's failing health once again forced him to step down. His term under Anderson had been brief but effective, with the Church investigation his most notable accomplishment. Such was his prestige that in early 1997, he was once again tapped to tackle a complex and intractable child-murder probe: this time of a six-year-old girl named JonBenet Ramsey, whose strangled and mutilated body had been discovered in the basement of her Boulder, Colorado, home on Christmas Day, 1996.

The sensational murder had immediately provoked international headlines and had drawn the obligatory media circus to the bucolic college town. Not the least of the lurid details that captured the public's attention was JonBenet's budding career as a doll-like contestant in the outlandish world of children's beauty pageants, with photos of her as the winner of the Little Miss Colorado contest, coiffed and made up like a miniature runway model, becoming shorthand for the whole bizarre milieu of the case itself. Cultural gadfly Camille Paglia would come as close as anyone to explaining the insatiable public appetite for the case, claiming that the murdered girl had become "a strange meditation device for American sentimentalists who can't let go of the pre-Freudian idea of childhood as a sexless paradise befouled by serpent adults."

"Precious, innocent little Jon Benet," wrote a gushing fan on one of the scores of Internet chat rooms devoted to the subject. "I believe that she is my angel." It was such ghoulish fixations that gave the case its creepy subtext, magnified by a rapacious press. According to Boulder Mayor Bob Greenlee, his community had been exposed to "a dimension of contemporary journalism that is quite troubling." His Honor, it seemed, had a gift for understatement.

No less compelling was the shadow of suspicion immediately cast over the little girl's parents, John and Patsy Ramsey. From almost the beginning, they were considered prime suspects, even as professional opinion was sharply divided on their culpability. On New Year's Day the couple appeared on CNN to give their account of the events a week earlier, but by that time many inside the investigation had already made up their mind. The parents were under what one official called "the umbrella of suspicion."

As the new year wore on, the glare of international attention grew exponentially brighter as various and widely reported breaks and leads ended up going nowhere. Months of rampant speculation and frustrating dead-ends had made a mockery of Boulder Police Chief Tom Koby's early assertion that JonBenet was "Not O.J. and it's not LA here in Boulder. Our guy won't walk." Despite the bluster, that seemed to be exactly what was happening. "This cannot go on forever," Mayor Greenlee plaintively stated. "There has to be an accounting for this." "My optimism is that we will have an arrest," confided another city official that summer. "But frankly I'm less confident than I was six months ago. We need some closure."

Smit would soon have the opportunity to change the internal dynamics of the case, applying his well-honed professional instincts to getting it back on the right track. It was in March 1997 that Boulder District Attorney Alexander Hunter announced that he had coaxed the detective out of retirement yet again, this time to work with prosecutors as lead investigator in what had been dubbed an expert prosecution task force. This novel formulation, modeled on O.J. Simpson's "Dream Team," was Hunter's way of drawing the best legal and forensic minds he could into the ever-widening probe, recruiting such high-profile talent as DNA expert Barry Sheck, ironically part of O.J. Simpson's storied legal crew. "We probably looked at over eighty-plus individuals," Hunter remarked on the process of picking Smit, "and found him to be very superior, with a tremendous amount of expertise. He still calls himself a street detective, but he has extraordinary talents."

He also had, from almost the first day, an extraordinarily personal connection to the murdered child and an unwavering commitment to the search for her slayer. He would eventually take to carrying a beauty pageant snapshot of the child in his wallet, calling her his "little sweetheart" and even framing another photo of the victim to hang above his home office desk as a constant reminder of whom he was working for. What in others might have seemed an unhealthy fixation was for Lou a way of maintaining focus and intensity, a constant reminder of the calling he was convinced God had given him.

After downplaying the high expectations that came with his appointment to the expert prosecution task force that spring— "I'll probably get settled in and just get busy," he remarked at the time—Smit squarely faced what had become a hopelessly snarled and compromised case, exacerbated by months of false leads and stalled momentum. It was a situation marked by a series of flashpoints in a long-simmering feud between those in the task force and the Boulder police department who had believed from almost the first day that John and Patsy Ramsey had killed their daughter, and those equally convinced that an as-yet-to-be-apprehended intruder was behind the horrendous crime. The authorities pointing the finger at the Ramseys had in fact been prepared to make an arrest as early as April, with Hunter announcing that the couple had become the focus of the investigation. It was due only to those who championed the so-called "intruder theory," most notably Lou Smit, that the search for other suspects continued. A month later, the Ramseys again made a television appearance, this time to proclaim their innocence. Hard on the release of the autopsy report that cited evidence of sexual molestation came news of an ambitious TV legal analyst, Darney Hoffman, who, claiming that lead detective Mark Beckner was "rearranging deck chairs on the Titanic," promptly sued the DA to force an indictment to be brought against the Ramseys.

The logjam seemed briefly to break in October with the announcement that a person of interest was being sought in Oceanside, a San Diego, California, suburb, where, thirty-two years earlier, the suspect had been arrested for indecent exposure. The fifty-four-year-old man had subsequently moved to Boulder and lived only a few blocks from the Ramsey house at the time of JonBenet's murder. A flurry of frenetic attention greeted the news and prompted the normally taciturn Smit to warn the public against jumping to premature conclusions. "It's a small lead and I don't know if it means anything," he cautioned. "It's nothing, really."

Running down long shots like the Oceanside sex offender was a waste of time and resources, according to the parents' accusers, and when the tenuous break turned up nothing, pressure on Lou and the handful of others who clung to the intruder theory only increased. But there was a divergence of opinion even among those who held John and Patsy accountable, with one half believing the father had done it and the other half that it was the mother. The generally poor quality of evidence-gathering that had compromised the case from the outset and now the contentious debate that divided the detectives were quickly spilling over into a vituperative public dispute.

The simple fact was that the wheels were coming off the entire case even as tabloid headlines screamed out weird theories and fresh suspects of their own: "JonBenet Killed Because She Wet the Bed!" read a typical example, while another claimed "Mom to Plead Insanity!" and still another, "O.J. Helping Dad Beat Murder Rap!" Grisly crime-scene photos were dug from the trash bin of a Boulder photo lab and sold to a newspaper. A week later, Boulder cops gave a vote of no confidence to Police Chief Koby, whose "this is no O.J." comment had come back to haunt him. By early that fall, Koby had announced his imminent retirement, the department's lead investigator had been replaced, and the FBI lab in Quantico, Virginia, had been invited to lend its expertise to an investigation mired in contradiction, controversy, and cross-purpose.

It would be almost another full year of pointless tail-chasing, behind-the-scenes bickering, and trial by headline before Smit finally threw in the towel. He had already reduced his hours of active investigation back in July, when Barbara took a turn for the worse. But it was clear even then that the lack of progress on the case and his inability to convince the Boulder police that they were after the wrong people had left him with no choice. "I had gotten to know John and Patsy," he remembers. "They were good people. They had nothing to do with the death of their daughter. But even without that personal conviction, there was just too much evidence pointing to an intruder. It was piling up and just being ignored. I could only push so far and it became a problem to try and move the case forward and turn it in the right direction at the same time." There was another layer of complexity to the case, as well. "The first rule I learned," Lou would say, "is that you have to work just as hard to find a person innocent as to find them guilty in a murder investigation."

In September 1998, Smit wrote a two-page resignation letter to DA Alex Hunter, which, like virtually every other aspect of the case, became instant fodder for the media. "I find that I cannot in good conscience be part of the persecution of innocent people," he wrote. "It would be highly improper and unethical for me to stay when I so strongly believe this.

"What a double travesty it could be," Lou continued, hardly mincing words, "an innocent person indicted and a vicious killer on the loose to prey on another child and no one to stop him." He went on to reiterate a promise he had made to the Ramseys to honor the memory of their slain child: "I intend to stand with this family and somehow help them through this and find the killer of their daughter." Then, lest anyone get the impression that he saw himself as a lone crusader in a lost cause, he singled out his colleagues in the prosecutor's office as "some of the most honest and dedicated people I have ever met." It was not, by implication, regard he extended to the Boulder Police Department, which persisted against his best efforts to believe that the Ramseys, singly or together, were responsible for the crime. "They are just going in the wrong direction," was all he would say.

Smit had made his feelings and findings about the case clear. JonBenet's parents, he wrote, "did not do it" and further, "there is substantial and credible evidence of an intruder." The evidence, of which virtually no one had a more comprehensive grasp, convinced him not only that John and Patsy Ramsey were completely innocent but that there was "a very dangerous killer who is still out there and no one is actively looking for him." Ironically, Lou's resignation followed shortly after another investigator on the JonBenet task force called it quits, but for very different reasons. In his letter of resignation, Boulder Police Detective Steve Thomas directly accused DA Hunter of bungling the case, protecting the Ramseys by sharing evidence with the family's attorneys, ignoring evidence, and refusing to subpoena key evidence. These were charges that Hunter would quickly label as false and misleading, and yet he made no comment on Smit's letter, leaving the impression that he was perhaps heeding the veteran detective's plea to "wait and investigate this case more thoroughly."

Even as he stepped down from active involvement, Smit would continue to promote and defend the intruder theory, marshalling an enormous amount of evidence to support his contention. "It's about the little details," he asserted. "They pile up; they won't go away." Indeed, even after resigning, he continued to follow leads and develop new ones in his home office after returning to Colorado Springs, as well as working from a small bedroom in a colleague's Boulder home, where he lived in spartan conditions several days a week for more than a year and a half. Now, without official resources and support, Smit recruited his family to help wrangle the sheer volume of new information that he was gathering. The whole Smit clan helped organize and file the evidence while many nights Lou and his wife, when her cancer allowed, would sit together in their matching recliners discussing the more arcane aspects of the case. "We're all fascinated with crime stories," Barbara Smit said at the time. "We're sort of living vicariously through him."

As a result of these tireless efforts, Smit became something of a living repository of all things related to the Ramsey case, and especially the chain of circumstantial evidence that pointed to a break-in by a vicious sexual predator. Lou had painstakingly constructed a chronology of the crime, mapping out the sequence of events to underscore the conclusion that an intruder broke into the basement on that Christmas Eve to perpetrate a crime of almost unbelievable cruelty. "There were cobwebs stripped clean from a seldom-used window down in that basement," Lou recounts, "and autumn leaves on the floor. There was a suitcase with a faint imprint on it that been left in the wrong place and could have been used to help the murderer make his getaway by climbing on it back out the window. We found a palm print we couldn't identify on the door to the wine cellar where JonBenet's body was found. We also discovered a metal baseball bat outside the home, with fibers on it that matched a carpet that was in the basement." He pauses, his pale-blue eyes flashing as he spoke with the authors. "But it was that little girl's body that was really the most compelling evidence we had for an intruder. He left his marks all over her: an intricately tied garrote imbedded in the flesh of her neck, the slipknot around her wrist, the male DNA under her fingernails and on her underwear, the torn hymen. It all points to sexual torture by an experienced predator."

It was clear that by publicly stating a conviction running directly counter to the official version of the crime, Lou was not merely embarrassing the powers-that-be but also putting his professional reputation on the line. Yet if anything, the high stakes only caused him to focus more intently on fulfilling his almost sacred obligation to the dead girl. Following a ruling by a grand jury, announced in late 1999 after a thirteen-month investigation, that there was not enough evidence to indict John and Patsy Ramsey, Lou upped the ante by participating in a flurry of national media appearances and interviews, promulgating his alternative account of the event. Against the backdrop of yet another sensational story in which a California woman claimed JonBenet was killed at a sex party where asphyxiation was employed to induce orgasm, Smit's appearances on *20/20*, *Barbara Walters*, *Larry King*, and elsewhere ratcheted up the deep internal divisions in the investigation.

Among Lou's many disputed contentions was that the girl had been subdued by means of a stun gun. Appearing on NBC's *Today* during a weeklong series on the case, he provided autopsy photos that showed a distinctive pattern of rectangular red welts on the dead youngster's face and back. "Stun gun marks are very, very specific," he insisted. "Once you know what they look like, it's not hard to distinguish what they are." It was an action that irked many on the other side, including Colorado Governor Bill Owens, who had earlier taunted the Ramseys to "stop hiding behind your attorney. Stop hiding behind your PR firm." Meeting with a group of newspaper editors, he added, "My concern is what Lou has done is to publicize evidence that should have remained private until the trial." It was proof of Lou's wry estimation of his stature within the Colorado law-enforcement family: "I'm like a nail sticking out of a wood plank," he told reporters. "They'll have to pound me down."

Among those who jumped to Smit's immediate defense was former Colorado Springs District Attorney Robert Russell, who told a national television audience, "You shouldn't believe Lou Smit. You should believe the evidence Lou Smit has collected." Also lining up in solid support was his old friend and former boss, Sheriff John Anderson, whose comments to the media claiming that the Ramseys had been falsely accused and that the killer was still on the loose prompted the newly appointed Boulder Police Chief Mark Beckner to demand an apology. "I'm appalled that a police executive would be so outspoken about another agency's ongoing investigation," he fumed. Anderson shot back, "To discount Lou Smit's opinion concerning any homicide investigation is not a wise decision. He has no equal when it comes to complex crimes." The detective himself was equally blunt. "If they're saying the Ramseys did it, then charge them. Don't just infer it and add to their misery. You've got to open new doors to solve this case."

As convinced as Smit might have been by the preponderance of the evidence, there were other troubling elements that made the intruder theory far from a lock in many minds. There was the matter of a paintbrush handle, used to tighten the garrote around the girl's neck, on which paint splatters were found that matched samples in Patsy Ramsey's art supplies. Then there was the vexing question of the ransom demand. Originally found by Patsy Ramsey on a staircase step, the note asked for the odd sum of $118,000 (later said to be the approximate amount of John Ramsey's Christmas bonus that year) for the return of JonBenet, who at that moment was lying dead in the basement to be discovered by her father a few hours later. Subsequent tests revealed that both the paper and the pen used to write the inexplicable note were from the Ramsey home. Handwriting tests ruled out John, but a match to Patsy remained inconclusive, with one expert suggesting a possible match. The discovery of what seemed to be a "practice" draft of the ransom demand was also found in the home.

Like everyone else following the case, Lou struggled to make sense of these incongruous elements. He proposed the notion that the intruder had started writing an undiscovered first draft of the note, a theory that drew more than its share of derision. John Suthers, a former Colorado DA, scoffed that "he had a real hard time understanding the position Smit has come to in this case." It was "highly unlikely," he opined, that anyone would take the time to write out two drafts of a ransom demand while lingering at the scene of the crime. "Lou's great strength is looking beyond the obvious," Suthers contended. "But in some things, you can look too far beyond the obvious."

Lou stuck to his guns. "He's a high-risk criminal," the detective insisted. "In fact, some people get extreme pleasure out of going through your house and watching you even while you're sleeping." It was an explanation of the intruder's punctiliousness that stretched credibility for many, but when it came to the critical consideration of motive, no one could improve on

Smit's conjecture. "JonBenet was a pedophile's dream come true," he stated unequivocally. In an appearance on the *Today Show*, almost sixty months after the crime had been committed, the detective reasserted his long held conviction that the killer had been acting out an elaborate sexual fantasy that included bondage as one of the elements of stimulation. "I have a little room in here," Smit would subsequently tell local newspaper columnist Lou Gonzales, as he tapped his bony forehead. "It's filled with horrors, and I'm the one with the key."

CHAPTER NINE

THE APPLE DUMPLING GANG

Along with his trademark sleuthing skills, Lou Smit had another handy resource to draw on as he navigated the torturous machinations of the Ramsey case. The name of that resource was Charlie Hess.

After arriving in Colorado Springs to care for the widowed Candice, Hess had made it his business to cultivate a circle of friends from the city's law-enforcement community. "After all that time in Mexico, I realized I missed the camaraderie," he admits. "As I got to know those guys, they kept talking about Lou Smit, telling me he was the best homicide detective in the business. I was naturally curious."

It was in 1994 that their paths crossed at last, and not surprisingly, they hit it off immediately, sparring at racquetball and meeting regularly to jawbone over coffee and pastry at the Old Heidelberg. "We talked about cases," Charlie recounts. "Ones we'd worked on and ones we were still trying to solve. It was common ground." It would also be the beginning of a friendship at the heart of some of the most remarkable achievements in either man's life.

Naturally, as Smit began his long and dogged involvement in the Ramsey murder, the veterans increasingly spent time trying to unravel the complex threads of the case together. "He'd commute regularly from Boulder," Hess remembers, "dividing his time between working the case and looking after Barbara, and we'd get together when he was back in town just to kick things around. I like to think I helped him just by being a sounding board. He had theories and conjectures that he was working through all the time. Bouncing them off me gave him a chance to see how the pieces fit together—or didn't fit together. It happened both ways."

Aside from being a good listener, Hess also served as invaluable moral support as Smit tried to stay above the fray threatening to engulf every aspect of the Ramsey investigation. "Charlie understands how an old-fashioned cop thinks," explains Lou to the authors. "He asked the right questions and made the right suggestions, but what really mattered was that we became close friends in the process. We liked the way each other's minds worked, the give-and-take. I could try things out on him without having to worry about the politics or the personal egos involved in the case, with people too busy defending their turf to actually try and solve the murder. Charlie was interested in the same thing I was: finding out who did it."

Eventually Smit would see his insistence on the intruder theory at least partially vindicated. Throughout 1999 and 2000 his ad hoc work on the Ramsey investigation continued, and he was eventually called back to Boulder to brief yet another new DA undertaking a review of the dead-ended case. The emphasis this time would be on a possible intruder. Shortly thereafter, U.S. District Judge Julie Carnes concluded that Smit's much-derided theory might just be correct after all. "The weight of the evidence is more consistent with a theory that an intruder murdered JonBenet than it is with a theory that the Ramseys did it," read a key passage in her finding. But even with these new developments, it was clear that Smit's role in the infamous case was coming to a rather arbitrary close. "Speaking personally, I was never going to give up," Lou confided. "I knew that, sooner or later, we were going to catch this guy. But I guess I had outlived my usefulness in an official capacity. It was right about then that Charlie told me what he was up to."

"He just walked into the cold-case room one day," Charlie resumes, "and said he'd come to join me. I pointed to a spare desk, and he took off his jacket and got to work." Lou, who had been re–sworn in as a police officer when he joined the Ramsey prosecution team, was still technically a member of the Sheriff's Department. Not only was he familiar with most of the cases Charlie was steadfastly wading through, but he had brought with him impressive organizational skills, sharply honed over his many years as a homicide detective.

Even more significant was the fact that the duo shared a particular fascination with the challenge of reviving cold cases. "More often than not the solution to the crime has already been written down somewhere in a cold-case file," Lou told the authors. "For whatever reason—time, resources, or just simple inclination—nobody has taken the trouble to read it, process it, and draw the right conclusions. Usually it's not a matter of new information coming to light. It's about old information being properly analyzed and applied."

Smit also lent invaluable credibility in the effort to reevaluate unsolved investigations. "Cops are naturally protective of their turf," he explains. "Some guys had worked on those cold cases for years and they weren't particularly excited about us sniffing around them again. I can't say as I blame them. There was always that possibility that we might blow a case by trying to open it up again or maybe, even worse, actually solve it, which wouldn't do much for the reputations of the guys who had initially worked on it. My hope was that I could allay some of their concerns."

Brad Shannon, then a lieutenant, had made a controversial decision by bringing on Smit. "It's very rare to use reserve officers to work a cold case," Smit tells the authors, "not to mention someone like Charlie, who had no official connection to the sheriff's operation to begin with. Usually anyone who gets access to an open case, no matter how old, is subject to strict criteria, expecially when it's a murder investigation. Something about homicide fosters a lot of secrecy. The last thing you want is someone looking over your shoulder. We had to reassure a lot of officers that we weren't trying to move in on their territory. Navigating the personal and professional intricacies of the department was a big part of our job early on."

It was a job that benefited enormously from the time the pair had to review and rethink each case. "When a murder is committed," Smit told the authors, "you may have five or six detectives working on it, each taking a different aspect of the investigation: working on the crime scene, talking to the family and friends of the victim, digging into the suspect's lives. At that point everything is run through the sergeant, who becomes the only one who really knows how the whole thing fits together. Once that case goes cold and the sergeant who was in charge has moved on to something else, there's no one who still has a grasp of the big picture."

"What Lou and I did," Charlie continues, "is to look at the cases together, talk about them, turn them over in our heads. After a while we both had the same working knowledge of the facts and evidence." It was a task that amounted to arranging all the available material—narratives, interviews, photographs, and physical evidence—into a coherent form. "We created indexes," Hess recounts; "we put together meticulous time lines. We wrote summaries of all the material in the files and listed leads that needed to be pursued in order of importance. Then we standardized everything in sequential volumes, sometimes as many as twelve binders per case. The whole point was to be able to get back into the case quickly and effectively, no matter who would be picking it up after we were done. And of course, we naturally kept our eyes out for the possibility of investigating something ourselves."

For Hess and Smit, the task of bringing order to the cold-case jumble could well have occupied the remainder of each man's restless retirement. While Charlie was in the habit of calling anything with a blinking cursor a "wamma-jamma machine," Lou's computer skills were adequate to the task of in-putting the enormous amount of data the pair was busy generat-ing. It was clear the duo was going to need more help. "There wasn't a budget to hire a secretary or data clerk," Hess contin-ues. "We had a do-it-yourself approach and we were getting some results, but it was very labor-intensive."

Shannon was aware of the problem, just as he was aware of the very real possibility that given their respective résumés, the grizzled veterans might make real headway on cases that in some instances had been on the books for decades. What they needed was some able-bodied assistance, and in the summer of 2002, it arrived in the form of a soft-spoken, barrel-chested for-mer newspaper publisher with a lifelong penchant for police work.

Scion of a fifth-generation New Mexico publishing dynasty, Scott Fischer's fascination with law enforcement began at an early age. "My father published the local newspaper in Clovis," he recounts to the authors, "and at the same time was the civil-ian head of the New Mexico State Police. I'd been interested in photography since I was old enough to hold a camera, so when I got to be a teenager, my dad let me take pictures for the paper." Starting out covering local sports, Fischer quickly made himself a fixture at the paper's crime desk. "My dad, of course, knew a lot of the local cops from his work with the state, and they'd let me ride along with them on patrol." As a result, Fis-cher became the de facto police photographer for Clovis and surrounding Curry County.

It was, he recalls, fascinating work. "In a small-town envi-ronment like that, there were times when you might actually know the victim personally and have a pretty good idea who the perpetrator was. I became pretty good at doing amateur in-vestigating on my own. As time went on, the photography be-came more of a hobby as I got more and more interested in the police work."

Eventually interviewing for a job with the FBI, Fischer instead opted for a more financially rewarding career in the family's burgeoning publishing company, subsequently managing newspapers in California and Florida before coming to Colorado Springs to assume control of the local paper of record, the *Gazette*. "Newspaper publishers get to stick their noses in everybody else's business," he says with a rueful smile. "It was as close as I could get to being a real cop. I got to hear about the important cases from the inside and get the lowdown on the latest tips and leads. It was kind of a vicarious thrill, but in the meantime I was getting a continuing education in law enforcement." As a result Fischer became an accomplished amateur forensic expert of no small skill. "It was an itch I never got to scratch," is how he explains it. "So after I retired from publishing, I started volunteering to serve on sheriff's posses. In order to qualify to work with active units, I had to train as a reserve officer, but the truth was I was getting a little old for that kind of duty and the last thing I wanted was to get in anyone's way. I needed something that was more in line with my age, my experience, and my abilities."

"Brad Shannon is a good friend of mine," Fischer continues. "He asked me what I wanted to do with myself, what was it I enjoyed doing the most. I told him that the times I had worked in law enforcement, even in an unofficial capacity, were some of the happiest in my life. He said, 'Well, as long as you don't mind not getting paid, I've got the perfect job for you.' "

Shannon had been quick to realize that Fischer, whose publishing career had given him considerable computer expertise, was an apt addition to the fledgling cold-case effort he had set in motion with Hess and Smit. "We immediately clicked," recounts Fischer. "I love characters, and the minute I met those guys I knew I was in the presence of two of the greatest characters I'd ever run across. Fortunately, I was also able to add value to their work almost immediately. Lou had gone a long way in designing the template for a cold-case database. And I was able to expand on his computer model with some tweaks of my own."

With Scott on board, the trio quickly came to be known as the Apple Dumpling Gang by Colorado Springs' law-enforcement professionals, taking the sobriquet from the 1975 comedy starring Don Knotts and Tim Conway as leaders of an over-the-hill gaggle of would-be gangsters. Considering the time Hess, Smit, and Fischer spent talking over cases in the wood-paneled breakfast nook of the Old Heidelberg, they might have better been called the Sacher Torte Team, but the import was clear either way: these three old-timers had joined forces to fight crime.

As their work continued at a steady pace through the later half of 2002 and early 2003, Fischer's growing friendship with Hess and Smit began to affect some of the conclusions he had come to over a lifetime of proximity to criminal mentality. "I used to think that a cop's job was to get rid of the bad guys," he explains, "but as I started hanging around Charlie and Lou, I began to understand it was just as important to bring comfort and closure to the victims and their loved ones. We weren't judge and jury. We just tried to bring things back into balance a little bit. Charlie and Lou made me feel more compassion and less condemnation. That sense of empathy was the driving force in the work we were doing."

In the meantime, the cross-referencing evidentiary techniques the trio was developing would turn out to be an exemplar in the systemization of cold-case work nationwide, a method Smit would subsequently teach to a wide range of law-enforcement agencies. "More times than you might guess, you can close a case if you can get a good grasp on the evidence and information already collected," he asserts. "We would develop an average of twenty or thirty new leads in the process of re-ordering those files. A lot of those investigations really cried out for follow-ups."

"If you don't catch these guys, they're going to kill again," Hess concurs. "We felt an obligation to be as thoroughgoing as we could. Behind each one of those files were grieving loved ones for whom the clock wouldn't ever run out. We knew from experience that circumstances change. A reluctant witness might finally be willing to come forward. New evidence might be uncovered or new technologies applied. Even the dynamics of the case itself changes. There's always a chance for a new direction to open up when you least expect it."

The cold cases that the Apple Dumpling Gang labored over represented a grab bag of unsolved homicides that took in a wide swath of central Colorado society from both sides of the tracks. "Our policy was to treat each victim with the utmost respect," Hess contends. "For example, several of the cases involved what I call 'ladies of the night.' I use that term because to me they're not hookers or whores or even prostitutes. They're people, no matter what kind of misfortune may have befallen them in life or death. Even the fact that they may have brought it on themselves doesn't mean they don't deserve common courtesy and respect."

Of the "ladies of the night" murders to which Hess refers, most took place in the mid-eighties. "We saw a link almost immediately," he recounts. "And going through the files, we were able to pinpoint who we thought might be responsible for at least two of them. Of course, proving it was something else. Just as it's always possible that a new clue might break a case wide open, it's just as true that witnesses die and evidence gets lost and people forget."

In one of the more bizarre cases the trio took a fresh look at, a dispute over a woman had led to a hand grenade being booby-trapped in the victim's mailbox. "The guy was killed instantly," Hess remembers. "His wife was partially blinded, and a Jehovah's Witness who happened to be passing by was wounded. At one point the FBI, the Bureau of Alcohol, Tobacco, and Firearms, and the Post Office were involved in the investigation. It was another case where, by looking at the files, it was clear enough who the perpetrator was. And, by the same token, it was getting a conviction that would prove to be the real challenge. In the end, we couldn't bring charges."

Still other cold-case homicides lacked even the most rudimentary leads. "There was the John Doe whose skeleton was found in a field," Hess recalls. "White male, five feet, five inches, wearing a pair of Calvin Klein jeans. He'd been shot. That's all we knew. Also, there was a soldier on leave, killed in his car on a lonely road. There was no other evidence except the body and whatever it wants to tell you. There was the guy they found frozen in the mountains out west of town, still pretty well preserved several months after his murder. There was the lady bartender who went missing until hikers found her body by the side of a trail, wrapped in a blanket. Most of these people had been all but forgotten: their names, their lives, the fact that they'd even existed once."

It was just such case—those that seemed to defy any attempt at a solution—that began to stir a common yearning in Hess, Smit, and Fischer. As useful as their cold-case database might prove to be, it was the desire actually to break a case, an important case, on their own that increasingly consumed them.

An opportunity would finally reveal itself when one afternoon at the old Heidleberg, Charlie casually suggested the trio turn their attention to a serial killer. "You must know a likely suspect," Scott said, turning to Lou. "Yeah," Smit replied laconically. "Robert Browne." A subsequent review of the Heather Dawn Church file uncovered an enigmatic letter written by Browne almost two year earlier, in the spring of 2000. It was addressed to "Whom It May Concern" at the office of the district attorney. *"In the murky placid depths,"* it read, *"beneath the cool caressing mire, lie seven golden opportunities. Missed opportunities?"* It was signed, *"Lovingly, Robert Browne."*

PART THREE

CHAPTER TEN

"HE DID IT"

As the Apple Dumpling Gang continued their connecting and corroborating in their cramped quarters, seeking all the while for a case to call their own, Robert Charles Browne had already served eight years of a life sentence without possibility of parole for the murder of Heather Dawn Church.

With punishment that seemed only too fitting for the child killer, Browne had been virtually effaced from all human contact, subject to twenty-three-hour lockdown in the maximum-security facility of a sprawling complex of state prisons an hour south of Colorado Springs near the town of Canon City.

A community that tried hard to downplay its proximity to one of the largest penal institutions in the nation, Canon City relentlessly promoted its middling tourist attractions, including the Royal Gorge Scenic Railroad, a decrepit fossil find called Dinosaur Depot, and a local abbey with a wine-tasting tour. But it was hard to deflect attention from the hundreds of acres of grimly guarded flatlands housing six separate penitentiaries on the outskirts of the town. It was almost as difficult to gain access to the Canon City perimeter as to the North American Aerospace Defense Command, the nerve center of America's nuclear arsenal, buried under nearby Cheyenne Mountain.

It was in the bowels of the enormous hive of caged humanity at Canon City that Browne spent his days and nights alone in a six-by-eight cell, visited once a day by two guards who escorted him to the shower room and a dog-run exercise yard. It was part of a system designed to obliterate any pretense of personal power, and the marks it left on the prisoner were plain to see: wan and sallow from constant exposure to artificial light, Browne had aged twenty years in the eight he'd spent behind bars. He still had a full head of dark hair, but his beard, now stained with grey, straggled uncut down to his sternum. His haggard eyes peered expressionless from a deeply lined face, and his wide mouth turned down into a tight-lipped scowl, leaving a perpetually petulant expression. At fifty-three, he already seemed like an old man.

The investigation that had finally put him behind bars had gained traction in late March 1995 with the breakthrough match of Browne's fingerprints to those found on the Church home windowsill. It was all but wrapped up three months later, a remarkably expeditious conclusion for a case that had up to that point dragged on for the better part of four agonizing years. That achievement was due in large part to the exemplary police work of the task force Lou Smit had assembled, most notably detectives Mark Finley and Michele Hodges. It was a painstaking procedural process that had begun on the very day of his arrest, when the duo began assembling a time line of the suspect's life, scrupulous in its attention to detail and utterly relentless in bringing to light the motives and methods of a man who had deliberately obscured his true identity with an array of alter egos and ever-changing personas.

It was, of course, standard police procedure, assembling every detail of a suspect's life by strict chronology in order to determine as far as humanly possible the cause and effect, the action and reaction that would lead to murder. In Browne's case, that chain of events was both tantalizingly suggestive and frustratingly elusive. What it would most resemble in the final analysis was the rootless wandering of a petty criminal at the margins of society.

Finley's and Hodges's investigation began back in Louisiana, where Browne had graduated from high school in Coushatta before joining the army in 1969. Assigned as a legal clerk at Fort

Polk in his home state, he was eventually shipped out for active duty in Southeast Asia. It wasn't until he actually arrived in country that it was discovered he was still only seventeen and legally too young for combat. Two days later he was transferred to Korea and shortly after turning eighteen, back to Vietnam, where he remained until 1972.

The detectives next tracked Browne's frenetic effort to ground himself in the stability of marriage and family. A year after he had enlisted, he married a local Coushatta girl named Terry Hetterick, whom he subsequently abandoned and divorced after ten months together. In 1973 he met and married a Vietnamese immigrant named Tuyet Huynh with whom he had a son named Thomas. Two years later, following his Army transfer to Hamburg, Germany, he once again filed for divorce. Huynh would subsequently remarry, giving up the boy for adoption to Browne's sister Mary, while Browne himself, after an eight-month fling with Marcy Miank, a married woman he met while in Germany, would quickly run through wives three and four, both young women from Coushatta.

Browne's career path, Finley and Hodges would learn, was similarly ill-fated. Leaving the service in 1976, he gravitated back to Red River Parish, where he would remain working variously as a bricklayer, a factory worker, and, briefly, on an offshore drilling rig in 1987. It was then, after serving a ten-month sentence for auto theft, that he was paroled to Colorado Springs.

"I knew people out here," he would tell Detective Hodges by way of explanation. "My brother Ronald and Marcy, who I'd shacked up with in Germany. She had a house out in Fountain with her husband Jon. So I stayed there for a while down in their basement. I worked at a convenience store and a gas station and delivered furniture until my back started acting up and I had to quit that."

Shortly afterward he met Diane Barclay, a widow, and in September of 1988 she would become his fifth wife, offering Browne the closest thing to an actual family he'd had since giving up custody of his son, Thomas. Diane had a daughter, Carrie, from her first marriage, and the notion of stepping into the ready-made role of protector, provider, and authority figure had a powerful appeal to Browne, he told the detectives.

But almost immediately he and his teenaged stepdaughter clashed. "She couldn't live by the house rules," was his taciturn estimation of the problem. "She's a lot like me in that way. She can never say she's sorry or that she's wrong, and pretty soon it was going to be either her or me." When Carrie began dating a black kid in her senior year, Robert and Diane drew the line, and when they eventually made their move to the Black Forest property, she did not accompany them.

As Finley and Hodges continued to probe the "murky depths" of Browne's past, another team of investigators led by Detective David Reisman took on the task of establishing the suspect's means, motives, and opportunity in the murder of Heather Dawn Church. Driving to Denver shortly after Browne's arrest, they interviewed his wife in a conference room at the U.S. West Airlines offices, located just across the street from the apartment she shared with three other women during her workweek. Although shocked and deeply shaken, she initially refused to believe that her husband was capable of the heinous crime. Even after the fingerprint evidence was carefully explained to her, she steadfastly stood by her man. "He's a good guy," she insisted, "a wonderful husband. He cooks and cleans all the time. When I get home from work on Friday, he's always got dinner waiting for me and the place is spotless." In response to Reisman's queries she admitted knowing he had been in trouble but that it had been a long time ago.

"It was some sort of robbery, wasn't it?" she continued when pressed for her knowledge of Browne's criminal background. "A car or something." She paused, as if seeking a way to clarify her own confused and contradictory feelings. "I don't really know Robert all that well," she admitted at last, her voice trembling. "He kind of keeps to himself. I know he's been married before, but I don't really want to know much more about that, either. Our life together began when we first met. What happened before just isn't that important."

Distraught and distracted, she nevertheless proffered an unsolicited alibi for her husband's whereabouts on the evening of Heather Dawn Church's disappearance. "We were home together, the whole night," she contended. "We live close enough to the Church house that if something bad was happening there, I'm sure I would have heard it. And I'm sure I also would have heard if Robert left the house for any reason."

It was a long time ago, Reisman gently reminded her. Was she absolutely sure of what she was saying? Diane didn't answer, and the detective changed the subject, asking if anyone else lived with the couple on the property. Not currently, she replied, but back at the time of the Church disappearance, Robert's son, Thomas, had stayed with them for a while before moving out to live with her daughter Carrie.

"After her dad died, I guess I must have spoiled Carrie a little," Diane continued unprompted. "Robert tried to put some order back into her life." She glared at Reisman. "I know what you must be thinking. But I'm sure that Robert never did anything to Carrie. I told her that if anyone ever tried anything, you know, sexual, she needed to tell her mother."

Moving gingerly back to Diane's crucial memories of that fateful September evening, the investigator asked her if she remembered the search that had occurred on their property the following morning.

"He did it," she suddenly announced.

"Who did what?" asked the puzzled Reisman, alert now to the possibility that the agitated women might actually be implicating her husband.

As if startled by her own words, Diane hurried on to explain that she clearly remembered Robert allowing the searchers onto the property. That's all she meant, she stammered: that she had been there and had seen Browne cooperating fully.

Reisman did a quick mental replay of the chronology of the case. The search had taken place on a Wednesday morning, he reminded her. How was it possible that Diane, who spent her workweek in Denver, could have been present when the searchers arrived?

She looked at him, flustered and increasingly unnerved, although in the moment the detective chalked up her inconsistent recall to the passage of time and the shock of the situation. "Maybe I was at home that day," she admitted at last, "or maybe Robert told me about it later. I can't exactly remember."

Reisman nodded sympathetically. Of course—most people can't remember what happened four days ago, much less four years ago. It's not surprising that some details would be fuzzy. Like the fact that she and Robert had been together the entire night of the seventeenth and that he hadn't left the house; maybe that recollection, too, wasn't quite as clear as she claimed.

"It's possible," she allowed, and the detective heard the slightest note of relief in her voice, as if the question and its implications had lifted the responsibility of proving her husband's innocence. Somewhere, beyond her panic and confusion, a corner seemed to have been turned. "A lot of times he took walks in the evening, and he'd never let me come with him. Sometimes he'd even get up in the middle of the night and leave, and I'd wake up to find him gone. He liked to roam around. He was restless that way."

A long pause ensued as the weight of her response began to sink in. Reisman wait patiently. However much sympathy he felt for Diane Browne as her world began to crumble around her, there was still work to be done. He reached into his briefcase and pulled out a photograph of the tattered pajamas that had been found next to the remains of Church at the Rampart Range dump site. He slid it across to Diane and asked her, his voice calm and uninflected, if she recognized what she saw.

She immediately nodded; the blue-on-white print pattern was familiar although she couldn't exactly say from where; maybe an old pair of curtains or something else that had once been in the couple's trailer.

"Could it have been a pair of pajamas that belonged to Carrie?" Reisman asked.

Diane allowed that it could: her daughter was a petite girl, under a hundred pounds and a little over 5 feet 1 inches. "I could have held onto them," she ventured. "But I can't be sure." She looked up at him again, a helplessness growing in her eyes, and repeated, "I can't be sure."

A picture was slowly emerging, that of a wife whose trust and faith in her husband was inexorably crumbling. Aware of Diane's deepening emotional vulnerability, Reisman took the opportunity to cut to the chase.

"Is there anything we could say to Robert," he asked, "that might cause him to tell us exactly what happened the night of Heather's disappearance?"

Diane sighed as if something inside of her was slowly deflating. "I don't know of anything that would get Robert to tell the truth," she replied, her voice barely above a whisper. "He lies to me all the time."

"About what?" the detective prompted.

"Little things," she answered, her eyes cast down to the conference room table. "Mostly about money. Sometimes he can get violent when you accuse him of hiding something. It's mostly just verbal, but he can be pretty scary when it happens."

"Did he ever hit you?" asked Reisman.

"Once he pulled my hair when we were fighting," she remembered. "He'd hit the doors with his fist and shout, but it never got too bad. He'd get drunk after we'd argue, but then he'd just leave the house and sleep it off in his truck. But there was one time when we had a big fight about something he'd bought, and *I* was the one that threatened to leave." She paused as the recollections began to gather. "Little things would set him off," she continued. "He'd get very angry if he was talking and didn't think you were totally focused on him." She looked at the detective as if trying to remember the reason for getting married to this strange and unknowable man in the first place. "I had just broken off an engagement when I met him, and Robert was the first man I ever knew who wanted to have a relationship and not just sex." She paused. "But he was always very exciting to me. You know . . ." she added with a shy smile.

"Things changed for the better after a while," she continued as her blush receded. "For the past few years it's been great. Ever since he started his tree farm, he's been feeling more independent. I think that's helped a lot, even though the business isn't quite off the ground yet. He's a good man," she wanted Reisman to know. "Very giving. He'd help the neighbors out and could be friendly if he wanted to. He even went to church once in a while. You know, the Mormon temple up in Black Forest."

In point of fact, detectives would soon learn of a disturbing pattern of incidents reported by Browne's neighbors on Eastonville Road. One of them, Doreen Donnell, recounted a run-in with the suspect in 1994 when her Labrador retriever had wandered onto Robert's property and she had sent her son, Simon, to bring the dog back. It was in the woods back behind the trailer that the youngster encountered Browne, who threatened to kill the animal if he ever caught it loose on the property again. A few days later, the Lab sickened and died. A veterinarian concluded that the dog had been poisoned. It was the same fate as that of another neighbor's dog, which had mysteriously died some six months earlier, and not long after the incident, Donnell and her son returned from a tae kwan do lesson to find the back door open and a pile of freshly plucked bird feathers on the boy's bed.

It was all highly circumstantial, as was Diane's insistence that her husband was a churchgoing family man at heart. What Reisman was looking for was something more substantial. "Do you think Robert could have left the house that night and not told you about it?" he prodded, sensing a new opening in Diane's ambivalent attitude.

She shrugged. "He could have," she allowed.

The detective pressed on. "So you would say that he could have left that night and you may not have known it? Is that a fair and accurate reflection of your feelings?" It was important now, to get the statement on record.

She nodded, the last of her resistance falling away, ready now, it seemed, to imagine the worst of a man with whom she had shared her life for seven years. "Yes. It is."

Essential to building the case against Robert Browne, imagining the worst was a point to which investigators would bring potential witnesses time and again. Even as Diane Browne was slowly coming to her horrific moment of truth, Michele Hodges was delving into the deeply mixed feelings of Robert's older brother Ronald toward his sibling. Ronald's wife, Rebecca was also present at the couple's Colorado Springs apartment during the interview, insisting that her husband should stop talking to the detective, until he ordered her to leave the room.

"I love my brother," he told Hodges when they were alone. "But if he's done anything, he's responsible for his own soul." He knew, he went on, what it means to lose a child: his son Alex had committed suicide three years earlier, but if they asked him straight up if his brother was capable of killing the Church girl, well, he just couldn't say for sure.

The mere fact that Ronald would have entertained any doubts at all was of compelling interest to the detective. Was there something in Robert's past or personality that might have alerted his brother to some dangerous tendency?

"Robert kept to himself," Ronald said, which sounded like the standard evasion, as if he, too, was getting nervous about inadvertently incriminating himself. "We never do anything together. He drops by once in a while but he never talks about his personal life."

Had Ronald noticed any change in his brother's behavior? "He's been difficult his whole life," was the prompt reply. "He was on drugs a lot. Cocaine, mostly. Donald, my twin brother, tried to help him out. So did I. When he first came out here, I put him up for a while." The words flowed more easily now, as Ronald began to put the facts together for himself, their sinister connotations emerging for perhaps the first time. "But he was partying constantly. When he wasn't high, he had a real difficult time in crowds, out in the everyday world. That's why he never kept a job for long. He's like me in that way. We don't put up with people's bullshit. He was calm when he was by himself, otherwise he'd get upset and nervous, real easy. Sometimes he'd get really depressed, too, but that runs in the family—me, my sister, we all have our bouts. But when it happened to Robert, you couldn't get through to him, no matter what. Of course, it's hard to get close to him, anyway. His wife, his family—he kept himself apart. In fact, Diane came to me a couple of times, asking me for advice about divorcing Robert. She wanted to get out of the marriage but said she was afraid he might kill her if she did. I thought she was just overreacting, but . . . who knows?"

Perhaps not surprisingly, Ronald's wife, Rebecca, had no problem expressing her opinion of her brother-in-law. "I don't hold him in high esteem," she sniffed. "He's just up there living off his wife's labors and providing nothing himself." She knew what she was talking about; she was a personal friend of Diane Browne and they had worked together at U.S. West. "She's changed so much since she's been with him," Rebecca maintained. "I've seen it. She's gained a lot of weight, and they started having, you know, bedroom problems."

That was putting it mildly. "At first Robert was a very gentle and attentive lover," Diane would tell Detective Hodges in a later interview. "He was never much on foreplay, but we used all sorts of different positions and he always made sure I was satisfied. Later on he was just getting his business over with, always missionary style. Then one day, he came home with a pair of tin handcuffs and used them on me, cuffing me to the bedposts. The first time I just sort of went along with it, but the second time he got really rough and I asked him to let me go. He teased me and wouldn't unlock the cuffs for a while, just watching me squirm. When I asked if we could switch roles and let me handcuff him, he absolutely refused. Sometimes we watched porn videos together, too, and he'd make a lot of derogatory remarks about the various women. He seemed to like slender, small women with little breasts, which is pretty much the opposite of me. His attitude was that love had nothing to do with sex. Sex was just sex, plain and simple."

"I don't think he was ever too interested in her in that way, to tell you the truth," Rebecca Browne would speculate. "She's kind of the codependent type, depressed all the time and shutting out her friends. What do you expect? She's living with a man with no conscience."

In point of fact, Browne's wife would later admit to being "extremely frightened" of her mercurial husband. "He'd get very angry with me because of my personality," she explained. "He didn't like it when I cried and told me that as far as he was concerned, all women were selfish users. When I asked him if that included me, he didn't answer."

Rebecca Browne, on the other hand, had no problem providing answers. When asked if she knew of any connection between Robert and the Church murder, the response was immediate.

"He did it." She answered flatly in a weird echo of Diane's slip of the tongue. "Of course, I can't prove anything. But I have psychic abilities. I don't particularly enjoy having them, especially with something like this, but I told my husband and my mother, even back then, that I knew he had done it. You can ask them."

And while they were at it, they should ask Diane about how her husband was always sneaking off in the middle of the night. "She complained about it all the time," Rebecca Browne recalled. "How he'd just disappear, sometimes all night, without telling her where." She paused, leaning in closer across the kitchen table. "I know where he was. I get these feelings."

CHAPTER ELEVEN

MIANK

A lot of people had feelings about Robert Charles Browne—hunches and suspicions and a lingering uneasiness that seemed to be common among all his friends and family. What trailed the killer throughout his career was an unpredictable potential, the possibility always lurking beneath the placid surface that it could all turn, on a dime, into something cruel and incomprehensible. While most of those closest to him never saw what he was truly capable of, few would deny that the man carried violence in him like an electric charge. It was part of his strange charisma.

Yet what Browne kept close to himself, that potent, warping rage, couldn't stay hidden from everyone. While perhaps no one could say that they really knew him—what made him tick, what set him off—there was one who knew him better than most, the closest thing he ever had to a friend, a confidante, and a partner in crime. His name was Jon Miank.

Slow and hulking, with a heavy head and piercing blue eyes, Miank himself was well acquainted with rage and the hard-core criminal life that it fuels. His connection to Browne was forged in the same crucible of disadvantage and dereliction and disappointment, a poverty of expectation and a dire prophecy of neglect that worked itself out in reckless self-destruction. It was along this exposed nerve of resentment and retribution that Miank and Browne made common cause, recognizing kindred spirits in each other and at the same time opening a space in each other's lives to reveal what they had kept carefully hidden from the rest of the world.

As the Browne investigation continued through late March 1995, Detective Finley would in due course interview Marcia Ann Miank, a petite woman with rich auburn hair and a dry, world-weary manner whom Browne had previously identified as his girlfriend while he'd been stationed at the U.S. Army base in Hamburg, Germany. Aside from the necessity of developing as thorough a case as possible, Finley's interest in Marcy Miank extended beyond her brief liaison with the accused some twenty years earlier. She had, as it quickly became apparent, a more recent, direct, and germane connection to Browne and his activities leading up to the Heather Church murder.

Yes, Marcy confirmed in the waiting room of A Classic Clip, the downtown hair salon she owned and operated, she had first met Browne in Germany while living there with her former husband, who was also in the army. Robert and Marcy had worked together in the prop room of the base theater, helping stage amateur theatricals, and their connection was immediate and intense. The young woman, who already had two small children, would soon leave her husband to cohabit with her new boyfriend, shortly afterwards returning to Colorado Springs, where Browne joined her after his discharge. They lived together for almost a year, with Robert even adding his four-year-old son Thomas to the impromptu family, until, in the late spring of 1977, the romance faded and he returned home to Coushatta, taking the boy with him.

Aside from the occasional phone call, Marcy, who hailed from Manitou Springs, Colorado, heard nothing more from her former flame for several years. In the interim she met and married Jon Miank, another Colorado native. Miank had spent his youth on a Michigan farm until his mother divorced his father and returned west with her son and his three younger sisters to remarry, this time to a career military man.

The next time Browne would make an appearance in Marcy's life was in 1985, shortly after her nuptials with Jon. He stopped by on his way to California in a brand-new truck, freshly stolen from a Louisiana dealership, and stayed for a few months with the newlyweds before eventually relocating to the nearby 4-U Motel. It was from there that he put together money for the next leg of his trip, offloading a few pounds of marijuana with Jon's help.

Detective Finley already knew the next installment: Browne's arrest and conviction for car theft, resulting in a prison sentence. After serving his time in Louisiana, he reappeared in Colorado, showing up in the suburban hamlet of Fountain, where Marcy and Jon, along with her two now-adolescent children, had rented a home. Browne had written earlier to ask if he could stay with them in their basement apartment until he got back on his feet, and Jon, who had established a quick and lasting affinity for the ex-con during the pair's previous pot-selling escapades, even wrote corrections officials requesting that Browne be paroled directly to their household.

The connection that Jon Miank felt for Robert Browne arced directly back to a hellish personal history that had commenced at age eight, when, he claims, his stepfather began a regimen of physical and sexual abuse that would continue unabated for most of the next decade. "I didn't know how to handle it," Miank told the authors, with a kind of utter and unflappable transparency. It is that rigorous honesty that has become his primary coping mechanism for a life that regularly plunges him into an abyss of dark depression and appalling self-destruction. "One way I tried was to do everything I could to please him," Miank continued in an interview shortly after his release from prison. "Like somehow it was my fault that he was treating me like this. But that only made the feelings of shame and worthlessness worse." It's the kind of concept that recurs repeatedly in conversations with the forty-six-year-old, the result of many years of intensive, court-mandated therapy that through an almost heroic effort of renewal has taught him to change everything about himself. "I was a master manipulator," he says, as if the admission is in itself an act of healing. "That's what drew me to Robert. I learned from him. He was the closest thing I ever had to a mentor . . . a friend."

At age nine Miank broke into a neighbor's house, embarking on what would become an extensive career in burglary and larceny. "I got caught," he remembers, "and the cop gave me a big lecture, but I didn't hear a word. I was getting a thrill from busting into houses while people were asleep, stealing their wallets and jewelry and then screaming as loud as I could to wake them up before I ran off. Eventually I got into killing their pets and nailing the carcasses to the wall, just to horrify them."

Driven by obsessions he had no way of understanding, much less controlling, Miank expressed his own self-loathing by cutting and burning himself, even as drugs exacerbated his profound alienation. "I started smoking pot when I was twelve," he continues, "then pretty quick I graduated to 'ludes and valium and drinking. I moved in with my aunt and uncle for a while to get away from my stepfather, but there was no way they could control me. I was drunk all the time and when I set fire to the school, they had to put me in a juvenile facility. I stayed there almost five years."

It was the first in a revolving series of incarcerations that would in the end account for almost half of Jon Miank's life. But it was as a teenager, deflecting the sporadic and ineffectual ministrations of the social workers that surrounded him, that Miank learned to become what he calls "an expert con artist."

"I'd get high scores in group therapy for being open and honest with my feelings and all that other bullshit," he recounts. "Then, as soon as I had them believing me, I'd laugh in their face and tell them it was all a lie. They'd end up locking me in my room for four or five days at a time because they didn't know what else to do with me."

"Incorrigible" hardly goes far enough in describing Miank's implacable hostility to authority in all its forms. At twenty-one, finally released from juvenile detention and all its lame attempts to rehabilitate him, he embarked on a crime spree that would last much of the next twenty years. "The day after I got out, I broke into another house," he continues, with the same uninflected earnestness. "I got busted, jumped bail and split for Georgia. I did another burglary and an armed robbery when I got there. They caught me again and I got a ten-year sentence that time and ended up serving five." He pauses for a moment, thinking back. "In a lot of ways that was one of the best times of my life. I was young and dumb enough that I thought I could take whatever they dished out, like constantly getting thrown in the hole. I just didn't give a shit. I joined the Aryan Brotherhood, and that gave me a family and a reason to do damage to other people, blacks and Mexicans . . . whoever wasn't white like us. I got stabbed twice and tried to poison a guy with mercury. It was all a game to me."

In late 1984, Miank once again returned to the Colorado Springs area, where he met Marcy Bustin at a job where they both worked. "I pointed her out to her son, Aaron, and said she had nice tits and ass," Jon recalls. "He told me she was his mom, then passed on the supposed compliment to her, and we kind of went from there." After a whirlwind courtship, they were married in February 1985. "Marcy was eleven years older than me," Miank continues. "I've always gone after older women, I think because there's less of a chance that they'll get pregnant. The last thing I wanted was to have a kid of my own to take care of. I knew, with the kind of life I lived, I wasn't going to be the best father. It didn't seem fair. Besides, Marcy had two kids of her own, Aaron and her daughter Stephanie, who was about twelve at the time. I figured we'd have our hands full just dealing with them."

For the first year of his marriage Jon tried his best to stay out of trouble, even while his drug use continued unabated despite his new wife's adamant disapproval. "I did a few landscaping jobs," he recounts. "I went to college to take some automotive courses but eventually got kicked out for getting high. Right around that time, Robert showed up again."

He was, as Jon Miank puts it, "very rememberable." "Robert was always laid-back seeming, but very smart. He came off debonair, and was careful to keep himself well groomed. He was constantly fooling around with the way he looked, letting his hair grow and then cutting it off, experimenting with different kinds of beards and mustaches."

It was an observation backed up by Diane Browne. "He'd have his hair in a ponytail," she recalled, "with a long beard. Then, one morning he came out of the bathroom with it all cut short and completely clean-shaven. It was like he couldn't make up his mind who he was from one minute to the next."

In other arenas, however, Browne was nothing if not utterly convincing. "He really knew how to put a con together," asserts Jon Miank. "He was like a mastermind in that way. We'd do some burglaries together, and even though I've always been afraid of heights, he'd talk me into doing these second-story jobs. He was very persuasive and very systematic. He'd do jobs in a kind of radius around wherever he was living. First he'd go out and case the neighborhood, making mental notes of the stuff he wanted to steal, then come back later and knock them off, one by one. Most of them were within a mile of each other. But he also figured out that we could make money stealing from the county supply depot down on REA Road, where they stored things like tractors and plows and fence posts and barbed wire. We had a deal where we could sell as much barbed wire as we could get our hands on, at fifty bucks a roll. One day we stuffed so many of them in the car that Robert had to walk home."

It was also Robert who came up with the scheme to kill and butcher cattle on neighboring ranches to keep the family supplied with fresh meat. "I'd poached deer when I was a kid back in Michigan," Miank explains. "So I knew how to dress an animal. We'd go out and hunt around for a cow to shoot. I had a shotgun but I wasn't too accurate. Robert could drop one of them with his .22, aiming right behind the ears from a long distance. He could really handle himself with a gun. Then we'd cut it in pieces there and then drag it home. Later we'd get rid of the hide by stuffing it in a dumpster and feed the bones to the dogs. Every time we did the slaughtering, Robert would have a cup with him that he'd fill with blood and drink it. I didn't know why. I didn't care. Most of the time, I was too high to care."

It was a condition for which Miank also had Browne largely to thank. "When he came out he brought five kilos of cocaine and fifteen pounds of pot with him. The coke was very pure and the pot was mostly bud tips. He wanted me to sell it for him, but he also wanted me to know who was in charge. He told me that he'd killed two dealers in Louisiana to get the stash. The implication was that I shouldn't be trying to cheat him."

With such a substantial cache of cocaine on hand, Miank was quickly and completely addicted, dealing from Browne's ample drug supply simply to maintain his own voracious habit. "Coke was it for me," he declares. "There was nothing else that even came close. Later, I'd try crystal meth and crack, but I'd never get to where I could go by mainlining cocaine. It was Robert who shot me up the first couple of times until I got the hang of it myself, then we'd go out together and tie off out on the Rampart Range or Gold Camp Road or in the parking lot of the Loaf 'N Jug or the Nazarene Bible College; anywhere but home, just because we didn't want Marcy to find out. It was bad enough that I started stealing from her, then pretty soon stealing from where she worked. But even with all that, I couldn't keep up and I got in pretty deep in debt with Robert. I thought of him like a brother, but the truth was, he treated me

141

like a slave, always ordering me around, out to get beers or needles or to do some chore for him. He said I owed him. I didn't
mind. I was glad to do it. I wanted to please him, just like I
wanted to please my stepfather. I'd never had anybody really
close to me and I figured this was how you got someone to like
you."

There was one demand, however, at which Miank drew the
line. "He wanted to have sex with me," he recalls. "It was something I just couldn't do. It hit too close to home. I'd flash back to
what my stepfather did and kind of freak out. Later they told me
it was pretty much the same as a posttraumatic stress reaction.
Like being in a war. So when I rejected his advances, I guess
Robert went looking somewhere else."

He didn't have far to go. "He liked little girls," asserts
Stephanie Bustin, Marcy Miank's daughter from her first marriage. "I was about fourteen years old at the time but very developed for my age and I remember that when he was living with
us that he used to watch me a lot. Doing the dishes or whatever,
I could feel his eyes on me. He was always really nice to me,
telling me how pretty I was and everything and then, one night
just before he moved out, he came into my room. He started
hugging and touching me, kissing me on the mouth, with my
mother in the living room downstairs. I was in bed at the time
and he was speaking very softly, telling me that everything was
going to be all right, that it was natural and a beautiful part of
life. Then he had sex with me. It was my first time. I remember
being so scared I didn't move or make a sound."

As time went on, Browne's malign influence began to per-
vade every corner of the troubled household. "He could freak
out at a moment's notice and go into a total rage," Miank recounts. "I remember once he was driving this old Datsun 210
with a bad clutch. He got so mad at that car, he just went
berserk and more or less took it apart with his bare hands. By
the time he cooled off it was so trashed, we ended up taking it
to the junkyard."

"He had a violent temper," Marcy Miank agrees. "He used to punch holes in the wall with his fist when he got angry, even over the smallest little thing. He had a real Jekyll and Hyde personality that way. Very mellow one minute, than he'd go crazy the next. He had a way with people and could get them to do pretty much what he wanted, but he didn't like to be around them that much. He was always talking about building an underground hideout in the mountains, where he could get away and not be bothered. He was a loner at heart."

"He had a fascination with fire," Jon Miank recollected. "He'd take a bunch of garbage out back and dig a hole. Then he'd pour in a gallon of gasoline and light it up just to see it burn. One time the flames shot up so high, the fire department got called out. After he started these blazes, he'd always come back later and sift through the ashes, like he was looking to see what the fire couldn't burn."

As the summer of 1986 likewise burned itself out, Miank and Browne plunged into a nightmarish frenzy of drug use. "Cocaine completely controlled me," Jon remembers. "At one point I was up to using a quarter-ounce a day, shooting up every fifteen minutes until most of my veins collapsed and I ended up with phlebitis. At a feed store we'd buy these big three-cc syringes that they used to give medicine to horses and cattle, with those sixteen-gauge needles so thick the blood would be running down your arm afterwards." At one point the pair even injected a bottle of lidocaine, a local anesthetic Miank had stolen from a hospital. "Cocaine, lidocaine . . . what was the difference, we figured."

Not surprisingly, they came close to overdosing on more than one occasion. "Robert told me about what he called 'hearing the train,' " Miank explains. "You'd do up a half-gram of coke and start hearing this roaring in your ears, like a locomotive coming straight at you. Then you'd go into convulsions and, when you came out of it, you'd be higher than you'd ever been in your life."

Together and separately, Miank recounts, the two "went off the deep end." "Robert would go out a lot at night by himself," he continues. "Sometimes, he'd come back just wearing his underwear, carrying his clothes in a bundle, all wired up with this wild look in his eyes. I never asked where he'd been. I didn't care. I didn't have what you'd call feelings back then: happiness, sadness, fear, or even any warning system. I'd see other people reacting to various situations, letting their emotions show, and it was like watching aliens from another planet. I though they were the crazy ones." Miank would later emphatically state that he was not involved in Browne's killing spree and had no direct knowledge of any of the murders.

As the manic summer melted slowly into fall, Miank found himself slipping into a hallucinatory realm of ineluctable violence. "Once I threatened Aaron, Marcy's son, and he called his father to come over," he recounts as if reciting a routine weather report. "He started waving a gun at me, but I wouldn't back down. I just kept coming at him, so he shot me in the face. Even that didn't slow me down. I went to a neighbor's house looking for a gun of my own. I fully intended to kill the motherfucker, but I couldn't see because of the blood running into my eyes, and in the meantime he got away." He displayed the jagged scar where the bullet ripped into his temple and lodged against one of the motor nerves that controls his facial expression. It's a grim explanation of his seemingly dispassionate affect. "It hurts to move my face too much," he says.

The pair meanwhile maintained themselves with a constant string of thefts and burglaries. "We'd do two or three every weekend," Miank continues. "I'd do even more when I didn't feel like sharing the haul or the drugs I got from fencing the stuff at some pawnshops downtown. I'd have people shoot at me, or try to run me down with their cars. It didn't matter. Once Robert's stash of coke was gone, I needed a constant source of money to stay high. I'd steal anything: jewelry, appliances, whatever we could cart away. The only thing I'd ever held onto was guns. I gave them to Robert. He had a thing about guns. He'd play with them, fondle them and pretend to take aim at you. He always carried a .22 snub nose around with him, tucked into his pants at the small of his back. In the end he must have had a stockpile of twenty or thirty."

The end, when it came, had both the inevitability of a runaway train and the finality of a brick wall. "In 1987 I got busted for stealing an engine hoist and selling it for two hundred dollars," Miank recounts. "I ended up doing four months on a one-year sentence before they put me into a community corrections program, which was kind of like a halfway house where they'd let you go to a job during the day. But instead of working, I'd go down to this auto body shop run by one of my buddies to get high. I just couldn't get off coke, no matter what situation I was in or whatever opportunity they offered me."

With his partner out of commission, Browne would eventually drift off to greener pastures, eventually marrying Diane and moving to her property in Black Forest. "He was good at that," Miank observes, "cutting his losses. He had a way of controlling his life, of doing things just the way he wanted and never looking back. I guess you could say that he was very goal-oriented."

CHAPTER TWELVE

"CALL ME WHEN YOU PULL THE SWITCH"

In early April 1995, Jon Miank was released from his Canon City, Colorado, prison cell to take a drive with Captain Lou Smit, Detective Michele Hodges, and Department of Corrections Officer Larry Rand on a tour of his old haunts: here was an auto supply store from which he and Browne had stolen engine parts; there, a community college where they had boosted computer monitors. They'd netted a coin collection from a ranch off Highway 85 and stripped the copper plumbing from an empty house on Link Road. "We really trashed that place," Miank would remember, and selling copper scrap had subsequently become a lucrative sideline for the team.

As they made their way up a scenic drive to the Garden of the Gods, a rugged national park frequented by the thieves, Miank talked freely about his malevolent mentor. "Sure," he remarked, "I was surprised when I heard that Robert was up for the murder of that little girl. It threw me for a loop. I started looking back at everything we'd done together, and saw it in a whole new way. He was capable of anything, and I think I knew that somewhere in the back of my mind, even then. I believed him when he told me he killed those two dealers in Louisiana. But as far as a child goes . . ."

As they climbed out of the car and headed through a fresh fall of snow to the Rampart Range dump site where Heather Church's body had been found, Miank expressed some uncertainty: he wasn't sure whether the spot had been one of the impromptu shooting galleries that he and Robert had staked out along the fire roads and backpacking trails snaking through the park. Then, as they stood at the steep drop-off looking into the garbage-strewn ravine, his thoughts circled back again to the proliferating possibilities Browne had left in his wake. "If I ever found out he did anything to Stephanie back when he was living with us, I'd fucking kill him." He paused, swallowing hard. "She was a beautiful little girl, and it was my job to protect her."

What Miank might have suspected had, of course, already been confirmed by the investigation, straight from the victim's mouth. But for the moment, it didn't seem to Lou Smit like the best time to let the convict in on the information. They still had work to do.

Back at the station, when Miank was shown photos of the crime scene where Heather Church's remains had been discovered, he was able to positively identify it as the location they had visited earlier that day. It was the rusting hulk of the car—in the pillaged back seat of which they used to get high—that gave it away. "There's a shooting range not far from here," he recalled. "We used to hear the guns going off all the time and then, naturally, Robert would pull out his gun and started shooting at things, too. He'd bring along some beer, but I always drank diet coke. I don't like beer."

He stared at the photo for a long moment. "If Robert did this," he finally said, "then he should pay for it."

Miank wasn't the only one learning new things about Robert Browne. Detectives Finley and Hodges, along with DA Investigator Larry Martin, had been dispatched to Louisiana that spring to complete their in-depth investigation of Browne's personal history and criminal career, conducting exhaustive interviews with friends, relatives, and former spouses.

Among the most notable was Terry Hetterrick, who, at age fourteen, had become Browne's first child bride. It was she who had the most direct contact with the sprawling family in whose midst Robert had grown up a victim, as he saw it, of cruelty and callous disregard.

"His dad was kind of high-strung," reported the soft-spoken redhead, "but the mother was just plain strange. She had a lot of emotional and mental problems. I guess that's what comes from having nine kids, what with three sets of twins and all. She used to tell me that raising them up, they were so poor, she'd have to stick their nightshirts under table legs to keep them from wandering off. They couldn't afford to buy enough playpens."

"There were mental problems on the mother's side," Red River Parish Sheriff Buddy Huckaby told the detectives. A family friend who in 1960 had briefly worked with Robert's brother Ronald as a deputy sheriff, Huckaby laconically recounted the Brownes' Southern Gothic background in a perfect *Heat of the Night* drawl. "They were squirrelly, all of them. Especially Old Man Bamberg, Robert's grandfather on his mother's side . . . crazy as a loon. He dug a cave under his house up there in the north of the county where no one goes and just hid out all by himself for years. Then one day, he wrapped a big logging chain around his neck, hooked the ends with a pair of vice grips and threw himself into a well. Suicide kind of ran in the family. Self-destructive behavior, I guess you'd call it."

"But they could also be very pleasant," Terry Hetterrick would tell detectives. "The whole family. They could make you feel like the most special person in the whole world, charm the pants right off you. And Robert was very magnetic. We used to drive up to the Dupree Gravel Pit, and the other one behind Garland's Kitchen Store, to make out. It got hot and heavy, but he never tried to force himself on me."

Contradiction seemed to prevail in townsfolk's assorted memories of the Browne brood and Robert in particular. Yet from those very anomalies a picture was emerging of an affable, engaging country boy who, for all his seeming self-regard and smooth manner, was periodically swept up in the dark currents that raged just beneath the surface.

"A week after we were married, he tried to strangle me," avers Rita Morgan, another Coushatta local interviewed by investigators, who married Browne in late 1980. "My larynx was bruised so bad I had to go to the emergency room. It was all because I'd picked up the wrong set of car keys. He was like that. He'd blow up over nothing."

For all of Browne's wives, but for Morgan especially, tying the knot had quickly become like slipping on a noose. They had met at a ball game and gotten married shortly thereafter, coinciding with a time when Browne, out of the army and without prospects, was at his most savage and unrestrained. "He beat me a lot," the tiny blonde with elaborately painted nails admitted to Finley. She would subsequently reveal to a newspaper reporter that she had begged him to see a psychiatrist after an incident in which he held a gun to her head. "He agreed," she recounts. "He said he knew he had a problem, but when we got to the Veterans Affairs clinic he had a whole different story. The doctor was very aggressive, kind of scolding him for hitting me, especially since I was such a little woman. Then Robert, who wasn't religious at all, started spouting all this stuff from the Bible about how Scripture said that I was his wife and he could do whatever he wanted with me.

"But it wasn't just me that he had a grudge against. He was always scheming, always figuring somebody owed him something. He had a plan to find a homosexual with a lot of money, a lawyer or something, then have sex and blackmail him. And he made me sign over all my property into his name; make him the beneficiary in case something happened to me, he said. I didn't have but my car and a trailer, but he made me do it anyway."

It would not, Finley already knew, be the last time Robert

would make a grab for the assets of his women. In a previous interview with Diane Browne, she had revealed to the detective that her former husband had also made her change her hundred-thousand-dollar insurance policy to name him as the sole beneficiary. When she balked, he accused her of trying to control his life and insisted that they open separate bank accounts and post office boxes. "He wanted his privacy," she said.

He had also wanted to instill an unholy fear into those closest to him. "He used to explain to me how easy it would be to kill someone," recalled Rita Morgan. " 'You just don't know,' he'd say. 'You just don't know.' " She could only nod when Mark Finley asked her if she took the words as a threat against her. "I was afraid of him all the time," she whispered. "I was sure that if I ever tried to leave him, something would happen to me. It spooked me when he'd get up in the middle of the night and just disappear for hours at a time. When he came back he'd tell me he just couldn't sleep, that he was driving around or drinking coffee at a diner. I honestly didn't know where he went."

Additional interviews by Finley and his team would reveal that Browne kept a coterie of girlfriends throughout the parish. "Maybe that was my fault," Morgan speculates. "I told him he'd have to find someone else. He wanted sex all the time, but mostly after he'd been mean to me or hit me. Then he'd get really calm and start kissing and petting me. It was like hurting someone turned him on."

"He thought he was great in bed," scoffed Brenda Herbel in an interview with Detective Hodges. In 1977, aged seventeen and still attending high school, Herbel had met and married Browne. "What did I know?" she shrugs. "I was a kid. I remember once he came down with VD and blamed me for giving it to him. When the doctor said otherwise, he tried to convince me that he'd gotten it off a toilet seat. I believed him." She paused before adding, "I consider him the reason I've never liked sex since."

Herbel's story had the same harrowing familiarity as the other young women in Browne's orbit: a beating when she forgot to put a spoon in the gravy; a stray kitten brought home that provoked a blind rage and a knife wound when he burst in on her as she sat taking a bath; the constant threats that if he couldn't have her, nobody could. "I've blocked a considerable portion of it out," she admits with a haunted look that she also shares with the others. "Especially that time out in the country, around Cannon Slew, where he kept me to himself for a couple days. He had a gun and he was using this special combination of drugs he liked. White cross speed, black beauties, LSD. He called it going to the max."

He was also, according to Terry Hetterrick, fond of maximizing the melodrama of his own life in incidents both real and imagined as well as in various combinations of the two. "We were living in San Antonio," she says. "He'd gotten back from Vietnam and was acting really weird. Very moody. I found a picture in his closet of this oriental girl: real small and skinny. I asked him who she was and he told me that he'd met her over there and that they had fallen in love."

It was a story he'd expand considerably by the time he retold it to Diane. "He didn't talk at all about his other wives," she recounts. "Except he'd get very nostalgic about this one he said he'd met over in Vietnam. They'd been married for three weeks, he told me, and were going to have a baby, but a bomb or something landed on the apartment and killed her right before his eyes." She shakes her head. "I never believed a word of it. It sounded like he was just making it up, like he saw it in a movie or something."

Browne would also claim that his mysterious romance with the waiflike Vietnamese girl was the reason he had eventually married Tuyet Huynh in Texas. "She was a lot like the one that supposedly got killed," Diane would explain with barely contained skepticism. "He said how gorgeous and intelligent she was and how much they loved each other." She laughed. "I always wondered if they were so much in love, how come she'd left him."

Brenda Herbel knew. "I met the woman," she told Finley. "The mother of his son. She said he beat her all the time . . . really went overboard on the whipping. She got away first chance she could, but had to walk away from her boy to get out from under Robert." She hesitated for a moment, weighing her words carefully. "He's the devil's right-hand man," is how she finally put it. "Call me when you pull the switch."

As Finley, Hodges, and additional Colorado law-enforcement officials continued to unearth incriminating new evidence in Louisiana, the case against Browne was taking on bizarre and menacing new dimensions in Colorado. In early May, District Court Judge Gilbert Martinez, who had earlier signed Browne's arrest warrant, received a letter from a distraught local father claiming that the accused had molested his preteen son on several occasions, starting three years earlier.

In subsequent police interviews, the alleged victim, now thirteen years old, related a highly detailed account of his encounters with Browne in the men's room of a restaurant where his family would occasionally stop for dinner after choir practice at their church. Rife with lurid particulars, the boy's story, which detailed successive incidents of anal rape, often at the point of a gun or a knife and with the threat of death if he ever talked, was duly added to the mushrooming case file. Included was the boy's statement that he had repressed all recollections of the serial assaults until Robert's face was shown on television shortly after his arrest.

As with so many reports of child molestation, it was maddeningly difficult for investigators to determine how much of the account was true and how much was in the vivid imaginings of a troubled teenager. Browne was certainly capable of sexual predation: the violation of his stepdaughter Stephanie had proven that, and it seemed clear that, indeed, *something* had happened. The boy had been seeing a psychiatrist for almost two years to help him deal with the resultant trauma, and it was the doctor himself who had recommended writing to the judge. But among the investigators, there was serious doubt as to whether it would be possible or even advisable to pursue the lead any further. "There is no credibility to this identification," wrote the officer assigned to the follow-up. "Robert Browne will not be pursued as a suspect in this case." The focus, from Lou Smit on down, was to bring home the Church case.

Nevertheless, it was difficult to discount the escalating claims made by those who knew the accused, however tangentially; harder still not to try to fit it all together in a pattern that shed light on Robert Browne's motive and opportunity.

Some incidents were downright weird. A neighbor just south of the Brownes' Black Forest property reported witnessing Robert placing large stereo speakers outside his windows and blasting what sounded like animal noises, including the growls of tigers, into the surrounding forest in regular thirty-second intervals. "I called over to ask what the hell he was doing," the neighbor reports. "But he didn't answer the phone, even though I could see him moving around in the trailer."

Then there was the long-distance girlfriend whose name had been discovered during the initial search of the trailer. She lived in Provo, Utah, and Browne would occasionally make the trip to see her, the rest of the time keeping up a frequent e-mail correspondence. "He used to tease me over how little I knew about him," she recalls. "He'd say that for all I knew, he was a serial killer with five or six wives chopped up and buried on his tree farm. I took it as a joke at the time. But he kept repeating it, and it started to creep me out."

Other episodes had an altogether more directly threatening aspect, such as the harrowing encounter experienced by Ron and Angela Pastor, who were neighbors of the Brownes during their stay in Black Forest. Angela had known Diane from their teenage years, growing up across the street from each other in a Connecticut suburb, and she and Ron had bought property from her shortly after the death of Diane's first husband. The couple had done what they could to help the widow through her grieving, inviting her to meals and occasionally babysitting her daughter. Like many others who had previously known Diane, they noticed a progressive and profound change in her demeanor after her marriage to Robert. According to Angela Pastor, who worked as a nurse while Ron bagged groceries at a local supermarket, she had often discussed with her husband the uneasiness she felt toward Robert. "There's something wrong with him," she remembered fretting after meeting him for the first time in the summer of 1988.

Eighteen months later, whatever it was that was wrong with Browne became frighteningly evident when he asked the Pastors if he could use the back end of their property to plant some of the trees he had purchased for his fledgling business. Ron was amenable until Browne hooked a hose into his well to irrigate the saplings, often for hours at a time. After repeated requests to use his own water—and as many promises from Robert to do so—Ron Pastor eventually put a lock on the wellhouse door. A short time later that same day, Browne came storming up the driveway with a hacksaw, intent on cutting his way through the padlock. Pastor confronted him, and the situation quickly escalated.

"You're a dead man, motherfucker," was the threat Browne repeated to his neighbor several times until the Sheriff's Department was summoned and deputies arrived on the scene to separate the two.

A few days later, Ron Pastor spotted Browne on his property again, this time back at the trees he had planted, spraying the ground with a pungent chemical. "He killed them all rather than run the risk of letting me have them," Pastor insists. "Nothing's been able to grow on that ground since."

Despite the close ties between the two women, the couples

broke off all contact as tensions continued to grow over the next few weeks. It was partially as a result of the hostile environment that the Pastors decided to put their property up for sale and move to New Hampshire. "We were both really afraid, although we didn't really want to admit it to each other," Angela recounts. "It was just an uneasiness, like that feeling something is going to happen that keeps you on edge. I remember Ron asked the realtor if it was really necessary to put a For Sale sign on the land, because he didn't want Robert and Diane to know that we were clearing out."

Later that week, Ron was startled to see a figure prowling across his porch. "I was looking out the bathroom window," he asserts. "I couldn't see his face, but I knew who it was. I started screaming: 'What are you doing here? What to do want?' What really scared me the most was that he wasn't more then a few feet from the bedroom of our kids. He just turned and looked at me and then walked away. I watched him go down the road and then got on the phone to report an intruder on the property to the cops. While I was talking, out of nowhere, my woodpile burst into flames. It was as if someone had poured gasoline all over it: flames straight up in the air. It was like a small explosion."

Shortly afterwards, the Pastors decamped, leaving behind, as Angela made sure Detective David Reisman made note, the family cat, which had mysteriously disappeared around the same time as the arson attempt. The sinister connection, in her mind, was beyond dispute.

As the investigation wound down after two frenetic weeks in late April, one piece of suspicious, albeit circumstantial, evidence caught the attention of investigators working the Louisiana end of the case.

The information had first come to the attention of Detective Finley during a routine interview with Red River Parish law-enforcement officials. As he put it in his subsequent report, he was attempting to "obtain background information on the suspect . . . and to ascertain additional contacts in reference to the case." On hand was Major Larry Rhodes from the Investigations Division of the Red River Parish Sheriff's Office in Coushatta.

Initially, it was simply more of the same. Sure, Major Rhodes stated, he'd known the suspect all his life. Finley was beginning to wonder if there was anyone in the town who didn't know everyone else all their lives. "Robert Browne was basically a loner," Rhodes would assert in what was becoming a by-now-familiar refrain, until, almost as an afterthought, he brought up two unsolved cases from a dozen years earlier that he thought might be of interest to the cops from Colorado.

The first was the disappearance of a local girl named Faye Self, who had last been seen in 1983 at a tavern on the outskirts of town in the company of an individual identified only as "Robert." The second was another Coushatta native, twenty-one-year-old Wanda Faye Hudson, whose corpse had been found in her apartment two months after the disappearance of Faye Self. The thing was, Rhodes continued, both of the victims had lived in the same cluster of clapboard cottages known as the Riverside Apartments, which at the time had been owned and managed by Robert's brother, Ronald Browne. He also seemed to remember that Robert himself had lived in one of the units at just around that time and was even working as a handyman on the property for his brother.

Finley was understandably thunderstruck. Two unsolved murders within two months of each other, both presumably committed in close proximity to Heather Church's accused killer. While it seemed fair to ask why Red River authorities did not follow up these extraordinary leads on their own, Finley restrained himself. They obviously did things differently down in those parts, and he was mindful of the fact that Ronald Browne had been a Louisiana state trooper until a bullet wound put him out of commission. It was perhaps judicious not to look too closely at that link, at least for the time being.

Finley had no such scruples, however, in following up the new clues on his own. Along with DA Investigator Larry Martin, he immediately summoned Donald Browne, Ronald's twin brother, to the county courthouse and put the question to him directly: To his knowledge, was there any tie between his younger brother and the events in and around the Riverside Apartments?

"He had nothing to do with it," insisted Donald, in a spirited defense that confirmed to Finley yet again that blood was thicker than water. "There was a pharmacist back in town who was carrying on with Wanda Hudson. He's the one that did her. As far as Faye Self, they never found her body, so how are they going to accuse Robert for a thing like that?"

So did that mean, in Donald's opinion, that Robert was incapable of murdering anyone? "That's not what I said," was his aggravated reply. "There used to be a rumor in the family that he had killed some guy back in Korea when he was in the service, but if you ask me, that's all it was: a rumor. As far as that little girl out in Colorado: he couldn't have done it. It just wasn't in him. Considering the crowd he ran with, it's more likely that he's been set up, if you ask me."

Bearing in mind the source, Donald's denials were not exactly a ringing endorsement of his brother's innocence. Rita Morgan, for her part, had a whole other story to tell. She was with Robert the night Wanda Hudson had been murdered, she told Finley. Although separated at the time, she had allowed herself to be talked into spending the evening with Browne. "He could convince you of anything," she ruefully admitted. They had talked through most of the night, drinking coffee in the cabin he occupied at the property, his kitchen window looking directly into the bedroom window of the victim. While professing uncertainty as to how the evening had actually ended, she remembered being there the next morning, with Robert cooking breakfast when the police arrived to discover Hudson's dead body next door. "He went out to talk to them," she recounts, "then came back and told me what had happened. I was shocked and upset and he tried to comfort me. A little while later, he told me that he was worried about another woman who lived at the apartments, that she had turned up missing and that he feared the worst." She pauses, a barely perceptible shiver running through her diminutive frame. "What got me the most, though, was a few months later. His brother Ronald was having trouble renting Wanda's old apartment. You know, because of what happened there. But Robert didn't have a problem with it. He volunteered to move in and never gave it a second thought."

CHAPTER THIRTEEN

CLOSURE

On April 11, 1995, just as the multistate investigation was concluding, a grand jury handed down a hefty twenty-six-count
indictment against Robert Browne. Foremost among them: two
charges of first-degree murder in the case of Heather Dawn
Church.

The first count against Browne alleged that the murder had
been committed during an act of either burglary, kidnapping, or
sexual assault. The second was a charge of premeditation. The
jury could reach a guilty verdict on only one of the two mutually
exclusive allegations. Also included were two counts of sexual
assault and two more of attempted sexual assault in the case of
Marcy Miank's daughter, Stephanie. There followed a grab bag
of burglary, theft, and arson charges stemming from the incidents on the Pastor property and other felonies that had
emerged over the course of the investigation. Included was the
theft of a Bobcat front loader that had been found on the Browne
property and false information provided to a pawnbroker to
whom Robert had hawked a pair of diamond earrings stolen
from his wife Diane. Finally two counts of cruelty to animals
were added for good measure, to cover the death of various pets
reported by neighbors, including Angela Pastor's vanished cat.

Jorge Sierra, Browne's public defender, did his best to avert
an all-but-certain death-penalty verdict, complaining about the
enormous amount of publicity that the Browne arrest and indictment had already generated. He pointed particularly to a
news conference held by Sheriff John Anderson that inter-

rupted prime-time programming on local television when the suspect had first been arrested. Even as Sierra was pleading with Judge Martinez not to "try Mr. Browne in the press," District Attorney John Suthers had likewise taken to the airwaves, asking for the public's help in adding possible new charges. "If anyone, particularly in the Black Forest area, was a victim of a burglary in 1991, we would sure like to hear from them," he requested.

Underpinning the indictment was the prosecution's allegation, codified in three additional counts, that Robert Browne was a habitual criminal. Under that proviso, Browne would automatically be given a sentence four times the maximum for each conviction stemming from the Church case, along with the other various and sundry charges. A final tally of the possible sentence was 576 years in prison, plus four life terms.

For his part, Browne seemed completely cognizant of the grim prospects facing him. Colorado had had a death penalty statute on its books since 1859, and since then, 102 executions had been carried out, most recently by lethal injection.

Yet for all its Wild West heritage, the citizens of the state had an ambivalent attitude toward capital punishment. Colorado had carried through only one legally mandated death since 1977 and had demonstrated a long-standing unease with the ethics of state-sanctioned execution. Eventually, in February 2007, a committee of the Colorado legislature would vote to abolish the state's death penalty and mandate that the millions spent battling death-row appeals be used to close the thousand-plus unsolved killings that moldered in cold-case files such as those that the Apple Dumpling Gang had been investigating. The same John Suthers who prepared the Robert Browne indictment would go on to be elected Colorado attorney general and speak out vociferously against the vote. "The social contract demands our response be greater than saying, 'We're going to take away your television privileges,' " he remarked acidly.

Yet in the spring of 1995, the Colorado death-penalty debate was only beginning to heat up. The state retained the right to put its worst offenders to death in cases of first-degree and felony murder as well as any kidnapping that resulted in the death of a victim. Robert Browne knew only too well that he fit those criteria exactly.

On May 24, fifty-eight days after his arrest, he passed a message to the court: he was ready to plead guilty to all charges stemming from the abduction and murder of Heather Dawn Church. His proffered plea bargain stipulated that in exchange, the state would not seek the death penalty and would drop all other charges not related to the case. With the deal in hand, DA Suthers immediately contacted the murdered girl's mother and father, as well as the other victims named in the pending charges. All agreed to accept the proposal.

The next day Browne appeared before Judge Martinez. In the courtroom were Mike and Diane Church, Heather's parents. "He stood up today and said he did it," the tearful mother later told reporters. "I saw it with my own eyes. It is a big relief. If he is willing to say he did it, then I'm willing to let him stay in jail for the rest of his life."

Mike Church didn't seem quite so ready to settle accounts with the murderer of his daughter nor to listen passively while Robert admitted his guilt. When, under questioning from the bench, Robert began delving into the grim details, Church put his fingers in his ears. "I didn't have to hear those parts," he said later. "I didn't want to."

In a session that lasted less than half an hour, Judge Martinez sentenced Browne to life in prison without the possibility of parole. The four-year ordeal was indeed over. Closure, that elusive point at which grieving gives way to getting on, had finally been achieved. "I know it doesn't bring back Heather," Mike said, speaking for many close to the case. "But I'm ready to move on with my life." Justice may have been delayed, but it was not ultimately denied.

Yet in the minds of the detectives who had worked so hard

to build the case, Browne's sudden and unexpected admission still left a lot of loose ends. Most notably, the fate of Wanda Faye Hudson and Faye Self weighed heavily on the investigators who had traveled to Louisiana. What authorities there had relegated to their own extensive cold-case repository had come tantalizingly close to being cracked by Finley, Hodges, and the rest of the Colorado team. The next step was to confront Robert himself. If he had decided to talk about Heather Church, maybe he'd be willing to keep talking. On the morning of June 1, a week after Browne's sentencing, Finley and Smit went to visit him as he underwent medical evaluation at the Department of Corrections Diagnostic Facility in Denver.

They would not get what they had come for. The prisoner declined to discuss anything having to do with events in Coushatta and registered no reaction whatever when Finley mentioned Hudson and Self by name. Instead he launched into a rambling colloquy on the reasons behind his guilty plea, insisting that his bad conscience had driven him to make a clean breast of it. He begged the detectives to assist him in getting a complete psychiatric evaluation before he was sent to the supermax security prison at Canon City. Finley assured him that his request was part of standard operating procedure for the Department of Corrections and that he would be sure to follow up on the findings of the evaluation himself.

True to his word, the detective had a conversation five days later with Susan Lawrence, a DOC placement counselor who had conducted Robert's psychological evaluation. It was an altogether chilling account, resolving many of the questions left in the Church case while at the same time posing many more. "Robert," Lawrence would later write in her report, "enjoyed roaming the neighborhood at night, looking for places to burglarize. He remembered that when he went to the Church house, there were two lights on and no cars in the driveway, which led him to believe that there was no one home. Surprised to find Heather in the house, he grabbed her, with one hand over her mouth and another around her neck." He had demonstrated the move on Lawrence, who went on to report that it had seemed to Browne as if he held the girl in his grip for only a few seconds. "He now believes it must have been for much longer," she continued. "He assumes he strangled her because she was dead when it was over. He also admitted that it was possible he had broken her neck. He placed her body in the back of his pickup truck and drove to the mountains, where he disposed of it. He said that afterwards he believed he was going to get caught but as time passed and nothing happened, he became more secure."

Of Robert's insistence that he had no sexual contact with his victim, investigators were understandably skeptical. "I think he kept her as a sex toy," Lou Smit would assert in a conversation with the authors. "I think he had her stashed on the property, probably in one of the outbuildings in the back, which is why he warned off the searchers with his story about the attack dogs. I think he held onto her for a while before he killed her and dumped her body."

Still, for all its still-lingering uncertainties, the case had reached a satisfactory conclusion, at least as far as it went. Whatever the actual events, the right man was now in jail for his entire life, or nine centuries, whichever was longer. The investigation into the death and disappearance of Hudson and Self ran aground on Browne's insistence, made again during his evaluation with Lawrence, that he had nothing to do with the missing and murdered women. "He seemed concerned about providing nontestimonial evidence regarding these cases," Lawrence would later tell Finley.

And that, largely, was that. But it wasn't long before Browne grew restless with the snail's pace of his punishment. Alone for all but one hour a day, he had an abundance of time to think and think again in his solitude undifferentiated by day or night or even the slow changes of seasons. It was during that first long year that his ruminations naturally turned to the expedited legal processes that had put him behind bars. That one, brief half-hour in court, he recalled, and it was all over for good and forever. If only he'd had a lawyer who knew what he was doing—who *cared* what he was doing—maybe he might have gotten some kind of break, some small wedge of bargaining power.

By the early autumn of 1996, Browne believed he'd discovered a way to beat the odds, or at least improve on them. The only reason he'd pled guilty in the first place, he reasoned, was for fear that he'd end up on death row. But in 1991, the year he had killed Heather, the death penalty had been repealed in Colorado for two short months while the legislature wrangled. In July of that year, the state Supreme Court reinstated capital punishment, but it was in that narrow window of time—three days before the death penalty was brought back into force—that Browne had killed Heather Church. According to his reasoning, honed over those endless lonely hours, the ultimate sanction could not be applied in his case. His lawyer had misrepresented the possible punishment Browne was facing. Through his new court-appointed attorney, Ed Farry, he filed a motion with the Fourth Judicial District Court to withdraw his guilty plea. "There was no death penalty," Farry wrote in the motion. "Therefore, to offer not to seek the death penalty was, in fact, no offer at all."

The DA's office wasted no time in refuting Browne's contention, with DA Suthers pointing out that there had never been a definitive finding on the actual time line of the murder. The only evidence that Heather Church had been killed in her home on September 17 had come from Browne himself. Indeed, there was at least some tangential evidence that he had actually abducted her and kept her alive for a few days, as Lou Smit conjectured. A few of the Churches' Black Forest neighbors had reported hearing screams the night of the seventeenth, which threw into doubt the strangulation account Robert had given, even given the fact that she could have cried out before he

choked her. There was also the discovery of the shredded pajamas at the Rampart Range dump site: if Heather was wearing
them at the time of her death, then they did not match the
clothing she had on at home on the evening of the seventeenth.

It was up to Judge Martinez to decide whether to grant
Browne's request to withdraw his plea, and he set a hearing
date for October 28, some two weeks after the initial motion
had been filed. At that point, Browne's lawyer Ed Farry intro-
duced more legal uncertainty: if the attorneys and the authorities could not agree on the essential sequence of events that had
led to the murder charge, then how could the judge be capable
of reaching an informed decision? It was a good point, and Martinez responded by moving the hearing date forward another
month.

As it turned out, five full months would elapse before the
matter was finally heard in a contentious six-hour argument before Martinez attended by Browne and both Mike and Diane
Church. As expected, Farry stubbornly contended that the DA's
agreement not to seek the death penalty in exchange for
Browne's confession was a bargain without substance: there
was no death penalty at the time. "There is no way I would
have ever pled guilty except for that one reason," Browne
would testify.

Deputy District Attorney Dan Zook was having none of it.
"When the court asked Robert Browne why he was pleading
guilty," he reminded Judge Martinez, "he stated, 'because I am
guilty.' "

On March 29, the principals were back before the court. In
giving the matter such a thorough hearing and deliberating for
so long a time, Martinez seemed to be giving credence to
Browne's hairsplitting contention. The fact that no clear con-
sensus had been reached regarding the exact time of Heather
Church's death made it impossible to determine what the law
might actually have been at that crucial juncture. It was a concern clearly reflected in the judge's remarks; since no one

seemed to be able to agree on when the crime occurred, he had no choice but to deny Browne's motion. The matter was one for a jury to decide, and that decision had been precluded by the defendant's plea. The loophole wasn't large enough for Robert to slip through. His plea would stand.

But not, as it turned out, his sentence. In his detailed examination of the applicable law, Martinez had discovered yet another wrinkle: at the time of the sentencing, a provision had been on the books allowing for possible parole in a life sentence under certain circumstances. Those circumstances were met in the Browne case. The law had since been changed, but Martinez chose to apply the provision retroactively. Robert Browne would now be eligible for parole after forty years, in 2037, at the age of eighty-four.

It was cold comfort to the convicted killer, whose subsequent appeals took the better part of the next year and a half. In late 1998, a two-to-one decision was handed down, again denying Browne's motion to change his plea. "In my view," wrote Judge Arthur Roy, the lone dissenting vote, "the defendant was not sufficiently aware and was not advised of the relevant law or how it might be applied to the facts of his case."

It was, in the profoundest sense of the term, an academic argument. None of the legal maneuvering, the precedents real or imagined, the arcane arguments and procedural niceties could bring back Heather Dawn Church. She would have been twenty years old at the time the final decision came down on Robert Browne's forlorn shot at freedom. Yet it was also true that justice had been served, albeit in agonizing fits and starts. Robert Browne was where he belonged and there he would remain— for forty years or four hundred, it didn't really matter. At long last a curtain had fallen over an incomprehensibly senseless crime committed by an unfathomably brutal killer. For Robert Charles Browne, there was no future.

The past, however, was another matter entirely.

PART FOUR

CHAPTER FOURTEEN

86504

It is hardly an unusual occurrence for law-enforcement officials—from judges and prosecuting attorneys to arresting officers and prison wardens—to receive copious correspondence from the criminals they have helped to send to and keep in jail. The effectiveness of putting a man behind bars lies in the hopeful if not naïve assumption that he will use the time to think about the error of his ways and ultimately resolve to do better if granted the opportunity when his debt to society is finally paid.

Of course, it rarely works out so neatly. While society's demand for retribution may be well and rightfully met through the penal system, remorse, repentance, and rehabilitation are rarely achieved by leaving a man alone with his roiling thoughts and feelings for years at a time. Instead, what might be considered a state of situational insanity often seems to ensue. The endless feedback loop of resentment and revenge played over and over in the mind and heart of the convict can drown out any impulse for self-examination and reform, and more often than not, the prisoner cultivates his grudges into a phantasmagorical garden of toxic fantasies. Loneliness, isolation, and the institutionalized violence of his diminished environment all contribute to the pathologies that put him in prison in the first place.

There are, of course, coping mechanisms—the endless legal appeals, the rigid internally imposed routines, the self-improvement techniques ranging from pumping iron to earning a degree—and occasionally a prisoner will almost miraculously regain his sanity and along with it control of his life through the very exigencies of his deprivation. Jon Miank, for one, would achieve a genuine understanding of himself in prison. Robert Browne, by contrast, seemed to have sunk deeper into delusion and despair and devious devices.

Familiar with the processes by which men in cages cope with themselves, cops and guards and those charged with achieving some semblance of rehabilitation are understandably dubious of any prisoner's attempt to alter the intolerable paradigm of their imprisonment. Bargains and deals of every description—offers to inform or spy on fellow convicts, hints and clues to unsolved cases, or simply unhinged rants—are all too common and all too commonly dismissed as the desperate ploys of men trapped in the tightening grip of their punishment.

It was hardly surprising, then, that whoever opened the mail at the office of the district attorney of the Fourth Judicial District on the morning of March 20, 2000, did not rush pell-mell into the boss's office with news that convict number 86504, residing at the Colorado State Penitentiary in Canon City, had written four lines of clumsy blank verse addressed to "Whom It May Concern."

Browne's missive, designated on the envelope as "Personal Mail, Not Legal Mail," came some sixteen months after his final appeal for a new trial had been shot down. He had in the interim effectively vanished from the face of the earth. The newspaper articles that duly reported his various legal maneuvers had ceased. Diane Browne and Jon Miank and Ron and Angela Pastor and all the others whose lives had been blindsided in his proximity were busy about the business of picking up the pieces. The memory of Heather Church faded for some and lingered for others, in much the same way as Colorado's spectacular seasons came and went and came again. Other murders were committed; other murderers paid for their crimes or escaped justice.

It was against this backdrop in the letter the Apple Dumpling Gang would discover two years later that Browne's spooky evocation of *"murky placid depths"* and a *"cool caressing mire"* sounded like echoes from another world in a voice that had been long and thankfully forgotten. While it is the stated policy of law enforcement to follow up on any suggestion of criminal intent or commission, the powers-that-be in the DA's office could be forgiven for not assigning Browne's vague intimations of "missed opportunities" the highest priority.

Yet if it was attention that Robert was after, he got it, at least in a desultory fashion. His letter, written in longhand on lined paper in a freestyle combination of printed and cursive letters, was passed on to Sheriff's Detective Mark Finley, who had been front and center for so much of the Church investigation. Three days later, he wrote back:

> Dear Mr. Browne:
>
> I placed this letter on plain paper rather than official stationary because I thought you would prefer it that way. Your letter was received at the District Attorney's office and forwarded to me for a response.
>
> I have tried to anticipate what you are wanting to do, and believe I have a general idea of at least some of the things you refer to in your letter. I have spoken to agencies in other states, who asked me to handle things on this end.
>
> Certainly I am willing to come speak with you if that is what you want. I will tell you up front, no other agencies are interested unless you are willing to provide bona fide information, which will be of assistance to them.
>
> I took the liberty of writing this letter, rather than making a visit, to access [sic] exactly what it is you want to do. It would be a waste of time to show up and speak in rhymes.
>
> Please let me know what you would like to do. I will try to accommodate you as soon as possible.

Finley did indeed contact Louisiana authorities, querying them on the cryptic content of Browne's letter. There was, to his mind, a tantalizing association between those *"murky depths"* and *"caressing mire"* and the endless miles of sodden bayou he had traveled over during the course of his investigations. Perhaps the police in Red River Parish might make a connection.

No such luck. As he half expected, no one back in Browne's home state had the slightest idea what the poem might be referring to and certainly did not consider it worth ransacking their cold-case file to come up with the *"seven golden opportunities"* to which Browne alluded. Yet Finley made the best of their obvious disinterest when writing back to the convict: if he came up with something "bona fide," authorities would be interested. It was another way of saying that no one cared much for Browne's poetic aspirations as they stood.

For that matter, neither did Finley. Risking Robert's ire, he had made the glancing reference to the futility of talking "in rhymes," even as he had gone on a limited fishing expedition by suggesting that he had a "general idea" of what Browne was hinting at. In fact, Finley had his doubts about all this sinister melodrama from the beginning and wanted Browne to know that, too. He was in no way inclined to play the killer's game.

Robert, on the other hand, had little to lose by being persistent. Two weeks later, the DA's office received another mysterious missive from the convict, once again addressed to "Whom It May Concern." It seems likely that it had crossed in the mail with Finley's response to the first letter, since there was no acknowledgment of the course of action the detective had suggested. Instead, what had been notable for its brevity and dreamy indolence the first time around had now become verbose and explicit, although still couched in an awkward doggerel. The free verse couplets would puzzle and intrigue investigators as they struggled to crack the code of its obscure imagery.

> *Foreign jurisdictions need not bother*
> *This seven concerns no other*
> *The seven sacred virgins, entombed side by side*

174

Those less worthy are scattered wide
No advantage will be gained
Until your minds have been drained
Once they're drained, it becomes clear
Dig in deep for the ones so dear
If this enigma is to be solved
Embrace the others who are involved
The High Priestess thought not of importance
Through practiced hysterical cries of ignorance
If you show no ambition
To pursue this to fruition
You obviously are not the ones
This communion is forever done

A postscript read, *"This is the last commune* [sic] *until results are seen,"* and once again, the correspondence was signed *"Lovingly, Robert C. Browne."*

With receipt of this lurid riddle, Finley could be forgiven for feeling both intrigued and frustrated. The seven golden opportunities had now become as many *"virgins."* The references to *"digging"* and *"draining"* once again summoned up the swamps of Louisiana, and the dismissal of *"foreign jurisdictions"* seemed to suggest that these murders—if indeed that's what they were—had occurred close to home, or at least in the United States.

On the other hand, hints of unsolved enigmas and a *"High Priestess"* smacked of cheap horror-movie clichés. If Browne really had more skeletons in his closet, figuratively or otherwise, he was being annoyingly coy about providing substantive facts. Even the most careful reading of Browne's communiqués left Finley with the distinct feeling that he was being jerked around. Adding to his ambivalence was the simple fact that Browne was already behind bars for what would certainly turn out to be the rest of his life. As much as Finley's professional pride would have been gratified to solve, at the very least, the

Wanda Faye Hudson and Faye Self cases, he had neither the time nor the inclination to be led around by the nose, playing Clarice Starling to Browne's Hannibal Lector.

While pondering his next move, Finley received another letter, this time addressed to him directly and written in an apparent lather over the thinly disguised skepticism the detective had evinced the last time around. Without so much as a salutation, Browne had launched into a scathing rebuke:

> The score is, you One, the other team, Forty-Eight. Are you willing to settle for this? You have the information to make the score Eight to Forty-Eight. Somewhat better, but you seem to not have the insight or ambition to score! In addition, if you were to drive to the end zone in a white Grand-Am, the score could be Nine to Forty-Eight. That would complete your home court sphere.
>
> Do you wish to retire into obscurity? Or, would you like to live a life of notoriety and wealth? Let's see if you have the insight, ambition and drive to be somebody!
>
> Again, you have your information! Do not contact me!!!

If Browne's intent was to raise Finley's hackles, he succeeded. The taunting tone of the letter, along with its cheap-shot references to retiring in obscurity or becoming rich and famous read like a mockery of all the dedication and idealism that the detective had invested in his long career. Browne's goading was way wide of the mark—Finley had been a cop long enough to know that there was no room for personal aggrandizement—but it still stung, especially coming from a convict that even other convicts considered the lowest of the low: a child killer.

Finley could hardly be blamed for taking the bait. There was, after all, at least one more intriguing clue that Robert had thrown out—that reference to a white Grand Am—which might well have been worth following up on. At the very least, stringing the killer along might have elicited more leads, aside from depriving him of the satisfaction of getting under the skin of the one man who had done more than any other to put him behind bars. Simply put, Mark Finley lost his cool.

After a long delay, during which he seemed to be nursing his grievances, he finally responded on September 20, with a quick rebuke of his own. The fact that he once again eschewed official letterhead and was now even writing in longhand seemed to underscore how personal this contest of wills had become. Yet at the same time, there was at least a modicum of strategy to his methods, a calculated risk that he could prod Browne into revealing more by refusing to play his game.

> *Robert,*
>
> *Your last letter reflects in-the-box thinking (no pun intended). It appears you believe that other people think in the same manner as you do. I don't believe that is true.*
>
> *I am sure it would please you to see news reports of me out hunting wild geese. It's not going to happen. Should you desire to provide some bonafide details so that I truly know that you are not just hallucinating, you will see me act accordingly.*
>
> *I find it interesting—the desire you place between yourself and the details I am sure you do know. It would appear to me that the star running back is afraid to play on the home field.*
>
> > *Cordially, MF*

Finley may well have been justified in taking this hard-nosed tack with his mercurial pen pal. Of the various vague references Browne had made in his last letter, one that attracted the detective's immediate attention was the number forty-eight. It was that precise number that had been given as the grisly body count of Gary Leon Ridgway. Over almost three years in the early eighties, the notorious Green River Killer had terrorized the Seattle and Tacoma, Washington, region, strangling prostitutes and teenage runaways and dumping their bodies in the nearby Green River. The sheriff of King County, where most of the killings took place, would eventually form the Green River Task Force, headed up by legendary detectives Robert Keppel and Dave Reichert, who had previously spent long hours with Ted Bundy attempting to coax additional information from the mass murderer.

Ridgway had been a suspect in the Green River homicides as far back as 1983, despite the fact that he passed a polygraph test at that time. It wasn't until 1987 that police finally gathered DNA evidence from Ridgway, a man who had once knocked on neighborhood doors evangelizing for his Pentecostal church, eventually using the scientific evidence to arrest and convict him. While the actual count of his victims hovered between forty-eight and fifty, even the lower number made Ridgway the most prolific serial killer in American history.

It seemed a little too neat for Finley that Browne seemed to be suggesting in an elliptical way that he, too, was laying claim to the number forty-eight. Was he in some twisted contest to match himself to Ridgway's ghastly achievement? It seemed a distinct possibility.

Yet even if it was true that Robert was out to lay his claim to fame, what remained inexplicable in Finley's response was that he seemed simply to ignore a second, sinister page that had been included in Browne's last letter. *"You have your information,"* Browne wrote, and indeed, he had handed Finley a crucial clue—a literal map delineating his ostensible crimes.

Hand-drawn and crudely rendered, Browne's map showed nines states in rough geographic proximity, starting with Washington in the upper-left corner, then skipping Oregon and outlining California further down the page. To the right, seven states were clumped together: New Mexico, Colorado, Oklahoma, Texas, Arkansas, Louisiana, and Alabama.

Within the outline of each of these states was a number: Washington had a 1; California, a 2; Colorado was listed with a

9; New Mexico and Oklahoma, 2 each; Texas, 7; Arkansas, 5; Alabama, 3; and Louisiana, an ominous 17. The total was forty-eight. The implication was clear.

Robert Browne had drawn a stark diagram of a killing spree that—if Finley counted from the deaths and disappearances of Wanda Faye Hudson and Faye Self in 1983 to the murder of Heather Church in 1991—had stretched over eight years. By his taunt he seemed to be proposing that if Finley could somehow crack the code of the white Grand Am, he would be on his way to solving the remaining eight cases that along with the Church murder made up the Colorado 9. It was a wide-open opportunity for a detective with the tenacity and time to sift through the unsolved-murders files of nine states looking for cases that Browne might have had a hand in.

Or was it? Finley was a working detective with a full case-load of active investigations to follow down. "Hunting geese" was a hazard of his profession, one to be avoided at all costs except, perhaps, that of solving the case. Finley had weighed out his options and walked away. Besides, Browne was where he belonged. Did it really matter what he was there for?

It did, of course. It would matter a great deal to the families of Robert's purported victims. Finley, who would later become an investigator with the Department of Corrections, had made a judgment call common to all cops. He decided Browne's mind games weren't worth playing.

Robert himself gave up the game after receiving Finley's letter. After all, the rules were clear: they would play it his way or not at all. The correspondence between Finley and Browne ceased.

But even as obscurity settled again over Robert, Lou Smit would file the enigmatic exchange in the back of his mind. He would recall it some two years later when, along with Charlie Hess and Scott Fischer, he perused the neatly filed shelf of cold-case files they had completely reorganized before wondering what they were going to do next.

"We had come up with a way of accessing information in

cold cases that could be applied by any police department any-where," asserts Lou Smit. Indeed, as the veteran cop would later demonstrate in his seminars on cold-case methodology, the referencing and cross-referencing of suspects, victims, evidence, locations, alibis, and other pertinent information had been fully digitized and logged into summaries, indexes, and calendars—a virtual table of contents for each unsolved crime. Along with Fischer, Smit had adopted computer templates to contrast and compare this welter of data, in the process providing an inestimable advantage to any investigating officer needing to get up to speed.

Those within the Colorado Springs Sheriff's Department immediately understood the value of what Hess wryly referred to as "grunt work." "Their system is a key for understanding and solving cases," enthused Support Service Bureau Chief Larry Kastner. "It's a road map for prosecutors and juries."

But that was all over now, a job well done for a trio of what Smit called "retired guys who want to help."

"It was hard to just walk away," recounted Fischer to the authors. "We'd gotten to know each other. Hell, we had breakfast together nearly every day and dinner at least three times a week. It's amazing to me that our wives put up with it. Once you get used to working together like that, as a team, you miss it when you're not together kicking around ideas and coming up with theories."

"We felt like we were part of something," adds Hess. "Brad Shannon, who had hooked us up in the first place, and guys like Joe Breister, a lieutenant in the department who was also a big supporter, came by a lot to see how we were doing. They became familiar with the cases as well and had ideas of their own to contribute. They hadn't just stuck us in a back room someplace. They knew there was a real possibility that we could help solve a few of those cases, some of which had been hanging around for decades."

It was Hess who first came up with the idea of carrying on

their work in another direction. "Actually, we all sort of arrived at the same place at the same time," he recounts. "We knew they wouldn't put us on an active case, which isn't what we wanted, anyway. We realized that the most valuable asset we could provide was our time. It made sense for us to go back and look at things that might have fallen through the cracks. There was no pressure, no trail to get cold. It was already cold. We could use the skills we had between us to pick it up again and follow it." He pauses to consider. "As much as anything," he adds at length, "we just didn't want to let our brains dry up."

The trio quickly set guidelines for themselves. First, they wanted a difficult case, one of those rare whodunits that would truly challenge them. They also determined they would go after big game. Many of the cold cases they had been working on had been just the opposite: crimes of passion in which the prime suspect had been more or less obvious from the beginning.

"We started talking about serial killers," continued Fischer. "We knew that most of them had been convicted for only a fraction of the actual killings they had committed. We figured that a good way to continue our cold-case work was to try and tie these guys to some of the murders and disappearances that were still on the books."

"We were too old to go chasing the bad guys from pillar to post," Hess admits. "I'd had two hip replacements, for Christ's sake. What appealed to us was someone who was sitting in jail with a lot of secrets. A lifer with nothing to lose."

"I thought of Browne immediately," Smit told the authors. "I had always known for a certainty that there was more going on in that case than just Heather Church. I knew what the team had dug up in Louisiana, and we learned that Finley had been writing to Browne, although I hadn't heard what had happened between them."

"It was a natural," agrees Hess. "Robert Browne was just who we were looking for. A guy with stories to tell. Maybe all he'd need was someone to listen."

CHAPTER FIFTEEN

"WHAT'S IMPORTANT TO YOU ISN'T IMPORTANT TO ME"

There are people who will claim that in one lucid moment of time, they have discovered what they have been meant all along to do with their lives. It's as if everything that has come before—all the seemingly random accumulation of knowledge and experience, the accidental expertise and unintended capabilities—suddenly lock into place for a specific purpose requiring their unique skill set.

Charlie Hess is not one of those people. Unlike his friend and partner Lou Smit, Hess is not one to assiduously seek divine purpose in the life choices that he has made or that have been made for him. Phlegmatic, even fatalistic, he has learned to deal with what comes his way by accepting it at face value. It was how he learned to cope with his drinking, accepting the things that he could not change—and how he had come to terms with such shattering events as the death of his son-in-law.

Nor was his sense of personal destiny heightened in early 2002 when Smit and Fischer volunteered him to write and introduce himself to Robert Browne in their attempt to draw the killer out. After all, Hess was seventy-five years old, with multiple open-heart surgeries and two bad hips to boot. It wasn't exactly the prime of his life. He had by and large been there and done that. As eager as the trio had been to find a case and keep their hand in catching the bad guys, Hess had no cause to guess that what could well be his last hurrah would become instead the high point of his career, bringing together a lifetime of learning and the distilled application of what he did best: talking and listening.

These were skills he had perfected in his years developing informants as an FBI agent, as a Phoenix operative in the CIA finessing double agents in the Vietnamese jungle, and as a master of the polygraph, charting the liminal zone between truth and lies. He had even accrued considerable previous experience in writing letters to open lines of communication with criminals and potential agents.

"Look," he says by way of explanation, "I'm not a big believer in fate. But the fact is, everything I've done all seems to add up to something. I was getting taught lessons all along that would come in handy later. I was figuring out how to motivate people, to get them to do something they didn't think they could do, or maybe didn't even know they wanted to do. In the process, I learned a lot about human nature. I made it my business. I studied how people lie, to each other and to themselves. And I tried never to judge them, because I knew what it meant to try to escape the truth, to avoid responsibility. I did it with drinking for thirty years. That keeps you humble. I'm no different from anybody else."

He pauses, squinting his left eye as he seems to search the empty air to find his thoughts. "What comes as a surprise to most people," he says at last, "is how much I've really liked some of the people I've dealt with in my time—the ladies of the night, the junkies, the killers." He smiles a craggy, knowing grin. "Some of the worst people can be some of your best friends."

Yet none of these hard-taught lessons—nor even the ability to hold their contradictions in balance—would necessarily avail when Charlie settled in to write his first letter to Robert C. Browne, Inmate 86504, Colorado State Penitentiary, Canon City, Colorado.

"There was no reason I could think of why he'd be willing to give me the time of day," Charlie admits. "He was serving a life sentence for murdering a little girl. There was nothing I could offer him that was going to change that. Any appeal to conscience was going to be totally futile. The whole idea that bad guys want to get it off their chest is pure Hollywood. In my experience, most of them are perfectly content to go to the grave with their secrets.

"On the other hand," Hess allows, "I kept thinking about that map he'd drawn for Finley, each state with a number written in it. At one point it seemed as if he'd really wanted to talk, or at least to bargain. It seemed like it was worth a shot."

By an extraordinary coincidence Charlie's hunch was confirmed when, on May 5, 2002, after a silence of almost two years, Detective Finley once again received a missive from Browne. The killer was picking up the correspondence as if no time, or bad blood, had passed between them at all, asking an intriguing question that seemed to suggest at least the outlines of a possible bargain. *"If a person were to identify a murder,"* he conjectured, *"and then pled guilty to this murder in exchange for a sentence of death, how long would it take for the execution to take place?"*

Finley would never receive the letter. In the many months since he had last heard from Browne, the detective had left the Sheriff's Department, landing a job as an investigator for the Colorado Department of Corrections, where he worked exclusively on crimes committed by the huge prison population of the state, both convicts and employees. The inmate's enigmatic query instead landed on the desk of Joe Breister, the lieutenant of the Investigations Divisions for the sheriff and an early champion of the Apple Dumpling Gang's cold-case project. On receipt of the handwritten single page, Breister immediately took two steps: he passed the letter along to Charlie Hess and responded himself to Browne.

"There is no simple answer to your question," he wrote

back, after introducing himself. *". . . If a person who committed the murder was hypothetically serving a life sentence for a previous murder, and provided credible evidence which led to the discovery of a body and evidence supporting such a crime, represented themselves at trial, pled or was found guilty, was sentenced to death and waived all appeals, the sentence could be fast-tracked and carried out within 18 months. However, before any death sentence is carried out, it is automatically appealed at least once to the Colorado Supreme Court. That's the best case scenario."*

The unintended irony of the last sentence reflected Breister's uncertainty as to exactly what Browne might be asking. Breister was well aware of the possibility that the convict might have any number of other crimes to his credit, and it seemed at least possible that they were at the tentative beginnings of a negotiating process. Was Browne suggesting that, like convicted Utah murderer Gary Gilmore, he was demanding to be put out of his misery by insisting on an expeditious execution? Or was this simply the opening gambit for a proposed deal, a teasing hint of information that might or might not be forthcoming? By connecting Browne's "hypothetical question" to the killer's own situation as a "person serving a life sentence for a previous murder," Breister was signaling that at the very least, he was willing to play the game.

Or rather, have Charlie Hess play it. *"Incidentally,"* Breister continued in his reply, *"you have probably already received a letter from a retired law enforcement officer who volunteers at the El Paso County Sheriff's Office. I thought you should know that he does volunteer his time and reports to me."*

Indeed, a week earlier Charlie had composed his first communication to Browne, introducing himself as *"a volunteer . . . mostly working on cold murder cases,"* and outlining his background as a *"Special Agent for the FBI, a CIA Agent in Vietnam and ultimately a retired polygraph operator."* He continued:

In my endeavors here, I had occasion to review certain details of your case. I must say I was very intrigued by the correspondence you directed to the District Attorney's Office here, subsequent to your incarceration. The information you alluded to brings to mind previous high profile matters I handled and [I] am wondering if you feel it in your interest to grant me an interview.

It has been my experience that intelligent, unique individuals often times are in a position to illuminate matters that could never come to light via any other avenue.

Hoping that you feel a contact would be of mutual value, I remain,

> *Sincerely,*
> *Charles J. Hess*

Even a casual parsing of Hess's prose demonstrates the full range of the specialized skills he had worked a lifetime to acquire. The nonthreatening tone, the aura of slight erudition, the carefully couched flattery and discreet deference—simply put, Charlie was in his element. "The first thing you have to do," Hess explains, "is get out of that cop mentality. Experience teaches most cops that a dirtbag is always going to be a dirtbag and should be treated as such. The quicker you let him know who's the boss, the better. But it was Robert who really held all the cards, and it was his choice to play them or not. There was no percentage in provoking him. What you need is a light touch, a little finesse. For instance, when you suggest that you've had a hand in "previous high profile matters" you're telling him that *he's* high profile. The truth is, that was pretty much bullshit. I just wanted him to get the idea that someone important was taking an interest in him, even if it was just some retired dude in the cold-case locker."

But it wasn't all bullshit. "I had reason to believe that Robert was intelligent," Hess goes on. "There was something in the tone of his letters that sort of put him above the limitations of his education and upbringing. As far as being unique," he adds with a laugh, "well, that all depends on your definition of the word."

Charlie's carefully crafted strategy yielded immediate results. Within a week of mailing the letter, he received a reply, confirming in no uncertain terms that the game between them had well and truly begun. Although Browne refused a face-to-face meeting, he did hold open the possibility of further correspondence, asking, *"What specifically were you intrigued by? What high profile matters were brought to mind? What matters would you like to be illuminated?"* Taking the stakes up another notch, he added, *"My perception (accurate or distorted) will have a great bearing on the amount of what I share."*

"As far as I was concerned, we were off to a great start," Hess observes. "At the very least we had a dialogue going. He was responding to my questions, even though it was with questions of his own. I didn't really expect that I'd get a chance to meet with him. At least not right away. That was a privilege that was up to him to grant. But at the same time, I had someplace to go with this, a way to maybe move him forward, if I was slow and careful about it."

"Thank you for answering my letter," Hess wrote back on June 11, picking up where he left off with a measured mix of compliments and points of common interest. It was all very conversational. Browne, in prison for life, had, after all, nothing if not time, and it was Hess's job to prove that he, too, was willing to spend as long as it took to gain trust and prove himself worthy to hear the dark tales that Browne could tell.

"I note too that you were in Vietnam. I directed the CIA Phoenix Program in III Corps. . . . I however, did not earn a Bronze Star, a worthy accomplishment."

"I may have been laying it on a little thick, there," Hess admits. "But, hey, he must have done something to deserve it, and there was nothing to lose by giving him a little credit."

The obligatory strokes dispensed with, Charlie got down to business. *"As to the questions you posed (1) I was intrigued by the unique manner in which you originally chose the communicate, the map, the poetic verse, etc. (2) The cases it brought to mind were Ted Bundy, Henry Lucas and Otis Toole."*

Hess, of course, had had nothing to do with "handling" the cases of Bundy, Lucas, and Toole. Perhaps the most infamous serial killer in modern American history, Ted Bundy would eventually confess to the rape and murder of thirty young women. Before recanting, Henry Lee Lucas claimed an astonishing total of 350 homicides, a figure later called into question as a result of sloppy police work and what was widely considered to be a hoax. Lucas's alleged partner, Ottis Toole, was reputed to have slain and eaten his victims and was convicted of two murders, confessing to four more before dying in prison. "It seemed like good company," Hess grimly jokes. "I wanted him to believe that he was right up there with the most notorious names I could think of."

But it was in answer to Browne's third query that Hess cut to the chase. *"In response to the question in your letter,"* he wrote, *"The matters where I sought illumination were those unsolved cases to which you alluded. It did appear that you wished to provide details, by virtue of the information you provided. I feel you have a desire to clear up some pending matters. I, of course, have no idea as to your goal."*

"He knew that I knew that I was just out on a fishing expedition," Hess admits. "Maybe he was just fucking with me. The only way I was going to find out for sure was to play it out as far as it went. Which meant I had to do my part."

His part was clear but by no means easy. "I wanted him to tell me his secrets," Charlie continues, "the most personal stuff he had. Which meant I was going to have to do the same."

"As to my goal," he wrote, *"several years ago our family experienced a tragic event. My son-in-law was murdered . . . The void created by his death can never be filled, but there is great solace in closure. I decided to do as much as I can to assist others in finding closure. I have wondered if you too, would experi-*

ence a form of relief by revealing information that would give peace to parties who have a relationship to any case where you have information.

Perhaps we can both achieve our goals. Mine, closure. Yours . . . ?"

A six-week silence ensued. "I was starting to wonder what it was I had written that might have pissed him off," Charlie recounts. "I started second-guessing the way I'd poured my heart out. This guy could be up there laughing at me. Later, Robert told me straight up, 'What's important to you isn't important to me.' I took that to heart."

Then, on a sweltering summer day in late July, Hess received another missive from 86504. It marked both a new dimension in their evolving relationship and an escalation in their high-stakes contest of wits.

The difference was evident from the opening sentence, a marked departure from the polite and mannered formulations of Browne's previous correspondence. The tone now was one of naked contempt.

"I must say," he wrote without preamble, *"I am dumbfounded that, with the plethora if information provided, that someone hasn't deciphered such a simple and obvious message. I can only infer that, to this point, no one has truly harbored a desire to do so.*

"Does this clarify matters?" he continued with an almost palpable sneer:

> *Location: Murky placid depth—cool caressing mire.*
> *Amount: Seven.*
> *Instructions: Drain—dig.*
> *Accomplice: High priestess.*
> *Motive: sacred virgins—less worthy scattered.*

"It didn't clarify shit," Hess snorts. "It was just a rehash of all the stuff he'd sent to Finley. To tell you the truth, I'd never really bought into the seven sacred virgins and the high priestess and all that. It was too much like a bad Hollywood movie. Besides, if he really had killed seven virgins, you'd think they might have turned up in missing persons reports somewhere.

"The high priestess reference also seemed a little dubious," he continues. "Was he saying that he has an accomplice? Was she real or imaginary? There was no way of knowing except to follow him down the rabbit hole."

And once Browne got started, the trail grew increasingly twisted. *"Something else that might be of interest to you,"* the prisoner wrote. *"Hypothetically, if individuals were held in a concealed chamber and their caretaker was incarcerated, thereby causing these individuals to succumb over time, would the caretaker be considered guilty of murder, even though their deaths were a direct result of actions taken by law enforcement officials? I suppose there should be three added to the nine."*

"I was beginning to understand how Finley felt," Hess confesses. "I had the distinct impression I was getting jacked around. But it was also possible that he was letting me in on something. I looked at that phrase 'three added to the nine' for a long time. Was he talking about three other murders added to the nine he had placed in Colorado on his map? Either way, I had no choice. It was going to be Robert's rules or no rules at all. So, despite my reservations, I tried to give it all equal weight."

Robert concluded, in his July 26 letter, by requesting Charlie to provide him addressses of the Product-Development Divisions of the Ford Motor Company.

CHAPTER SIXTEEN

THE WHITE GRAND AM

"See what I mean?" Hess asks laconically. "The Ford Motor Company. He obviously dreamed some high-concept monster truck and convinced himself he was going to revolutionize Detroit. It's amazing where you can take yourself when the only place you can go is inside of your head, that echo chamber in your skull. It's a form of insanity, and in order to get what I was after, I needed to take on a bit of the craziness myself. He wanted to talk to the Ford Motor Company? Why not?"

As Robert Browne's mood took a wide swing to petulant derision, Hess would maintain a steady focus on his ultimate goal. "Even though he hadn't responded to my personal information," he explains, "I had the feeling there was still a way to build some mutual trust. I emphasized the positive, the experience we both had in common: Vietnam."

Charlie became downright philosophical as he looked for a chink in the killer's emotional armor. *"What a peculiar world we live in,"* he mused in a letter dated August 5, in which he duly supplied the Ford Motor Company address Browne had requested. *"About thirty years ago we were both trained to dispatch human beings and sent 12,000 miles away for that purpose. Now you are being incarcerated for just that, and I am investigating the who, what and where of it. The gods must be bewildered. Is it a stage on which we each have a role to play, or is the complexity of it beyond our comprehension?"*

"It seemed like a legitimate question," Hess asserts, "especially for someone in his position. What I was trying to say was that taking a life is relative to the situation you're in. We'd both been soldiers, trained to kill—we had that in common. The difference was that I had a pretty good idea how much he enjoyed it."

"In an earlier communication," he added, by way of reminding Browne that he was willing to swap his own private revelations for those of the killer's, *"you inquired of an investigator if he was interested in notoriety and wealth. At age seventy-five neither of these elements were of importance to me but before I leave this planet I would like to 'make a difference' in at least a few more instances."*

Hess then circled back around to the as-yet-unspoken agenda of their correspondence. *"I am hoping we can discuss these matters on a factual basis,"* he wrote. *"Permit me to pose a hypothetical. If an individual provides very cryptic information leading to the discovery of human remains, is that person less culpable than someone who gives precise detail? I believe you are trying to reach out to us and believe me, we are trying to reach out to you. You know what our interest is. What is the quid pro quo?"*

"I wanted to step it up a notch," Hess reveals. "I knew from experience that I could easily end up as his pen pal for the next several years, running down addresses for him or giving him free legal advice. It was a calculated risk based solely on the feeling that he somehow *needed* to talk to me. I wasn't sure why. Maybe he was just lonely. But whatever it was, there had to be a mutual benefit in keeping it going."

To soften the implicit challenge to Browne's meandering missives, Charlie ended his letter with the most concrete offer of friendship to date. *"Since I am aware of your appearance,"* he concluded, *"I am enclosing a photo so that you know mine."* The snapshot he tucked into the letter had been taken on a recent deep-sea fishing trip and showed Hess proudly displaying a large yellowfin tuna, its scales sparkling against the cloudless sky and a deep blue sea.

"That had to get him," he says with some small satisfaction. "I knew that he thought of himself as an outdoorsman. But as much as anything, I wanted to stir him up a little bit, give him a glimpse of the freedom he'd never have again. I'd been around criminals long enough to know that they're a lot easier to talk to when they're feeling sorry for themselves."

The ploy paid off spectacularly. Two weeks later Browne replied, and this time it was his turn to pour out his heart. "I'm not sure what did it," Hess admits. "It could have been the picture. Or it could have been me telling him it was time to cut bait or fish, no pun intended. Or maybe it was just that we'd reached critical mass. All of a sudden, I was his bosom buddy. He wanted to tell me everything, and he had a lot to say."

He did indeed. In a four-page handwritten letter dated August 26, 2002, Browne, in total fulfillment of Charlie's prediction, launched into a long lament over his poor health, the cruelty and stupidity of the justice system, and, for good measure, a virulent rumination on the human condition.

"That's a nice yellow fin in the picture," he observed, going on to complain about the heavy diet of carbohydrates he was forced to endure in prison and how the picture of the fish set off an acute craving for protein. *"Did that tuna taste as good as it looked?"* he asked plaintively. The subject of food elicited an excoriation of the prison bureaucracy. *"This place is overrun with simpletons who believe their employment makes them righteous beings,"* he ranted, but the real purpose of the letter seemed to be a wide-ranging and bitter philosophical screed, revealing more of Browne's mindset than even Hess had bargained for. *"Rage motivates murder,"* he asserted. *"Most homicides are crimes of passion and the passion of anger. Sometimes it's specific. A man murders his cheating wife. A son kills his sadistic father. Sometimes, its more general. Everybody deserves to die. It's up to you to settle the score."* After I read that letter from Robert, I felt as if I had tapped into the full force of his grudge against the gods and man. There was no room for mercy in his

world, no advantage to being kind and good, It was dog eat dog and he was determined to eat his share."

"You mentioned 'the gods must be bewildered,'" wrote Browne, reminding Hess of his last letter. *"I beg to differ. The gods must be ecstatic. I think the gods, at least the ones I am aware of, are taking great pleasure in the misguided squirming of humanity, which has created its gods to mirror itself. For example, the god of the Old Testament time and again killed thousands upon thousands of men, women and children and even their livestock. In addition, he had others kill, in his name, time and again, thousands and thousands of men, women and children."*

"Maybe I was just reading into it," Charlie ventures, "but the way he kept repeating that phrase about killing thousands upon thousands of men, women, and children, it was like a chant almost. Later Robert would tell me that his problem was not that he had killed so many people. It was that he had to show great will power to keep from killing so many more. When I read those lines in his letter, I got my first inkling of what his capacity for murder really was. Even that mention of livestock: I couldn't help but remember what Jon Miank had told the detectives about how he and Robert had gone out and slaughtered cattle and how Robert drank their blood, straight from the severed artery."

"It eludes me how humans can worship such an evil vindictive creature," Browne continued. *"Maybe it's as simple as [that] humanity is in denial. Maybe Jack Nicholson's line 'You can't handle the truth!!!' encompasses all of humanity."*

"Maybe so," Charlie allows. "He certainly had a point, at least as he had learned from hard experience. I'm not a religious man, but you've at least got to believe in the basic goodness of man. Even in my line of work, I cling to the idea that, under different circumstances, everybody has the chance to make something of themselves, to serve their fellow man. Robert didn't see it that way and it wasn't for me to tell him he was wrong. My job was a lot simpler: I just had to figure out what he'd done once he'd thrown off all the restraints that he claimed were nothing but society's lies."

Having to live under the rule of those ostensible lies was at the root of Robert's resentment, dug deep into his troubled childhood in Coushatta, inexorably connecting him to a family that, according to his bruised memories, ruthlessly exploited his youth and innocence. It was an all-too-familiar story to Charlie. "Most of us have childhood traumas, I would venture," he says. "From what I could tell, Robert had a hard life, sure, but it wasn't any more damaging, in my opinion, than half the walking wounded you meet out on the street. The fact was, he nursed his grievances, stored them up and rehearsed whenever he needed to remind himself that he'd gotten a raw deal and was owed some kind of recompense. He wanted you to believe that he had a special reason for being who he was, that the cruel world had driven him to it."

That was certainly the import in the closing pages of Browne's August 26 magnum opus, which consisted of his self-pitying account of childhood deprivation which would subsequently provide valuable corroboration of the investigative work of Mark Finley, Michele Hodges, and others on the investigative team who had gone to Red River Parish in the first days after the Church case broke. What Browne would describe to Hess, with withering scorn, as "the endless joys of my childhood," only confirmed for the veteran detective the lethal mix of rancor and revenge that seemingly motivated all of Browne's human interactions. "I kept trying to read between the lines," Hess recalls. "Here he is talking about how he cries and cries because they took away his bed. Look, when you've got murder on your mind, any excuse is good enough. He needed to believe he had a reason for being mad at the world. Maybe he did, but I never quite got it."

"I don't plan to be around much longer," Browne concluded at length, a kind of morose disregard settling into his writing.

"So the quid pro quo, whatever it could be, is probably insignificant in my motive. I'm fatigued so I guess I'll close for now."

"I pictured him turning out the light and pulling up his blankets under his chin with the noises of the cellblock around him," Charlie says. "Then I thought of the people who'd crossed his path who weren't ever going to see another light or hear another sound, and I remembered all over again what I was doing this for."

Hess was also only too aware that if he didn't finish the job, it might not get done at all. "Lou and Scott were with me all the way," he explains. "Scott even typed up my handwritten letters to make them legible. But I was really carrying the ball on this one. And right around this time, I started having more health problems. The doctor told me I needed another hip replacement operation. I knew at my age that there was always a chance that I wouldn't pull through. In my last few bypass operations I hadn't responded to the medication, and they'd had a hard time bringing me back. I started wondering if there was some way I could move things along with Robert. I also had this feeling that a lot of dead people were depending on me."

For his part, Hess was determined to keep the lines of communication open with Browne. The convict's revealing letter of August 26 was delayed in the mail, and in September, before it finally arrived, Hess had already written back.

"Ordinarily I would await your reply to my last letter," he began, *"but in this instance I thought I would contact you.*

"Even though I do not have any idea of your intentions, I am hoping we can accelerate the process in which we find ourselves." After explaining his upcoming surgery, Hess asked if it wouldn't be possible to *"get something tangible underway before I enter the hospital? I realize that if in fact the matters to which you have hinted have merit, that you may have some apprehensions as to how information you may furnish may ultimately affect you. Any questions you may have, we believe we can answer."*

"I was really grasping at straws," Charlie admits. "If Browne were to admit to killing Heather Church, there was nothing we could do to protect him in prison, where a child murderer is considered the lowest form of life. Besides, he was serving a life sentence. Nothing was going to change that. Maybe we could make his time a little easier, but there was really no incentive we could offer him that would really make a difference. If he wanted to tell us where the bodies were buried, he'd be doing so for his own reasons. The reality was, for all the progress I'd made, I still had absolutely no leverage with Robert except whatever friendship was between us."

"I have thought of a couple of possibilities for communicating information to us," Hess would continue in the same hopeful vein. *"Suppose someone would provide us with information on a specific matter, i.e. name, location, date, etc . . . and do it in some anonymous form such as through a third party, or some other such vehicle? I, of course, would pay you a visit and would naturally come alone. Would this allow us to establish the actual bona fides and help to formulate a mutually acceptable course of action? I realize that we are not necessarily on the same schedule, but I hope you will give some consideration to the above."*

For Robert, the whole notion was unworthy of even mentioning. In his reply, dated September 6, he seemed more concerned about his last lengthy letter, which had crossed in the mail, blaming the delay on the Department Of Corrections.

"My heart sank a little," Charlie confesses. "He was back to using me to vent his spleen. I wondered if he was going a little stir-crazy. He was starting to ramble, to string his ideas together in a disjointed way, just assuming that I was willing and able to follow along. Of course, that was part of the impression I had wanted to make in the first place: that I was on his side; that I was interested in anything and everything he had to say. But maybe I'd succeeded a little too well."

The rest of Browne's letter did nothing to improve Charlie's outlook, with the prisoner launching into one of his trademark tirades against the inequities of society in general and the prison system in particular. *"Most inmates will someday be released,"* he wrote. *"Regardless of their mental state before incarceration, they will be angry, vicious, vindictive creatures because of the routine and continuous abuse inflicted on them by the evil, sadistic, sanctimonious police and their guards. The seeds sown by this treatment will reach fruition after the inmates are set loose on society. Societies [sic] own creation will be societies [sic] demise. What do you think about this?"*

"At that point I pretty much felt like giving up," sighs Hess. "He was just playing with me. It was obvious that Robert was trying to make some point about how he'd been put in jail for the wrong crime, as if it really mattered. As far as society breeding vengeful monsters in jail, I got a real kick out of that, the whole idea of Browne warning the world about homicidal maniacs. In the end, I guess I didn't know whether to laugh or cry."

In the end, however, Hess did neither. Browne closed his letter with the hope that *"your surgery goes well."* Then, below the signature, he added a PS:

December or January 1987 or 1988 (about then maybe?)
White Grand Am
Colorado Springs

"I looked at that for a long time," Charlie recounts. "It rang a bell, somewhere in the back of my mind. I'd heard that bell before. It usually comes when you're about to get a break in a case, just about the time you've given up hope."

CHAPTER SEVENTEEN

DERKESTHAI

For the next nearly two years it was if the Apple Dumpling Gang had slipped imperceptibly into the strange twilight world of prison time, with days and weeks and months falling like a row of slow-motion dominos toward some inevitable extinguishment. Up in Canon City, Robert Browne unwound his centuries-long sentence in a numbing routine of crushing boredom, futile scheming, and institutional dementia. That same malignant penumbra had seeped into the cramped neon-lit confines of the cold-case office, turning it into yet another kind of prison.

"We ran that Grand Am lead into the ground," Lou Smit recounted to the authors. "We reviewed all our cold cases, had a look at the active homicide investigations, scoured the missing-persons files, looking for something, *anything*, that could connect that make and model car to a murder, solved or unsolved. Then we did the same thing all over again, with neighboring sheriff's departments and city police up to Denver and beyond. We pretty much scoured the state and at the end of a couple of months of hard work had exactly nothing to show for our efforts. We just sat there and looked at each other, wondering what to do next."

With the Grand Am investigation grinding on, Hess made sure to keep the lines of communication open with Browne. "I didn't want to reference the fact that we were looking high and low for an incriminating Pontiac," he explains. "Until we had something solid, I didn't want him thinking he could get us jumping through hoops. In the meantime, I went back to the earlier letters, really pored over them, trying to figure out if I was missing something. The last thing I wanted was to let my own perceptions and prejudices color the investigation. I didn't believe there was a real high priestess, but I had to keep an open mind, so I started checking sources—books on the occult and magic and the supernatural."

"I must admit that your references to the High Priestess have my mind awhirl," Hess wrote on September 12, after finally receiving the waylaid letter Browne had written some three weeks earlier. *"In reviewing Tarot depictions, the Magician and the High Priestess are balancing forces that make up the perceived world: the Priestess is the negative side . . . our unrealized potential waiting for an active principle to bring it to expression. Are you that active principle?*

"Robert, are we talking about a real person, or is the High Priestess allegorical?" Hess went on, trying once again to cut to the chase. *"I continue to feel that you are trying to provide me with specifics, but for some reason we don't get over that last hurdle. . . . Our relationship has now covered a long period of time but I feel we have begun to establish a level of trust. Do you feel that a face to face is appropriate? As I mentioned in my last letter, I go in for surgery November 4. What are the chances we can talk prior to that date?*

In a mutual search for life's answers to our existence, I wish you well."

Three weeks later, Browne would receive a birthday card from Charlie depicting a regal snowy owl with a piercing yellow-orbed stare. "It was all part of the charm offensive," Hess says. "I wanted to send him a present, too, and did a search of prison records to see if I could come up with something appropriate." A list of books Browne had checked out from the library included titles from the *Grandmaster* fantasy series, written by the team Warren Murphy and Molly Cochran, but Hess was told he could not send anything except letters directly to the prisoner.

The books would not have bolstered Hess's hope that sooner or later he and Robert could stop talking in riddles. Murphy and Cochran had concocted a blend of potboiling mysticism and international espionage, lurid ongoing adventures best summed up by a blurb from the series' 1984 debut: "Two men, born on the same day on opposite sides of the world, driven to oppose each other—for only one man may be the Grandmaster!" It was a description that in itself would have certainly elicited a groan from the stymied detectives.

As it turned out, however, Browne's literary tastes had turned to the somewhat more elevated realms of the *Earth Children*, another fanciful series, this time penned by Jean M. Auel. Beginning with the best seller *Clan of the Cave Bear*, featuring a Cro-Magnon heroine named Ayla, the five *Earth Children* books served up heavily researched prehistoric epics replete with survival tips on everything from medicinal plants and herbs to constructing a snow cave—perfect fodder for Browne's rugged wilderness fantasies. In a return letter to Hess, he even devised a way to get *The Shelters of Stone*, the last in the series, past prison authorities. *"You might consider contacting the library here to see if you could donate the book,"* he suggested, *"possibly with the hope that it could be checked out to me first."*

"The guy was always thinking," says Hess with laugh. "I guess where there's a will there's a way." Locating a copy of the book, he dutifully set about the arduous process of getting it to the inmate.

It was on October 29 that Browne replied to Hess's request for more specifics with a letter that in the end did little to move the process forward. Thanking Charlie for the birthday card and noting that he took "solace" in the "elegant and stoical beauty" of the snowy owl, the killer next took a decidedly disingenuous tack.

"I am just a simple uneducated country boy," he coyly wrote. *"Much of what I write is very simple and plain. One*

should take care not to over analyze my writings. To do so could easily obscure their simplistic nature."

"I guess I had only myself to thank for that," Charlie sighs. "I spent so much time trying to convince him I was fascinated by everything he said that now he was giving me his rules of good literature. Not that it helped much. He was off again on the high priestess, and when he got to my 'active principle' theory, it really got him wound up."

"As far as being the 'Active Principle,'" Browne theorized, *"this depends on the aspect of one's view. Would you consider the procurer, caretaker and disposer to be the 'Active Principle?' Disposer, not dispatcher. I suppose to be a procurer, caretaker, and disposer would make one an enabler, thus making one the 'Active Principle.' You can look at it that way if you so choose."*

"I kept having to remind myself that I was dealing with a very dangerous individual, who was probably a hell of a lot smarter than I was," Hess says. "He wasn't just some harmless crank with some crackpot ideas. I'd been hoping to build a bond, something I could use to get next to him. But he just kept ducking in and out of the shadows, playing hide and seek. I felt like I was running circles down a cul-de-sac."

It was at this point that Browne again shifted tack, returning to the self-pity that always lurked just below the surface. *"Trust is something that has been hammered out of me,"* he wrote. *"Maybe in time I could cultivate some semblance of trust. Maybe."*

"I wondered what kind of in-depth conversations he had had with his victims," Hess remembers with more than a trace of scorn. "To tell you the truth, I was pretty much at the end of my rope. We'd been at this for six months and now we were back to Robert feeling sorry for himself all over again."

Hess's frame of mind was hardly improved by the sign-off of Browne's late October letter: *"Sincerely, Derkesthai."* "I checked it out," Charlie continues. "Apparently Derkesthai was a name he found in a book called *The Dragon Legacy: The Secret His-*

tory of an Ancient Bloodline by a guy who actually called himself Prince Nicholas de Vere von Drakenberg. When I saw that, I
was really ready to throw in the towel."

"The three of us got together," Scott Fischer recounts to the
authors. "Between us we decided that it was time for a 'put-up-
or-shut-up' letter. We left it up to Charlie to figure out how to do
that without shutting down Browne completely. It wasn't going
to be easy, but at that point we had nothing to lose."

Hess decided to return to the Grand Am puzzle to see if he
could pry loose another clue. *"Dear Robert,"* he wrote on November 2. *"Perhaps you give us too much credit. In searching
available records regarding the use of vehicles involved in
cases, we are unable to locate any reference to a white Grand
Am."*

At the same time, he made sure not to neglect the requisite
flattery:

*"Robert, your letter of 10/29 surprises me. First of all, you
are not a simple country boy. You are obviously intelligent and
have shown great initiative. . . . Your understated sophistication
reminds me of the guy who sits down at the poker table and
says, 'I'm not good at this. What's higher, a straight or a flush?'
and promptly takes everyone's money.*

*"Further, I wonder why you feel it necessary to write in enig-
matic terms. After all, you were the one to initiate communication back in 2000. If you were just trying to tantalize those
responsible for your incarceration, I can understand that, but I
can't understand why you would want to 'run me around the
bush.' After all, I've put all my cards on the table. You know my
objectives, which do not include causing you any discomfort.*

*"Frankly I'm about the only one here that believes that you
can really put some cases to rest. Won't you consider laying out
just one verifiable instance? If you have reservations about being
open, please express them and I will try to resolve them. If this is
just a game, tell me, and we can continue to exchange philoso-
phies. You say that you find a face to face unacceptable, as you*

have not had a meaningful conversation in some time. . . . A visit is not a test, it's an exchange between two people.

Now it's my turn. I'm just a simple country boy from Wisconsin who needs your assistance." He signed off, *"Charlie, the Elder Dragon."*

"I made a mistake going in," Hess confesses. "All this time our communication had been personal, just between him and me. Now, I was talking about 'we,' which must have given him the impression that there was a bunch of cops standing over my shoulder. And that was true, as far as it went. The Sheriff's Department certainly kept tabs on what I was doing. He'd picked up on it right away . . . and he didn't like it one bit."

"In your previous letter," Browne wrote on December 16, in reply to Hess's November correspondence, *"you said . . . 'you give us too much credit.' I beg to differ. There was at least one case handled by 'us' where evidence was found where none existed. With police work like that, one cannot give 'us' too much credit. It seems that where legitimate information has been provided on several cases 'us' should have no problem completing the puzzle, if 'us' has any real desire to do so! I will not hand it to 'us' on a golden platter with nothing to gain for my efforts. What I could possibly gain eludes me for now."*

For all his anger and disdain, Hess picked up a ray of hope. "He was indicating, as least to my way of reading it, that he actually *had* something to trade and was at least willing to consider what he wanted in return."

It was a conjecture emphatically underscored as the letter continued. *"There are eight other states that may be interested,"* he wrote in an obvious reference to the nine-state map he had sent to Mark Finley back in 2000. *"Colorado has only nine points of interest. Louisiana has seventeen. The food in Louisiana prisons is far superior. There are also states with mutual interest in many of the Colorado twelve. Dispatch and disposal may have taken place in Colorado, but procurement may have taken place elsewhere. With procurement in play, the*

*number of states that may be interested more than doubles.
Also, how much prestige would come to an individual or office
that could solve at least 51 cases?"*

"This was a breakthrough," says Hess, recalling the excitement with which he and his partners mulled over the implications of Browne's chilling words. "For the first time I sensed the
true dimensions of what we were dealing with. But at the same
time, it was hard to know exactly what Robert might actually be
suggesting. It was obvious to us that he would have a lot to tell
us if we could ever get him to open up, but some of it was confusing and contradictory: Were there nine cases in Colorado, or
was it twelve? What was the difference between 'dispatch' and
'disposal'? What did he mean by the reference to the food in
Louisiana prisons? Was he angling for some kind of transfer?
The big question in my mind was that number 'fifty-one.' Was
he really saying he killed fifty-one people? Suddenly, the whole
case took on a new importance. We weren't just three old guys
out on a fishing expedition. If we could prove that what Robert
seemed to be saying was true, we'd be on to the biggest mass
murderer in American history." He shrugs. "Or it could all just
be pure bullshit.

"At the same time," Hess continues, "we made sure to keep
each other's enthusiasm in check. All three of us had had
enough experience with men behind bars to know that there's a
fine line between reality and fantasy. Robert was no fool, but
that didn't mean he wasn't crazy. Convicts make up shit all the
time just to have something to do. We still had our work cut out
for us, just to prove that Robert wasn't sending us out chasing
geese."

Birds seemed to be on Browne's mind as well, as he returned again to the image of the birthday greeting Hess had sent
him back on Halloween and lingered on the hoary image of the
snowy owl from the card. *"Nature is something I sorely miss,"*
he wrote. *"Through this small slit of a window I can see a wall
about 30 feet away. A wonderful view."*

Before 2002 was out, Browne would provide Hess with another view, this one of a moonlit forest glade blanketed with snow and traced by a meandering stream. *"In this spirit of renewal and reflection,"* read the treacly sentiment on the inside of the Christmas card he sent to Charlie, *"may our spirits wake to the beauty of life—may our hearts awake to the joy of love!"* Below it Robert had added his own holiday greeting: *"Have a merry merry and a happy happy."*

The elliptical negotiations continued in early 2003 when, on January 7, Hess replied to the tantalizing implications of Browne's last letter. *"You know Robert, I agree with you. I do not believe I would put the details on a gold platter without first receiving the assurances you consider important. On the other hand it makes one wonder why you wrote in the first place? You must have been moved by something."*

"I was starting to get the hang of dealing with Robert," Hess contends. "It was a real balancing act, because I needed to strike up a friendship. Whatever else he might have been, Robert was a smart guy with an interesting point of view. I never really stopped to consider whether I was faking being his buddy or not. I just did what came naturally, and the connection took its own course."

As the new year commenced, Hess began to push the boundaries of that connection. "I told him early on that I'd never lie to him," he explains. "It seemed like the time was right to give him the benefit of my point of view, regardless of how he might react to it. I felt like I'd earned the right."

"The following came to mind," Hess wrote in early 2003, *"when I tried to answer the question of why you had written in the first place; (One), you were angry at the outcome of your case and wanted to put those who worked the case through frustrating and maddening scenarios; (Two), that by using large numbers of victims you could heighten the level of interest; (Three), that in reality there are no unsolved cases, but you received satisfaction in the consternation which would arise;*

(Four) that there are other cases out there that you truly wish to set straight; (Five), due to the lassitude of incarceration you keep your mind alert via this correspondence.

So, Robert, where do we go from here?"

To soften his implied ultimatum, Hess wandered off into safer territory, describing his experiences hunting and fishing up in Northern Wisconsin and a trip he had once taken to track geese in Lake Charles, Louisiana. Yet of many ancillary topics the two traded—including the sinking fortunes of the New Orleans Saints in that year's football season—none seemed to interest Browne more than the possibility of writing a book of his life and crimes. "I did my best to encourage him," Hess recounts, "helping him get in touch with a writer and doing research on how to get published. If he was serious about writing his life story, it might be another potential source of information."

The lure of authorship, for Browne, seemed to loom large and he announced that he was planning to write a book in a letter to Hess dated January 16. *"I would like the world to understand how monsters are created,"* he revealed. *"They are a product of society."* He also let it be known that he had *"no incentive to reveal this information to other sources. Time is short. I need to get my affairs in order."*

Excoriating society for its callousness and maintaining the value of his "product" weren't Browne's only preoccupations during the long months of that frigid Colorado winter. With his revolutionary automotive design apparently now on the back burner, he was instead anxious for Hess to forward him the addresses of *"tree hugger companies or organizations."* His purpose was to get them interested in a utopian device that would produce a virtually *"endless supply of energy with absolutely no cost."*

The two had been down this road before, but Hess had learned his lesson. He was getting information, albeit in dribs and drabs, and the price was to entertain some of Robert's more fanciful notions. "It was like he was testing me, to see how far I would go with him," he explains. "My rule of thumb was: 'As far as it takes.' "

"Am I delusional?" Browne asked rhetorically, still on the subject of his ostensible energy breakthrough. *"Is this akin to the dreams of a perpetual motion machine? I don't think so."*

It was only after he'd laid out his plans to furnish the world with abundant clean energy that Browne finally deigned to address Hess's pressing questions directly: *"You are wondering 'why I wrote in the first place.' I don't know if I could answer that to your satisfaction. What my thoughts were at the time, I do not recall."*

Hess had gotten his marching orders and duly hunted down a contact for Dean Kamen, the inventor of the IT, a clean-energy scooter, as well as supplying addresses for various ecology publications. "Meanwhile," he recounts, "I had gotten a hold of a writer who showed some interest in doing Robert's life story. I was hoping to use the possibility of a book as leverage to start him talking."

"At the present time we are actively, but quietly, working on setting up procedures to work out logistical matters with the DOC," he wrote on the subject of a possible collaboration in a letter dated January 21. *"Since this is not an everyday event and very strict rules are in effect, quite a few aspects will have to be considered. One thing [that] was made very clear to me is that they are reluctant to make any changes unless they are convinced that I am convinced there is substance to the activities you have alluded to."*

"That was no lie," Hess explains. "Robert seemed to understand that, given the precedent for the Son of Sam laws, which prevented convicted criminals from capitalizing on their crimes, he wasn't going to be seeing any money from having his story written. And I had a pretty good idea that he wanted to give the money to Thomas, the kid he'd had with his Vietnamese wife, Tuyet Huynh. And given all the regulations about

visitations and access to inmates, it was going to be a complicated proposition to arrange. The Department of Corrections
was going to want to know up front whether it would be worthwhile bending the rules to let a writer in or in any way sanction
a relative of Robert's profiting from a publishing deal."

"*Robert,*" Hess prodded, "*what is your suggestion as to how
we obtain something tangible that will give us what we need to
influence them that there really are cases out there?*

"*Prior to you giving serious thought of a book, it was premature to pose the following questions, but it appears the situation
now makes it prudent for you to consider such things as: 1. If
the District Attorney is willing to work with the Colorado authorities concerning Colorado cases, what would you expect us
to do, and what are your expectations? 2. As to other states,
what would you expect us to do, and what are your expectations? 3. Are you willing to just lay it all out and let the chips
fall where they may?*

"*This would be the most expedient method of helping you
get things rolling. There are probably a dozen or so other points
for you to ponder, and I would help facilitate matters if you
could give us some direction.*

"*Who knows what opportunities will present themselves as
your story unfolds?*"

PART FIVE

CHAPTER EIGHTEEN

FLATONIA

"It really felt as if we were closing in," recalls Hess of the situation at the end of January 2003. "In one important way, Robert had tipped his hand. He wanted a book. That meant he needed some favors from us: to make the financial arrangements for his son; to intercede with the prison authorities to allow a writer access and time. Suddenly, I had a bargaining chip."

Yet Robert was not about to be so easily swayed. On the last day of January he penned a lengthy screed that seemed both to foreclose the possibility that he was taking the book bait and at the same time to open up some intriguing new possibilities.

But first things first: responding to Hess's offer to forward information to Dean Kamen, inventor of the IT scooter, Browne testily replied, *"Due to patent issues, it is not appropriate at this time . . . if much more was said about it, the 'light' in someone's mind would snap on and I would be left in the dark (no patent, no money)."*

As for his publishing prospects, Browne suspected that *"'the powers that be' are trying to conjoin the 'book deal' with a prosecutorial faction. I think not!!!"*

But Browne was just getting started. The whole idea that he was somehow being manipulated swelled into a spitting rage that he made no effort to contain. "Quite the opposite," contended Charlie. "He got more articulate than ever. I'd obviously hit a nerve."

That was putting it mildly. *"I'm not really concerned with who may or may not be prosecuted,"* Browne claimed. *"No, I'll not just lay it out and let the chips fall where they may. I'll take it all to my grave before I do such! I will not be abused!"*

"It was all pretty pathetic," Charlie observes with a dispassion borne of long experience. "I heard it a million times or more, from every con who wants to blame society for everything that's gone wrong with his life. The amazing thing is that they're so adamant about their rights. Once they have to pay for their crimes, suddenly they want everyone to play by the rules. Nobody is more insistent on the letter of the law than the guy who's broken it.

"Robert claimed he was being tortured," Hess observed. "I guess he was, if you consider that he was stuck in a tiny cell day and night with bland food and no amenities and minimal contact with other human beings. Look, it's obvious to me that putting someone in a cage is more about punishment than it ever is about rehabilitation. The idea that a guy like Robert could even *be* rehabilitated is absurd. The only thing left was to make him pay for what he did, and for a guy like Robert Browne, that *is* pure torture."

Not that you could tell it to the murderer of Heather Dawn Church. *"Wrong is wrong and right is right,"* he ranted. *"I ask nothing more than to be treated in a manner that is legally required."*

As depressingly familiar as it all might have been for Charlie and his partners, Browne, with characteristic offhandedness, closed his letter by once again paradoxically leaving the door open. It was as if, for all his talk of going to the grave with his secrets, he just couldn't help himself.

"As far as something tangible that will convince someone that there really are cases out there," Robert wrote, *"I tried before with the white Grand Am. I guess some cases (people) don't rate. Also, the sanitation companies do a great job of disposal.*

Hess was running out of options. His doctors had told him he needed another hip operation following his November surgery and he was starting to feel the strain of trying to stay one step ahead of Browne. But he couldn't afford to back off at this critical juncture. The fact that the killer had referenced the white Grand Am again, adding to it another cryptic clue with his mention of the Sanitation Department, suggested that there was substance behind the taunt. Smit and Fischer started combing through all the available records again as Hess sat down to write another letter.

He had now been corresponding with Browne on a nearly weekly basis since the autumn of 2002. On February 11, 2003, Charlie upped the ante. *"Robert,"* he wrote, *"you admitted in open court to the most serious of crimes. You should be receiving the sentence and conditions associated with that act. If you are being tortured, mistreated or abused, give me the specifics and I will bring this to the attention of the proper authorities."*

But at the same time, Hess was hardly in the mood to coddle the convict. *"I spoke with the previously mentioned author,"* he announced, peremptorily playing the book-deal card and ignoring Browne's virulent reaction the last time he had done so. *"He said he was not interested in spending time on such 'a dark project'—his words. His position is just about the same as that of the prison authorities, to wit: until they are certain that I am certain that there are cases out there, neither is interested in doing anything. A true 'Catch 22.' Frankly, I'm afraid we may lose the author's interest."*

But he was just getting warmed up. In his sternest tone to date, Charlie implicitly called Browne's bluff. There was more than a last-ditch tinge of desperation to his words. *"Robert,"* he wrote, *"the poems, the Grande Am, etc., etc. are just over my head. I told you I was not that smart. I can handle a name, a place, or some set of facts and possibly put that together. Since 1952, I have spent countless hours investigating everything from shoplifting to espionage, but at seventy-five, the mere mention of a type of automobile is beyond my capacity. I freely admit to my limitations. My successes have not come to pass because of any genius, but because I was trusted. I never 'hung anyone out to dry.'*

"Here is a thought. Suppose you provided me with enough information to verify one single case and I promise not to pass this information up the line until you become involved with a writer. You would continue to have a volume of other information, but at least we could get over the hurdle of getting this off the ground.

"You see, Robert, it really is all up to you. I agree that it is your right to take any information you wish to the grave. I promise to never again mention the subject of 'your cases' unless you initiate the topic . . .

"In closing, let me say this. If there is information or an address or the like that I can obtain for you feel free to write. If you wish to discuss your situation there with specificity feel free to write. If you wish to validate your contentions feel free to write. If you just want to communicate with someone feel free to write."

"I honestly didn't expect to hear from him again," Hess admits. "I purposely didn't leave him any wiggle room, which was the one thing he needed. I kind of resigned myself to the fact that we'd reached a dead end."

Not quite. Charlie's last-chance tactics paid off in spectacular fashion when, in March, 2003, he received Browne's latest missive.

"I thought I would throw a couple things your way in hopes of adding credence to the whole shebang," Robert wrote. *"The first is just in addition to what has already been said about the white Grand Am. I find it difficult to believe that a connection has not been made in this matter. I tend to believe that you are just fishing for more in hope of my hanging myself."*

"That struck me as pretty funny," Hess says with a grin. "*Of course* I was just fishing! What did he think I was doing? Robert had a way of pretending innocence: all that 'simple country boy' shit. But this time around, I got the feeling there was more going on. Like he'd given up, or was just curious, like me, about where all this was going to take us."

"Here goes," Robert wrote, a sigh of resignation almost audible in his cramped handwriting. *"Try the missing person's file on a young army wife. I know the report was filed. The husband was very unhappy with the police response. He was even more unhappy when he himself recovered the white Grand Am. If that doesn't ring any bells than nothing will."*

Now that he had gotten started, Browne seemed unable to stop. "I think he finally realized that, more than anything, he wanted me to believe him," Hess conjectures. "After all that letter-writing back and forth, it was important for him to convince me—not that he had a great truck design or a pollution-free invention but that he was a stone-cold killer. Part of it, I'm convinced, was that he wanted to show me that I hadn't been wasting my time."

"The second matter is from elsewhere," Browne continued. *"In addition to bolstering credence, I am mainly curious of the outcome [sic] of the following. I thought long and hard about an incident that would not be lost among the others. A 'very' small town seemed to be my best bet. Small towns don't forget such rare happenings. The town I choose is Flatonia, Texas. They don't get much smaller. The year was approximately 1984 or 1985. A young woman was killed and her body was found near this town. The last I heard was that the husband was being charged with her murder. I'm curious as to the eventual outcome. Please let me know. Afterward we may talk some more on this. Texas does like to kill people."*

"It was clear enough that Robert wasn't telling me any of this to relieve his conscience," Charlie asserts. "I believed him when he said that, as much as anything, he was curious. It was like an unfinished story, and he wanted to see what consequences he'd had on the lives of other people. If he'd actually killed some woman in this little Texas town, it apparently didn't bother him that the husband had come under suspicion of murder or even that he might have been convicted, for all Robert knew."

To whatever degree and for whatever reason he had finally unburdened himself, Browne was equally preoccupied with the usual mundane housekeeping issues. He reminded Hess of is promise to get a copy of Auel's *The Shelters Of Stone* through the DOC's bureaucratic maze.

The Apple Dumpling Gang at last had a reason for guarded optimism. After sifting through books on tarot cards and witchcraft, they at last had respectable leads to follow. They had, of course, already chased down the well-worn clues as far as they could, but Robert's insistence that they were overlooking the obvious fueled a new determination.

Their first step was to get in touch with the authorities in Flatonia, Texas. For all of Browne's assertions that homicide would be a rare and memorable occurrence in any small town, Flatonia, by virtue of its very isolation and anonymity, seemed like an ideal spot to get away with murder. Dangled in the scrubland of Southeast Texas in Fayette County, its fifteen hundred inhabitants were hunkered almost equidistant between San Antonio and Houston on a desolate stretch of Highway 10 and a spur of the Union Pacific Railroad.

"What interested us the most," Hess recounts, "was the fact that Flatonia also happened to be right along Robert's artificial-flower delivery route in the mid-eighties—back when he was out doing what he called his "rambles," those aimless road trips that sometimes took him two hundred miles or more in a single day. But we were going to need a lot more than that to tie him to a murder. Lou contacted the Sheriff's Department down there with what Robert had given us. They'd said they'd check it out and get back to us."

Work on the expanding investigation was interrupted in March when, after delaying the procedure once to continue his cold-case work, Hess finally returned to the hospital to have his hip replaced. Almost a month passed before he was able to write back to Browne. In the meantime, interest within the Sheriff's Department in the progress of the cold-case team had heightened. "All we needed was to make a few links," Smit told the authors. "Once we could establish that it was at least possible that Browne might have been responsible for other murders, they opened up more resources for us. On the Grand Am case in particular, a sheriff's office detective named Rick Frady was particularly helpful. An expert on auto-theft investigations, he would eventually put together a list of 170 stolen Grand Ams and sifted through them one by one, trying to tie a single car to a homicide."

Hess, considerably more limber with his newly implanted hip, was back in the fray on April 9 with a new letter to Browne. "I took my cue from Robert," he explains. "The last thing he had mentioned was wanting to get a hold of that Jean Auel novel, so that was the first thing I'd brought up. Now that the case was beginning to show at least some tentative results, we were also getting more cooperation from the DOC. I had a friend in the department who agreed to pass the book along to Robert. So at least I could claim I was coming through for him, like he was beginning to come through for me."

Meanwhile, the police in Flatonia had come back with a possible match for the murder Browne claimed to have committed there: a twenty-one-year-old dancer named Melody Ann Bush, whose body had been found in a highway culvert on the outskirts of town in 1985. The autopsy report listed the cause of death as "acute acetone poisoning." "It was still pretty vague," Hess remembers, "but at least the time frame and the location of the body seemed to fit."

"The Texas authorities have provided us with some interesting details which appear to apply to the case you mentioned," he would go on to write to Browne. *"So that no one can ever say that I fed you any details, any specifics you can add will*

help solidify that it is indeed a case in which you have first hand knowledge. The case is still open. The husband was a suspect at one time but never charged. Any information you could provide regarding cause of death, more precise details on body location, clothing, etc. would be helpful."

But Browne would not take the bait. Instead, in what was quickly taking shape as a race to stay on top of his tantalizing but still frustratingly obscure revelations, he threw out even more information, about yet another murder, this one with a particularly grisly distinction. Around the time of the Flatonia incident, he wrote on April 30, *"A body (in parts) was discovered off US Highway 59 in the Southwest Houston area. You would think someone would remember that."*

Meanwhile, he wanted Charlie to know that he had at last received *The Shelters of Stone. "It will be a nice escape,"* he ventured. *"I will try to ration the reading time so as to prolong the pleasure of the book."*

It was in this letter as well that Browne would make mention for the first time of his increasingly parlous health. Indicating that he was not feeling well, he managed to get a dig in at the prison medical facilities, grousing that *"They do a good job of giving the appearance of adequate medical care."*

"I know what it's like to have health worries," Hess avers. "It can take up all your attention, become your entire focus, especially if, like Robert, you didn't have any confidence in your doctors. At the same time, I knew that the care he was getting—that any prisoner gets in the system—is of a pretty high quality. But in the end, I couldn't help but be at least a little sympathetic. Real or not, I could relate to what he was going through."

"I received your letter indicating that you were ill," Charlie wrote back on May 4. *"I'm sorry to hear that and hope you are on the road to recovery.*

"Robert," he continued, after promising to follow up on the latest clue involving the dismembered body on Highway 59, *"I appreciate the fact that you have provided some relevant de-*

tails. But it seems that we are at a place where we need more than a date, a body, etc. In order to convince our DA and the others, who will play a role in the unfolding of the Robert Browne Story, I think we need an actual, specific case with the details. Maybe this is a good time for a face to face."

But for all his gentle prodding, Charlie Hess was still many miles from finding his way to Robert Browne and the cache of awful secrets over which he presided.

CHAPTER NINETEEN

THE TRIP

"There is a critical mass that comes with any criminal investigation," Charlie Hess explains. "Tips turn into leads, leads turn into evidence, and evidence proves the case. The picture often doesn't become clear until all the dots are connected in the right order. And sometimes you don't know what the order is until you've tried every possible combination.

"It takes a lot of patience," he continues. "You've got to be willing to let the process unfold at its own speed. You can't hurry it, or push it into premature conclusions, even when there seems to be so much at stake."

He pauses, with that familiar searching squint in his eye. "Robert tested that process to the max," he says at last. "As the months and the years went by, the only thing I was absolutely convinced about was that this guy had done some very bad things to a very large number of people. That added a sense of urgency to my work, thinking about all the people who might be out there in unmarked graves and the people who were still looking for them or maybe had even given up hope. But I still had to take things slowly and deliberately. There were times when I would have preferred to choke the information out of him. But he'd already made it clear that he was ready to go to the grave without saying another word if things didn't go at his pace. I couldn't let that happen."

Not letting that happen required Hess to engage his adversary fully, utilizing the strange mental and emotional compartmentalization that he had practiced throughout his career.

"Sometimes I hear people say that if they were to have met a bad person under different circumstances, they might have been friends. I didn't have that luxury. There were no different circumstances with Robert. I had to deal with the person he was, then and there. Like I said, I was convinced he was a certified serial killer. But he was also a bitter, self-pitying loner with health problems and a grudge against the world. At least some of that I could relate to personally. When I looked at it that way, I could have empathy. It might not have been as strong as my feelings about what he'd done, but it was still there. I could relate, and I used that to get my work done."

"It's good to hear you are doing OK after your surgery," Browne wrote back, some two weeks after Charlie's letter of early May in which he had mentioned his wife Jo's recent heart operation. *"I hope your wife has equal success with hers. I can only imagine the attachment one has to a life-partner. My best wishes to both of you."*

"Sure, Robert had lots of chances to find out what it meant to have the attachment of a life partner," Hess points up. "Sure, he was feeling sorry for himself. That was second nature to him. And, sure, he was just being polite. But I think there was also something real in those sentiments, like maybe he was reaching out for what he had denied himself."

"Again, I would like to thank you for the book," Browne continued, referring to the Auel epic. *"I managed to stretch it out for a week. I enjoyed it, but it didn't match my expectations."*

It was at this point that Browne ventured into a literary conceit of his own in what was, to Hess, the most surprising turn in their long correspondence. "It was a real flight of fancy," Charlie acknowledges with a touch of admiration. "I had to admit that Robert always kept me guessing. He had a very vivid imagination and all the time he needed to indulge it fully. He knew I was looking for hard facts to put together a substantive case. But he'd already said he wasn't just going to hand them to me on a silver platter. I guess he still wanted to make a game out of it."

A game or—in the case of Browne's fascinating letter dated May 20—a journey. *"Before I depart, I would like to continue the trip we are on,"* was his typically enigmatic introduction to this next phase of this long, teasing contest of wits in which the two were engaged. *"We started out in Colorado Springs. From there we went to Flatonia. From there we went east to Houston. Let's continue east on Interstate 10. New Orleans was very fertile ground. Let's go back to 1975 or '79 (approximately). Left inside a room, inside a Holiday Inn, about five minutes from the French Quarter. This lady claimed to be from South Philly.*

"Let's continue east along Interstate 10. We are now in Mississippi, but just barely. We are very near the Alabama border. There is a swampy area just north of the Interstate. There, two bodies were dumped. In parts (for ease of transport). Both of them were male. I made a point of stating that they were male so you wouldn't dismiss the incident. It was around 1980 then.

"Let's move north now. How about Arkansas? This is just across the Mississippi River from Memphis. I believe it is called West Memphis. There is a marshy area a little southwest of there. That is where this lady was laid to rest. Also 1980.

"Now let's go west to Tulsa, Oklahoma. Just southeast of there, along the south side of the Arkansas River is a flood plain. Lots of water grasses. There is also a male in the muck. This was in 1985.

"Let's go northwest. Way northwest. Washington State is our next stop. On the north side of the east-west Interstate (I believe it was Interstate 94) is a scenic overlook. There is an extreme drop-off over huge boulders. There is a mountain range to the north. The lady that was dropped over the precipice would probably never be found due to the terrain unless there was an intentional search of the area. This was 1986.

"Let's go south now. We are in California now. We are on the Pacific Coast Highway about 200 miles north of San Francisco (approximate distance). There is an exit to a sandy beach where there are areas with lots of driftwood among boulders to

the north side. Among the driftwood and boulders are two bodies. One male and one female. This was 1986.

"Let's go east now. We are in northwest New Mexico. I'm on an east-west highway. The number I don't remember. However, to the north of another scenic overlook is a tremendous rock face, grey in color. It can't be missed. Once again, there is a body over the precipice. This one is male. This was in 1993."

"The body count was starting to pile up," Hess remarks laconically. "By the end of our little trip, we had eleven potential new cases, not to mention whatever did or didn't happen in Colorado. From one perspective it was a giant step forward. He'd given me all sorts of detail, especially in the physical and geographic descriptions of where these crimes had occurred. The very fact that he'd been so specific about the locations gave him a lot of credibility. But it was typical that when Robert held the truth out in front of me, the closer I looked, the farther it seemed to be. I mean, how many swampy areas on the Mississippi-Alabama border were there? How many sandy beaches with lots of driftwood and boulders along the Pacific Coast Highway? How many scenic overlooks in Washington State? He was still taunting me and knew exactly what he was doing, giving me just enough information to keep me interested but never enough to come to any definitive solution."

Still, the "trip letter," as the team came to call it, offered a wealth of information, some of it lying just below the surface. They now had the means of narrowing down the numbers on Browne's map to something considerably more specific. Washington, for instance, was listed as the site of one murder. Now, instead of trying to run down every unsolved homicide in the state, they could concentrate on incidents that had taken place at a scenic turnoff overlooking a mountain range to the north. What would be required now was a lot of old-fashioned leg-work—or, rather, phone work.

"We'd have to get in touch with all the various jurisdictions that might possibly match Robert's description and get them to take a look at their cold-case backlog to see if anything might fit the bill," Hess explains. But even that wasn't as simple as it sounded. On certain key points, Robert's recall was hardly infallible. Interstate 94, for example, runs west from Detroit. Hess knows it well, since it winds through Wisconsin, where he grew up. But the highway terminates in Billings, Montana, a good four hundred miles from the eastern border of Washington State. The locations simply didn't add up.

In another example, Browne had provided a four-year spread—from 1975 to 1979—in the New Orleans case. "That's a lot of ground to cover," says Hess, "especially in the Big Easy. And there was always the possibility that he had forgotten or misremembered significant details or he was just fucking with us."

There were other, singularly disturbing hints and suggestions the team uncovered in Robert's lethal travelogue. Prior to this point, he had identified his targets exclusively as women. It is critical, of course, to establish the modus operandi of any suspect—the methods he uses to commit his crimes and his victims of preference. It can be a powerful piece of circumstantial evidence, and in the case of serial killers, it is usually true that a particular type of victim and a specific choice of weapon are favored.

"Not Robert," asserts Hess. "Here he was suggesting to us that he'd thrown somebody off an overlook, chopped up two others and tossed their bodies in the river, and in the case of Melody Ann Bush in Flatonia, poisoned her with acetone. Then there was the fact that the victims were both men *and* women. Of course, if you counted in Heather Dawn Church, that would make men, women, and children. That's highly unusual. If we were to accept what he'd written, there was apparently no discrimination in who he'd selected and no particular reason for doing so. He was an equal opportunity killer."

The impact of the "trip letter" was quickly felt throughout the offices of both the El Paso County sheriff and the district attorney. Terry Maketa, who had succeeded John Anderson as sheriff, would provide the Apple Dumpling Gang with additional resources, including a skilled investigator, Jeff Nohr, who, in the tight family of Colorado Springs law enforcement, was a former son-in-law of Lou Smit. Nohr would eventually be assigned to the Browne case full-time, with his first task being to assist Rick Frady in the continual search for the elusive Grand Am. The investigation was beginning to heat up.

Yet the task of keeping the fire burning still largely fell to Charlie Hess. "I was the only one Robert would communicate with," he states flatly. "And it continued to be touch-and-go with each letter. Taking that imaginary trip with him was the biggest break we'd gotten up to that point, but as much as it moved the ball forward, what was really important in that particular letter was what came at the end. I was constantly looking for leverage, a way to bargain with Robert, exchanging what he knew for what he might conceivably want."

Hess thought he saw an opening in the May 20 letter, when Browne suddenly and imperiously demanded to know, *"Now, what could I gain from giving more complete detail? Would the abuse stop? Would I be provided with legitimate health care? Would my physical pain be abated? Would my emotional pain be alleviated? 'Onward Christian Sadists, Marching as to War.' I thought I would throw that by you before I leave."*

"I don't know where he thought he was leaving for," Charlie remarks dryly, "but I suddenly could see what had actually been staring me in the face for some time." Hess spent the next few days carefully composing a response before handing it over for Fischer to type.

"Dear Mr. Robert," he wrote in a letter dated May 28th, *"I regret that the book fell short of your expectations, but we know that some writers only have so much to give, and then get by on their previously earned reputations.*

"Thanks for your kind words concerning the recovery of my wife's and my collective surgeries. Now we will do some planning for a trip or two this summer and fall.

"*Speaking of trips, my guess that if 'higher powers' see your information to be credible, it may be that you would be asked to actually take us to some of the places you mentioned. I don't know what you would think of that, so please give me your thoughts. If we do any traveling, I am sure there would be steaks, Big Macs, tacos and protein galore. Certainly better than the empty carbs you speak of.*

"*We are trying to check on a few of those things you pro-vided,*" he continued, circling in now on his primary intent, "*where there is sufficient information to conduct an investiga-tion. What are your feelings about coming down to Colorado Springs for a few days for a face to face between you and me? . . .

". . . The information you provided certainly puts us a long way down the road, and I believe we are about to 'move some of the big boulders.' Robert, we still need a local case or two where we actually find a body, and hopefully some attendant facts. The Grand Am thing may be a good place to start—I mean, all the specific information so we can use our time efficiently. Or, if you prefer, any other case or two where we can actually locate remains. It is necessary that we have these local cases, since we're nearing a point where this data is crucial, if we are to keep all parties interested.

"*Incidentally, if you came to the Springs we could do it under the pretext of having to have special medical attention or some sort of court proceeding.*"

As much as possible Hess wanted to assure Browne that his welfare was of primary importance. But most of all he wanted to dangle the possibility of "special medical attention."

"*Do you care to be more explicit as to what you need and are not getting?*" Hess continued, baiting the hook. "*Is the med-ical problem one that is continual or is it is series of different is-sues? Would a specialist be beneficial?*"

His concern about being provided with improved health care and having his physical pain and emotional pain alleviated was the closest Browne had come to expressing a legitimate need since their correspondence had begun. It was something Hess might be able to directly address with the cooperation of the DOC. *"We have traveled a long way together,"* he reminded Browne in his carefully constructed letter, *"and I hope there is some way I can make the rest of the trip easier for you."*

"I was feeling pretty confident," he recalls. "We'd been at this a long time and gotten past a few milestones in our relationship. I'd come through for him on a few small things, proving good faith at least, and could now make him an offer of help that might make a real difference in his quality of life. To a certain degree, Robert had reciprocated, complying with my requests for more and better information. But there was no question that he was still the 'grandmaster,' calling the tune and watching me dance."

Then as the blazing Colorado summer of 2003 began to crank up, the music abruptly stopped. Hess and his partners waited anxiously for word from Robert all throughout June, even as Detectives Frady and Nohr continued to plow through their list of stolen and missing Pontiac Grand Ams with no discernible results. Increasingly nervous that their quarry was slipping away, Hess, Smit, and Fischer decided to take the chance of writing again, without waiting for a response.

"Not having heard from you made me wonder if you are ill," Charlie inquired in a short query dated July 8, almost six weeks after his previous correspondence. As well as including a copy of that letter, Hess again underscored his latest proposal by asking *"Are your medical needs being attended to?"*

A week later Browne responded, although he hardly seemed in the mood either to carry on with the negotiations or to entertain their obvious implications.

"Yes, I have been and still am sick," he announced in a huff. *"Therefore I am not up to any trips or interrogations. Are you implying that if I agree to such, I will receive appropriate and adequate medical care?"*

"At least we weren't beating around the bush anymore," remarks Charlie with grim humor. "He knew exactly what I was offering and had figured out exactly what it was going to cost him. I didn't blame him for not liking it much. In his mind, I was trading his health and well-being in exchange for him incriminating himself."

"By now you should have been able to verify at least some of the incidents I alluded to," Browne concluded with the same aggrieved air.

He closed the letter with a pair of postscripts. The first requested the addresses of the Democratic National Committee and of Jim Gordon, an inventor and product developer he had seen interviewed on a talk show.

The second addendum brought him and Hess directly back to square one, again referencing the obscure *"seven virgins"* couplets he had written over three years ago to Mark Finley: *"You say you need bodies for local cases. Go back to the poem."*

While Hess was grateful that contact had been reestablished, the letter felt like a definite step backwards. "It was worrisome not to hear from him after such a long time," Hess remarks, "and it led me to believe what he was saying about his health. He was apparently suffering enough not to be able to continue writing. Of course, when he finally did, he didn't mince words. He understood the deal I was offering, and now I had to be very careful. I'd told him I'd never lie to him, and the truth was, he wasn't going to get the help he needed without coming to the table with something more substantial. My best move was to keep the focus on what most might benefit the both of us.

"I didn't even ask what he wanted the addresses for," he adds with a laugh. "The Democratic National Committee? Maybe he was thinking of running for president. I even dropped my embargo on plural pronouns. It was clear enough that it wasn't just me cutting these deals anymore."

"You asked about appropriate medical care," Hess reminded Browne on July 17. *"I have been advised that when we actually find the 'Seven Sacred Virgins' or any other body you*

can pinpoint, we are prepared to bring you here, have you properly diagnosed and properly treated according to the diagnostic findings."

Now that the quid pro quo was out in the open, it was time for Charlie to lay down a few conditions of his own. *"Robert,"* he wrote, *"going back to the poems to try and solve the puzzle is really not sufficient. We need a map, specific directions or definite locations in order to effectuate the matter discussed in the paragraph above.*

"As to the information you provided concerning other jurisdictions, it has been met with little or no interest. The authorities with whom we have spoken say they won't budge an inch without the same sort of specificity we need here."

It was true. The authorities the team contacted in California, New Mexico, Washington, and especially Louisiana all but laughed out loud. With the information being generally so vague, it proved difficult if not impossible to motivate them to dig for matching murders from their cold-case files.

"As you can appreciate, we have no control over their actions or lack thereof," Hess reminded Browne in his letter. *"We, on the other hand, are very interested in the cases here."*

"It was time for my 'Come to Jesus' pitch," Hess recounts. "We were past making allusions and metaphors. I finally had some leverage and I was determined to use it."

"I know you are disenchanted with the 'system,' " he wrote, *"and I truly sympathize, but I am trying to rectify your health needs. But it requires your input in terms an old guy can understand. Robert, it really boils down to whether or not you really want help. I have been honest, respectful and direct with you and would hope you will reciprocate. As I see it, you have nothing to lose and a great deal to gain. Correct me if I'm wrong."*

No correction was forthcoming. In fact, three months would pass before Charlie Hess was able to make contact with Robert Browne again.

CHAPTER TWENTY

"I DON'T DO NAMES"

"I have reviewed our latest correspondence and tried to deter-mine if I had in some way offended you," Hess would write after a three-month silence from Robert Browne. *"But I honestly do think we were getting on the same wavelength."*

After their final, highly charged exchange in mid-July, the question of corresponding wavelengths had taken on an omi-nous import. As weeks stretched into months without further word from the convict, the team began to fear that they had somehow blown their best opportunity to connect Browne to a homicidal spree that had covered thousands of miles over more than thirty years. "I wondered if by telling him he had nothing to lose and a great deal to gain, he hadn't gotten spooked," Hess reflects. "It seemed at least possible that the whole thing had been moving forward precisely because Robert *hadn't* been se-riously considering the consequences of opening up to me. As long as I could appeal to his sense of self-importance, the aura of mystery he liked to wrap himself in, then he could just pre-tend he was like one of the characters in those books he read. It wasn't quite real. But once we got down to hard bargaining, maybe it all got a little too real. Suffice it to say, I did a lot of second-guessing while I waited to hear from him again."

From Charlie's practiced point of view, it is hard to over-state the delicacy and finesse it took to keep Browne talking while at the same time steering the conversation where it needed to go. "Look," he says, "Robert had this stuff locked away in his head for decades, stuff no one could ever guess if they passed him by on the street. What was his incentive to expose those things? I was asking him to turn a light on and I never thought for minute he'd do it just to purge himself of his sins. A part of him lived in that world he'd created, where he had all the power and could make people suffer at will. Why would he want to give that up?"

With the unsettling lack of response casting a pall over the investigation, Charlie and his wife took the opportunity for a visit to friends and relatives back in Minnesota. *"I was hoping to have a letter from you on my return,"* he wrote when he got back in early September. *"As to medical treatment, etc., the offer still stands. I thought that I might have put too much pressure on you for details. . . . If that is the case, I would appreciate it if you would just tell me to 'buzz off' and I will not bother you anymore.*

"Regardless of your decision I sincerely hope that things are good for you. A friend of mine who pulled twenty plus years for a couple dozen bank robberies in the fifties once told me, "It's difficult to do hard time if there is nothing to look forward to."

There was still no response. "Lou and Scott and I talked it over," Hess recounts, "and decided there was only one thing left to do. We'd try a cold-shot visit. I'd just show up at the prison, see if he'd agree to meet with me, and we'd go from there.

Hess had asked for a face-to-face meeting with Browne in nearly every letter he wrote but had always been turned down. In 2000, after Browne's initial teasing correspondence, Detective Mark Finley had actually gone to Canon City to interview the killer but was greeted with a stony silence. Browne refused to even look at him, and Finley gave up after a half hour. Hess had reason to believe he might have better luck, based on the connection he had painstakingly cultivated.

Gaining direct access to the prisoner proved less difficult than might be expected, given Charlie's contacts within the Department of Corrections. "I was just a volunteer," he says, "one step up from a civilian. I had no real official capacity, and no real reason to be there. But I had a friend in the Department of Corrections who helped smooth the way. Since I was the one who had been writing to Robert, it was natural that I should go see him by myself. Anyone else might scare him off."

Hess got up early on the morning of September 9, 2003, to make the one-and-a-half-hour trip in his GMC Yukon to Colorado State Penitentiary—Scotts—in Canon City. There he was ushered into a small room, approximately six-by-six, just big enough for a table and two chairs for meetings with inmates and their attorneys. It was windowless except for a four-inch slit in the door where the guards could keep watch from the outside corridor. "This was definitely going to be a one-on-one," Hess quips. "There wasn't much room for anyone else.

"After a few minutes, they brought him in," he continues. "He didn't look so good. He was very disheveled and seemed a little disoriented, like someone had turned bright lights on him in a dark room. He was wearing the standard-issue orange jumpsuit with flip-flops and he was limping slightly. He had a scraggly, salt-and-pepper beard down to his chest that looked like it had never been trimmed. But what really caught my attention was all the hardware. They had him handcuffed from behind, with a chain around his waist and his ankles shackled. He must have been carrying an extra twenty pounds of steel and he was obviously uncomfortable."

Hess formed a number of significant impressions at first glance. "I knew he hadn't been lying about his health issues. I'd seen what prison could do to a man, and it had really done a number on Robert. Cooped up all the time, breathing that recycled air, eating that heavy, starchy food. It really takes a toll. He was pale and puffy and had that fifty-yard stare of most hard-time convicts. He was a big guy, over six feet, and I could tell he'd once been pretty fit. No earrings or tattoos, none of that shit. But after all those years in lockdown, all you could see was the ghost of the guy who must have once been there."

In person, Browne seemed no more or less a likely candidate for a serial killer than anyone else. There was no maniacal gleam in his eye, but Hess had been around enough murderers to know that standard stereotypes simply didn't apply.

"Do you know who I am?" Charlie asked as Browne lowered himself awkwardly into the straight-backed chair.

"I have no idea," Robert replied, and from the tone of his voice, he hardly seemed to care.

"I'm Charlie Hess, the guy who's been writing you the letters."

"How's it going?" Browne replied in a soft-spoken voice, as if this unexpected visit had been anything but a surprise. "I'd shake your hand, but you can see," he added wryly, "that might be difficult."

Charlie nodded. "Maybe we can fix that." He crossed to the door and tapped on the slit window, asking the guard if it was possible to remove some of Browne's restraints.

"He was having a hard time just sitting down with all that stuff wrapped around him," Charlie recounts. "I could see by the way he was squirming that he wasn't going to be able to take it for too long. I'd hoped to get as much time as possible with him and I knew he'd have to go back for a head count at 11 AM, so it was in my interest to make him as comfortable as possible. I also wanted to let him know that I was on his side. I got up and asked the guards to take off the chains, but they refused: it was against regulations. But at least I was showing Robert that I was trying."

Settling back in the chair across the table from Browne, Charlie asked how the inmate was faring.

"Not good," was Robert's terse reply, and proceeded to rattle off a litany of woes that included incipient arthritis, general headaches and back pain, a throbbing in his kidneys, and bone spurs in his feet.

Charlie nodded, regularly and sympathetically. "I got worried when you stopped writing," he managed to interject at last.

Browne shrugged. "I didn't have anything left in my com-

missary fund." For inmates receiving a daily stipend of thirty
cents, the simple necessities of life must be carefully rationed.
"With two dollars ten cents a week, they've got to buy everything," Hess explains. "Toothpaste, toilet paper, corn chips and
soda, and, of course, stamps and paper. Even if they want to go
to the doctor, it costs five dollars; twice that if it's an emergency. After all our second-guessing, it turned out that he just
couldn't afford to send me a letter."

It was the opening Charlie took immediate advantage of.
"How about if some money turned up in your fund?" he asked.

"That'd be nice," the killer replied impassively.

It was at this point that Hess made a strategic decision. "I
didn't know what to expect going in," he explains. "The response might have been anything from refusing to see me to
signing a full confession. Now that I was sitting across the table
from him, I considered that just by reestablishing contact, I'd
done a good day's work. It didn't seem right to string it out any
longer than necessary. I'd given Robert a chance to size me up,
to see that I would treat him with respect, as an equal. The rest
could wait."

"I hope I haven't caused you any distress by just showing up
like this," he said, after exchanging a few more inconsequential
pleasantries.

"No problem," was Browne's reply.

"I appreciate that we were able to finally get to talk," Hess
continued. "Do you think we can start up our communication
again?"

"Sure," Browne shrugged. "Why not?"

"Any objection to me coming back here again?"

"No," Browne answered evenly. "Come back anytime. I'll
tell you anything you want to know."

Charlie nodded and rose. "Then I'll see you soon," he said.

Browne gazed up at him. "He seemed bored," Hess recounts.
"Like he'd already lost interest. We looked at each other for a
minute, and I was thinking about all those letters we had writ-

ten, all the things he claimed to have done. Even though we were meeting for the first time, it really seemed as if we had this whole long history between us that had been left unspoken."

"Don't you want to know about any of the cases?" Browne asked at last, his low voice only faintly traced with his Louisiana accent.

Hess stopped, then sat back down and folded his hands on the table. "Sure," he said, hardly believing this latest turn. "What do you want to talk about?"

In what he would later characterize as "the moment of truth," Hess confesses to an utterly unprofessional flutter of excitement. "Robert had made a choice. He was ready to share his secrets with me. He'd clearly decided I'd earned the right to know. It was like a gift."

"How about the Grand Am?" Browne suggested.

"Great," Hess said, keeping his voice steady.

"It was back around eighty-seven, give or take, I guess," he began, in the same casually modulated conversational tone. "I was working as a clerk at a Kwik Stop in the Springs. There was this couple that used to come in to rent videos. The woman— she was small, very petite—used to like to flirt. We kind of had a little thing going."

"Do you remember her name?" Charlie asked.

Browne shook his head. "I don't do names," he replied. "I'm the world's worst with names. Let's just call her the Grand Am lady."

"The Grand Am lady."

Browne nodded, warming to his story. "Her husband was in the army out at Fort Carson, Spec Four or something. I didn't think they were getting along too well. It was just something I picked up. Then one day she came in by herself, and we got to talking, and I asked her if she wanted to go to a movie. I really poured it on, letting her know that I knew she was interested. She gave me directions to her place, and I picked her up that night."

"Where did she live?" Hess wanted to know.

"It was close to Murray and Pike's Peak," Browne replied after a moment, naming a busy intersection just east of downtown. "Not more than a couple of blocks from where I had an apartment, just across the street from the Kwik Stop."

"Would you know her place if you saw it?" pressed Charlie.

"Sure," Browne replied. "I think it was on the first floor, I'm pretty sure."

"So you showed up for the date," Hess prompted. "Where was her husband?"

"He was gone," Browne recalled. "She told me he'd gone to New Orleans or maybe Miami—that sticks in my mind—and taken their kid with him."

"They had a kid?"

Browne shrugged. "That's what she told me. Anyway, they were supposed to be getting a divorce." He smiled, flashing a set of pearly dental plates. "Like I said, I'm a pretty good judge of human nature."

"And you went to the movies . . ."

"Yeah, except, instead of taking my car—all I had was this little Datsun—we took her husband's. He had a white Grand Am. Couldn't have been more than a year old. Low mileage, four-speed, blue interior. Kept it immaculate. Very sweet ride."

"What happened then?"

"We went back to my place. We did our thing. Then I strangled her."

If there was a beat between the two men, it was imperceptible. A lifetime of training had kicked in for Hess. What was important now was not to blink, not to blanch, not to show the slightest shock or surprise. This was routine. This was all in a day's work—for both of them.

"What did you do with her then?" was Hess's next eventoned question.

"I covered her up with blankets," was Browne's equally phlegmatic reply. "I was pretty tired after all that and I needed some time to figure out what to do with her. So I left, took the Grand Am, and drove around for awhile."

"Where'd you go?"

"I ended up back at her apartment. I let myself in and looked around for something worth stealing."

"Did you find anything?"

Browne shrugged. "There wasn't much, except for this new nineteen-inch Sony TV. So I took that and also this pretty good-sized cluster ring with a lot of little diamonds on it that I found on the dresser."

"What you'd do with them?"

"The ring I gave to an old girlfriend who sold it for me. I kept the TV." It was in fact the same television that sheriff's detectives had inventoried at the Eastonville Road property in the course of the Heather Dawn Church investigation. The ring would later be identified as a gift given by Browne's former girlfriend to her daughter at her wedding.

"On the way out I got stopped by the security guard," Browne continued. "He asked me if the TV was mine and I told him it was." He smirked. "That was good enough for him."

"What about the car?"

"I drove it around for a couple of days, took it up to the mountains, just to wind it out, then parked it in a lot near the Kwik Stop, where I figured her husband could find it if he looked hard enough."

"So what did you end up doing with the . . . Grand Am lady?"

Browne seemed to be looking at a spot on the wall over Charlie's shoulder. "I put her in the bathtub," he said. "Then I dismembered her, or disarticulated her, or whatever you call it."

Hess could hear the murmur of the guards trading prison gossip in the hallway outside the door. A moment passed as he stroked his small goatee, trying to figure out what his next question might be. "How does something like that go down?" he asked at last. "Did you climb into the tub with her? Were you wearing gloves?"

"Of course not," Browne replied dismissively. "You just reach in and do your thing. You know, the body's not pumping blood anymore."

"Right."

"You just sever at the joints. Pop them out and take it apart."

"Right."

"Of course, there's naturally going to be a certain amount of blood, even after the heart stops pumping," Browne allowed, "but it stays in the tub. If you're careful, nothing spills. It's minimal cleanup."

"What did you do with the parts?"

"I put them in plastic garbage bags along with the knife and took them out to the dumpster, bag by bag."

"You mean your own dumpster? The one for the apartment?" That explained, Hess now realized, the written reference Browne had made to the efficiency of the sanitation company.

"Yeah. It was the closest one."

"Wasn't that taking a pretty big chance?"

Browne gave him an appraising look. "Rational people wouldn't do what I do," he acknowledged. "Sometimes the most obvious things are the easiest to get away with."

CHAPTER TWENTY-ONE

ROCIO

Her name was Rocio Chila Delpilar Sperry, and if there was ever proof required of the concentric mayhem spread by Robert Browne, then the fate of this fifteen-year-old Panamanian immigrant and her young family offered it in tragic abundance.

A round-faced brunette with dark eyes and a tentative smile, Rocio had already had a life marred by violence and displacement when she first met twenty-one-year-old Florida native Joseph Sperry, whom she married to escape an abusive foster mother in the home where she had been placed. For his part, Sperry was drawn to what he would call "her beauty and her sweetness."

Within months of their wedding in late 1986, Rocio had given birth to a daughter Amie, named after Sperry's mother. The couple relocated to Colorado Springs, where Joseph joined the army, hoping to carve out a career in the military, and was stationed at Fort Carson.

But trouble followed Joe and Rocio west as the child bride struggled to care for her infant and they tried to make ends meet on Sperry's meager salary. The marriage quickly soured, and in early November 1987, Sperry arranged with his mother to take charge of baby Amie while he and Rocio tried to settle their differences. He left for Florida with the child and a few days later received a late-afternoon call from his wife back in Colorado Springs.

"She told me she loved me," he would later tell investigators. "It was the last time I ever spoke to her. I called her later, but there was no answer." When Rocio failed to meet him at Denver's Stapleton Airport on November 14, Sperry knew something was wrong. Returning to the apartment, he found the place in disarray and his wife nowhere to be found. "All her stuff was there," he would later recall, "her clothes, her toiletries and makeup. The only thing I could see that was missing was the TV. I was going to go out looking for her, and that's when I realized my Grand Am was gone, too. So I started out on foot around the neighborhood, and when I couldn't find her, I stopped by the convenience store down the block to call the police and file a missing person report. They told me they couldn't officially list her as missing until she'd been gone forty-eight hours. I also told them my car had been stolen, but that didn't seem to make much difference either." Eavesdropping on the frantic phone calls was the store clerk who in happier days had often rented the couple videos. The clerk's name tag read Robert Browne.

"I went back to the apartment and started knocking on doors," Sperry recounted to detectives. "A neighbor told me that she had seen Rocio walking down Murray Boulevard toward the Kwik Stop, so I went back out and looked around some more."

His search would continue for the next two months and during his systematic canvas of the neighborhood, he finally came across his Grand Am, the keys still in the ignition, parked at an apartment complex less than a block from his home.

"I was pretty much on my own," he remembers. "After awhile, when she didn't show up, the police got involved, but they made it clear from the beginning that they considered me the number-one suspect. I'd be reporting for duty at the base during the day and at night I'd drive around the bad parts of town, showing her picture to prostitutes or anyone else I could find out on the street who might have a clue. Finally, I just cracked. I started yelling at the first sergeant and was called up on charges of insubordination. They discharged me."

Meanwhile, the police suspicion of Sperry was picked up by his friends and family. "They thought I'd killed her, too," he recounts bitterly, "and wouldn't let me even see my daughter. She grew up thinking that her dad had murdered her mother."

From that point on, Sperry's life spiraled completely out of control. He returned home to Florida, and it was there, in 1993, that he was convicted on a charge of aggravated battery. After the death of his father and the suicide of a close friend, he fell into heroin addiction and over the next several years struggled to overcome the habit in a methadone treatment clinic. Beginning at last to pick up the shards of his life, Sperry remarried and had a son, although he remained estranged from his daughter Amie. Rocio's disappearance remained unsolved.

It would be eighteen years between the time Browne strangled Rocio and when the Apple Dumpling Gang were finally able to close the case, a virtual eternity through which Joe Sperry had to live without knowing who had killed his wife or why. It was a wait that destroyed him. But even the ghastly details of Rocio's murder revealed to Hess in his first face-to-face meeting with the killer were not by themselves enough to decisively render either justice or peace.

"Now we had the story," Charlie explains, "but we needed the time, the place, and the name to go with it. The trouble was, for all the information Robert provided me, we still didn't know who the victim was. We'd already scoured the missing persons and stolen cars files and couldn't find even the slightest reference to a case that might fit. We were still groping."

There was, however, a key piece of data that had come to light. "Robert had named the intersection where he thought the Sperry apartment was," Charlie recounts. "Pike's Peak and Murray. Now, at least, we had a physical point of reference."

Returning from his September 9 meeting with Browne, Charlie debriefed Lou and Scott in a conference that was also at-

tended by a variety of sheriff's officers, who were now beginning to evince all-too-typically bureaucratic anxiety over the escalating implications of the case. "It was bullshit," is Charlie's
description of the three-hour summit that ensued. "The brass
got very hung up on my offer to give Robert some money to buy
stamps and stationery. Their concern was about the advisability
of paying for information and the fact that it might contaminate
the case, but as far as I was concerned, we were playing by
Robert's rules, not theirs. They kept hemming and hawing, until
we finally settled on a compromise. I'd initially asked for
twenty dollars. They agreed to give him ten. It had become a
major issue."

Meanwhile, the Apple Dumpling Gang got busy. With Scott
Fischer in tow, Hess and Smit went to the intersection of Pike's
Peak and Murray and watched as Scott the shutterbug took a
360-degree photographic view of the buildings. The plan was to
show the pictures to Browne in hopes that he might positively
identify the apartment where he'd picked up Rocio Sperry.

The cat-and-mouse contest between Hess and Browne continued apace. In the three weeks since their prison visit, the correspondence had resumed. *"I'll get down to business,"* Browne
wrote in mid-October, shortly after the arrival of the ten-dollar
money order that Hess had fought so hard for. *"I require medical
attention and relocation. I would like a thorough examination
by a real doctor. This includes any surgeries, medications,
follow-ups and therapies (physical and mental health).*

"On the relocation," he continued, *"Since I must remain in
confinement I would like a fire watchtower in a remote wilderness area where the only way in or out is by helicopter. Supplies could be dropped off to me once a month if necessary. I
would need reading material, television and a radio."*

"I laughed out loud at that one," Charlie remembers. "It confirmed to me that Robert was going stir-crazy. But I guess he
figured he'd never get what he didn't ask for. It was a place to
start a negotiation."

"Now you know what I want," he concluded. *"If this can be facilitated, we can deal. If you think this is impossible than [sic] please tell me and I won't waste either of our time."*

Then, as if to underscore his willingness to horse-trade for the right reward, Browne included a separate piece of paper on which he had written in block letters the words: "FLATONIA ETHER/ICE PICK."

"We took it as some kind of down payment," Hess remembers. "What caught our attention was the fact that down in Flatonia, they had told us that Melody Ann Bush had been killed by 'acute acetone poisoning.' Was somebody getting acetone confused with ether? It was hard to know for sure."

Charlie's search for certainty continued in October as shadows of the Rocky Mountain autumn lengthened and he arranged for a return visit to Browne. He had in the meantime been busy making arrangements through the DOC to have some of Robert's restraints removed, requesting an outside doctor to evaluate the prisoner's physical condition, and exploring what it might realistically take to get him transferred to a single cell in another facility.

Hess made his next trip to Canon City in the company of his wife Jo. "She came down just to keep me company on the drive. I left her in the waiting room, and I have to say it was a little strange. Jo stood for everything good and positive in my life. Robert represented a whole other side. I'd always tried to keep those parts separate. Now, suddenly, they were in close proximity."

"I was always fascinated by Charlie's work," avows Jo. "All his friends were either cops or criminals. It was exciting to be involved in what he was doing, and I think if he hadn't asked me to come, I would have invited myself along anyway."

Hess's primary purpose on his return visit was to present to Browne the photographs Fischer had taken of the Pike's Peak and Murray intersection. The meeting was again staged in the attorney-client conference room, and Charlie was gratified to see that Browne had now had his leg shackles removed and his hands cuffed more comfortably, locked in front of him instead of behind his back.

"You're looking better, Robert," he said after the prisoner had been escorted in. "Your color, I mean."

"I guess," was Browne's noncommittal reply.

"His hair was combed and his beard was trimmed," Hess recounts. "Instead of flip-flops he was wearing a pair of boots polished to a mirror shine. It must have been something he learned how to do in the army. But he also seemed much less responsive than when I last saw him. He talked slower and was generally less animated. I knew they had him on psychotropic drugs, and at various times had been adjusting the dosage. I figured this must be one of those times. So I tried to adjust accordingly, too."

With that in mind, Hess opened the conversation by reporting on the progress he'd made in securing outside medical attention for the inmate. "The guy I've got lined up is the personal physician for one of the brass in the sheriff's office," he told Browne. "He looked after his wife and kids, his whole family."

"Okay," Browne replied in the same subdued tone.

Hess forged ahead. "He's been in practice for thirty years. He also used to be the doctor down at the county jail. He knows what he's doing and he's promised he's going to review all your previous medical records."

"Okay."

"I was feeling a little unappreciated," Hess remarks with a slight smile. "The truth was, the whole thing was a major pain in the neck. The jail doctors don't want other guys coming in and second-guessing them. I can't blame them. And the last thing the prison administration wants is to establish precedent for this kind of thing."

It was time to take a sterner tack. "Robert," Hess said, "you understand he's coming here because we're paying for it. This is what you indicated you wanted."

"What about my transfer?" Browne responded. The prospect of a renewed round of bargaining seemed suddenly to have perked his interest.

"We're going to see what we can do," Charlie assured him. "We've already told them what you asked for."

"You mean minimum security someplace?" Browne asked, his fire-tower fantasy apparently gone by the wayside. "A single cell?" He sighed. "You know, I've never in my life been a social person. I have a hard time tolerating someone in the same cell with me. No more celly cells," he insisted, using the prison lingo for a bunkmate. "It takes too much effort."

"I told them," Hess repeated.

"A place I can walk around?" Browne pressed.

"That, too."

"What did they say?" he shot back with a mix of wariness and anticipation.

"They're going to do their level best."

"Yeah," Browne replied with heavy sarcasm. "I could tell you everything and then they'll just renege on it."

"That's not going to happen," Charlie insisted. "A deal's a deal."

Browne paused now, and Hess could see the gears in his head turning, taking him someplace far away. "I'd like to go where it's warm," he said at last, in a low voice. "This cold is killing me nowadays. When I was young I loved it, but now it's just tearing me up. My joints hurt when I get cold. They just scream . . . I need to go where I could do my time and not be bothered, you know, where it's warm and balmy."

"I don't like the cold either," Charlie agreed. A long silence followed as Browne actually seemed to transport himself to that warmer place, basking in the glow of a tropical breeze. "Robert," Hess said at last, "can I show you something?"

Browne blinked, returning to the harsh, neon-lit confines of the cramped room. "Sure thing," he said. He seemed refreshed, back to his old self.

Charlie produced a manila envelope of the photos Fischer had taken and laid them out on the table. Browne pulled a pair of reading glasses from his jumpsuit and perused the shots carefully. "This is the one," he announced when he got to a view of the southeast quadrant. "I'm almost a hundred percent sure." He pointed to a nondescript apartment building. "This is the place."

"And you said the apartment was on the first floor?"

Browne nodded. "We went down three doors, maybe four, flat off the street."

"You're sure?" Charlie pressed, and when Browne snorted impatiently, he began to gather the photos from the table. "Thank you, Robert." he said. "You've been a big help."

The killer regarded him quietly for a few moments. "That's it?" he asked finally.

"For now, I guess," Hess shrugged. "Unless you got something else you want to tell me."

Browne didn't hesitate. "I'll give you three," he said.

"Three what?"

"Three cases. You get me what I want—a doctor, a transfer—I'll give you three cases."

Hess considered the offer. "A transfer may take some time, Robert," he replied at length. "I'm not getting any younger. How about I get you the doctor, you give me the three?"

It was Browne's turn to weigh the options. "You get me the doctor," he countered. "Then we'll talk."

"I'll take that as a yes," Charlie said.

"You can take it for whatever you want," Browne shot back, getting up from his chair.

Hess was content to bring the interview to a close. "I figured I had a key piece of the Grand Am puzzle," he recounts. "I went back and got Jo, and she drove home while I wrote up my notes."

"I never write down anything while I'm talking to a subject," Hess adds. "No one's going to like having a conversation with someone taking down everything they say in black and white."

Hess had a growing conviction that they were closing in on Browne's first verifiable homicide since they'd begun the investigation. He returned to the cold-case room, where the team matched Browne's positive ID of the photo with a low-end apartment on Pike's Peak Avenue, euphemistically known as the Viewpoint. "The first thing we did was ride out and take a look at it," Hess remembers. "We checked a residential database called Cole's Directory, which is used by a lot of law-enforcement agencies and which gave us a list of the former tenants. We took that back and showed it to Rick Frady, hoping he could finally get a match between someone who had lived there at the time and the owner of a missing Grand Am."

Of course, Frady had already combed his lengthy roster of stolen Pontaics, but with the Apple Dumpling Gang's list of Viewpoint tenants, he was able to zero in for a closer look. "That's when he found it," Hess continues. "The car was registered to Joseph Sperry, and the reason it hadn't turned up before was because someone had transposed a couple of numbers on the police report."

At last they had a name, something to call the Grand Am lady, with all the belated dignity and humanity that would come with that discovery. But a question still remained: What had happened to the missing persons report Sperry had first tried to make from the phone at the Kwik Stop, with Robert Browne listening in? "We went back and checked again," Lou Smit explains. "We discovered that it also had been misfiled."

Eighteen years after the fact, the victim had at last been identified. All that was left was to inform the man whose life had been destroyed by the killer's savagery. "I got a number for Sperry," recounts Jeff Nohr, who would shortly be assigned to work full-time on the Browne dossier. "I called him at his mother's and told him that we'd found out who'd killed his wife."

"I want them to put me in a little closet with him," Joe Sperry would later say, when asked about his feelings toward Robert Browne. "Three minutes is all I'd need."

PART SIX

———◆———

CHAPTER TWENTY-TWO

SNAKES AND SNAILS

Browne spent the early months of 2004 waiting for the arrival of the outside doctor Hess had promised him. "I finally got the sheriff's office to sign off on the medical expenses," Charlie explains, "but the doctor had other obligations and he made and broke appointments a couple of times. I'd show up occasionally to keep Browne up to date, and if he had any doubts about me coming through for him, he didn't let them show. Of course, he wasn't giving me any information, either. It was more or less a standoff."

The two passed the time swapping stories and handicapping the upcoming NFL season. "I told him about my time in Baja California," Charlie recounts. "I showed him pictures, talked fishing and camping. Eventually we got around to his past, to the way he felt that his family had mistreated him.

"When you were three years old, they took your crib away from you," Hess reminded Browne during a meeting in March of 2004. "That must have been pretty gruesome for you."

Browne nodded vigorously. "It was very traumatic for someone that age: to have to deal with having no place to go. It was that and the abuse . . . physical and verbal."

"Sexual, too?" Charlie asked.

Browne seemed to bristle at the suggestion. "No," he replied sharply. "There was no sexual abuse."

"Just the physical then."

"Isn't that enough?" he shot back angrily. "I mean, the constant beration [sic]. Being berated by my brothers and sisters. I was their whipping post. They all did it. Shit rolls downhill.

And I was at the bottom of a very big hill. Plus my mother would not intervene. She was my mother. But she was abusive, too. Something would happen, and she'd grab anything within her reach and beat me with it. Clothes hangers, broomsticks . . . everything was allowed. Nothing was stopped. You know, a mother is supposed to stand up and protect her child."

"So my question would be this," Hess proffered gingerly. "Is your mother the reason there were more women victims than men?"

Browne shrugged. "The opportunity just presented itself more often." He paused, mulling over the implications of Charlie's query. "I've been disappointed with women my whole life," he continued at length. "Women—girls—are supposed to be made out of sugar and spice and everything nice, and boys are made of snakes and snails and puppy-dog tails. Women are portrayed as being more valuable and morally right. Then it turns out they're not loyal. They're users. They attach themselves to whatever male they think they can get the most from. And they call it love." He looked across the table at Hess, as if for all the world he needed more than anything to be understood at this moment. "That's what triggers my disgust," he explained. "The lack of morality. You know, women try to present themselves to be one thing and they always prove that they're something else."

It would be late spring before Hess was finally able to deliver on his promise to provide an outside physician for Browne. "As soon as I got a firm promise from the doctor," Charlie remembers, "I went back out to Canon City. By that time he'd been transferred out of the Colorado State Penitentiary to another facility up the road a bit, a place called Fremont. The idea was to see if they could integrate him back into the general population. He had a cellmate there, but the guy was another lifer, too, in for murdering his adoptive parents. Not exactly a role model for a well-integrated life."

Hess continues: "Out in Fremont he attended classes, went to group sessions and was slowly working his way back into prison society. When he made the move, I'd also arranged for him to get a single cell, like he wanted, and when we met, he wasn't wearing any hardware at all. I made sure he knew that I'd really delivered for him and gave him my personal guarantee that the doctor was coming on a certain date." It was only then that Browne reluctantly acknowledged the assistance Hess had provided.

"So," Hess would go on to prod. "How about it?"

"How about what?" was Browne's immediate deadpan reply.

"You said you'd give me three murders if I got you a doctor."

"I haven't seen the doctor yet."

"Robert," Charlie sighed, "have I ever lied to you?"

The two exchanged a frank look.

What the killer didn't know was that in the aftermath of resolving the Sperry case, the Apple Dumpling Gang had gained considerable credibility with both the Sheriff's Department and the District Attorney's Office. "We had solved a real-time murder," Hess asserts. "They were taking us seriously now. In one way that was very gratifying but in another way it made things a whole lot more complicated. Jeff Nohr, who had been working with us for a while, was put on the case full-time, and he didn't want me meeting with Robert on my own without supervision. He insisted I be wired for all the interviews going forward. I really fought the idea. It seemed really underhanded to me. I'd always told Robert I'd be straight up with him, and going in with a little 'joey' under my shirt felt like a deception. The thing was not only hooked up to a recording device but ran right into another room, where Nohr and a DOC officer were listening in. But I did my best to make it seem like it had always been—just the two of us."

"So," Browne would ask, after Hess made it clear what was now required. "You got anything particular in mind?"

Charlie nodded. Ever since Finley's initial foray to Red River Parish at the time of the Heather Dawn Church investigation, the unsolved murders of Wanda Faye Hudson and Faye Self had been on the team's to-do list.

"How about we start back at home?" Hess suggested. "Weren't there a couple of women that lived in that place your brother owned? You know who I'm talking about?"

"I told you," Browne replied, "I'm no good with names."

"Wanda Hudson," Charlie reminded him. "And Faye Self."

If Browne was surprised by his interlocutor's detailed information, he didn't show it. "Yeah," he murmured. "Those two."

"Which one came first?"

Browne shifted uncomfortably in his seat. "Look," he said peevishly, "it's not like this stuff happened yesterday. For me to remember what I remember I have to rack my brains for a long time. I have to relive it over and over until the little details start coming back. It's exhausting."

"What about your map?" asked Charlie, referring to the nine-state diagram Browne had sketched out for Mark Finley, each with what the detective had assumed were the number of homicides written in each region. "You did a pretty good job on that."

"That took me weeks," protested Browne. "Some of that stuff happened twenty years ago. Do you remember where you were twenty years ago?"

"Sometimes I don't remember where I was twenty minutes ago," joked Hess. "Just do the best you can." He settled back in his chair. "What about Wanda Faye Hudson?" he repeated. "What happened with her?"

"She lived next door to me," Browne began. "Out at the place my brother owned, the Riverside Apartments. They were little cottages, or cabins, or whatever you want to call them, these duplexes, and my kitchen window overlooked her bedroom. I'd . . . see her sometimes."

"So you picked her out?"

Browne shook his head. "It wasn't like that. It was more spur-of-the-moment. Spontaneous. That's the way I do a lot of things."

"No particular reason, then?"

He shrugged. "It was an opportunity. That's all. I had the

key to her place. I used to do maintenance work, you know, to earn my keep. I'd replaced the lock there. That made it easy."

"So it happened in her apartment?"

"Yeah. It was late, after midnight. I'd been out partying with my ex-wife. We were divorced, but we used to get together once in a while, just for fun. We came back to my place and she passed out. But I couldn't sleep. I'd been drinking, but I was also pretty cranked."

"Meth?"

"Right. I didn't do much of it, generally. Kind of rough on your body, but that night was different. Like I said, it's hard to remember exactly what I did, or why."

"Can you take it from where you let yourself in?" Charlie prompted.

Browne looked up at the ceiling, trying to summon back the humid evening over two decades earlier. He folded his arms over his chest and leaned back in the chair, its legs scraping loudly on the institutional tile. "It wasn't that easy," he recalled. "I got the door open with the key, but there was a chain on the inside. But I had a screwdriver. Oh yeah, and the red ant stuff."

"Red ant?"

"Yeah, you know, insecticide. I'd brought that with me, along with a rag. The stuff was really strong. You'd pour it in an anthill, and the fumes would kill them. I was going to use it to put her out."

"Then what?"

Browne gave Hess a search-me look. "I'd improvise."

"You were going to have sex with her?"

"Maybe. But it didn't get far."

"She put up a fight?"

"You could say that. I soaked the rag in the ant killer. She was lying in bed, in her nightie, but as soon as I put it over her mouth she started struggling. She was grabbing at my face, my hair. We both slid off the bed. It seems like it took a long time. Finally, I had to hit her in the jaw to keep her from fighting back, and she passed out. I guess I'd gotten kind of worked up. I took the screw-driver and stabbed her a bunch of times, in the chest and, you know, the groin area. I had to do it a bunch of times because it was blunt. It really didn't penetrate that well."

"Did you do anything to her after that?" Hess asked.

"She was dead," Browne protested, feigning outrage at the mere hint of necrophilia.

"So you left her there?"

"Basically," Browne replied. "I washed up first. Reattached the chain to the door and went back to my place. I think I had a couple of drinks, put my clothes in a plastic bag in the closet. I was finally tired enough to go to sleep, so I lay down next to Rita. Next thing I knew, the cops were knocking on the door. They wanted to know if we'd heard or seen anything. I played dumb, told them we'd been partying the night before, but I think it was Rita that really convinced them. She looked totally frazzled and hung over. Besides—" Browne hesitated.

"Besides what?"

"They were pretty sure they already had their man," the killer continued. "Her boyfriend, Higgs, the local pharmacist. I heard later he'd been by that night, I guess before I showed up. In fact, he'd been the one to find her when he showed up that morning for a cup of coffee. They never looked any further, even though she had strands of hair in her hand that didn't match his." He snorted derisively. "Typical top-notch police work."

Throughout Browne's matter-of-fact account, Hess had been mentally comparing the details with what he knew of Finley's investigation and subsequent report. Except for a few minor discrepancies—the fact, for example, that the corpse had been found naked with no nightgown and on the bed—it was a near-perfect fit. The thirty screwdriver puncture wounds in the chest and vagina, the traces of chloroform, an active ingredient in ant killer—Browne knew facts no one aside from the police had been privy to.

Hess also knew something else that Robert didn't: Wanda

Faye Hudson had told her uncle the day before she died that she suspected Robert of having a key to her apartment. "She said she was scared to stay there," the relative of the dead nineteen-year-old had told investigators, "because of what had happened there in the past."

Charlie also had a pretty good idea of what she'd been talking about: two months before her own brutal murder, the Riverside Apartments had been the site of yet another incident, that of a young single mother by the name of Faye Aline Self, who had disappeared.

"You know, there's a tendency to go numb," Hess admits. "You hear about so much bloodshed and after a while you just sort of tune out. It happens all the time in my business. But I didn't let it happen this time. These people had been living, breathing human beings. They were real, no matter how much Robert had tried to turn them into just 'opportunities.' "

Yet there was an undeniably deadening sameness to Browne's account that long afternoon, and not simply in his monotonous intonation or rote recitation, as if filling in blanks on an insurance claim. It was a droning equivalence that also seeped through his methods and motives, the cycle of misogyny and grotesque satisfaction he took in his handiwork.

Did any of his victims ever get away, Hess asked at one point? "None ever got away," Browne responded. "They never had the chance. If you're going to do it, just do it."

Faye Self certainly never had a chance to escape her terrible fate. Shortly before dispatching Wanda Hudson, Browne had encountered her at a Coushatta roadhouse called Alice's Wagon Wheel some time in March 1983. He knew her from his brother's cluster of cottages, where she lived not more than ten feet from the duplex where he lived adjacent to Hudson.

After Faye left the Wagon Wheel that night, telling friends she had to get back to her mother, who was babysitting for her infant daughter, Browne had stayed to dance with another patron of the nightclub before heading home sometime after midnight.

"I like to walk," he told Hess. "I'd roam around the parish, sometimes all night long. It was peaceful then, very quiet and lonesome, the way I liked it. Once in a while I looked for places to break into and, if I felt like it, go in and steal stuff, odds and ends, just for fun. That night when I got back, there were no cars or lights on at her place. I thought I'd check it out. It was another impulse-type thing."

Yet Browne's actions were not quite as premeditated as he would have Charlie believe. Before entering at an unlocked side door, he had gone back to his own cabin and poured the chloroform-based ant killer into a rag, which he placed in a plastic bag. Inside the apartment he found Self asleep on the living-room sofa, and in what amounted to a ghastly rehearsal of Hudson's murder some eight weeks later, placed the reeking rag over her face.

"It put her out immediately," he remembered, "so I left the rag over her face and went over to my place again to get some rope so I could tie her up. When I got back, she was already dead." Dragging her corpse into the trunk of his car, he drove to a bridge over the Red River and threw her into the swift flowing waters. Her body was never found.

Once Browne began his litany of random murder, he seemed to almost enjoy dredging up bodies from the murk of his memories. "I got another one for you from Louisiana," he told Hess without prompting. "This one I even have a name for. They called her Fuzzy."

"Why's that?" Charlie wanted to know. This was a new one, not included on Finley's list of possible victims from Red River Parish.

"I have no idea," Browne replied. "This had to be six or seven years before the others. I met her down at Uncle Albert's Chicken Shack in Coushatta, although I'm pretty sure she wasn't from town. It was late, and the place was starting to close up. She was with two other guys in a car, but when I came by she said she wanted to go with me, that she didn't have any place to stay . . . real high-class lady. She couldn't have been more than sixteen."

She was in fact fifteen, and her real name was Katherine Jean Hays, a runaway from nearby Natchitoches. Browne had taken her back to his apartment, and the two had sex. "It's gets a little fuzzy after that," he said, smiling. "No pun intended. We got in a fight about something, she was a smart-ass to begin with, a born troublemaker, and I think she must have been half drunk, because after a while she fell asleep on the bed. I looked around for something to do her with and found a leather shoelace. I used it to strangle her."

"Like the Grand Am lady."

"Yeah, only I didn't cut her up. I just loaded her in the car and drove up to Highway 71 out around Clarence until I found a bridge I could dump her off. Later on I heard a couple of hunters had found a skull out that way. I guess some dogs must have got to her, scattered her bones."

He stopped then, and rubbed his face in his hands, his energy flagging. When he looked up again, he fixed Charlie with a look that combined a sort of infinite weariness with a thin and brittle defiance. "That's three," he said. "That's our deal." He rose suddenly and winced with pain. They had been sitting together, uninterrupted, for several hours. "Don't bother coming back until you've got something for me."

CHAPTER TWENTY-THREE

SUGAR LAND

As Hess had promised, the doctor arrived a few days later to give Browne a thorough going-over. "The doctor confirmed the diagnoses of the DOC," says Hess. "I don't know if Robert was disappointed or not. He really believed he was being neglected and abused by the prison doctors. What he found out was that he had the aches and pains that come with getting old. Hell, *I* could have told him that."

For his part, Browne seemed if not exactly chastened, then at least a bit chagrined. Aside from the doctor visit, Hess had continued depositing money in the inmate's commissary account, often from his own wallet. He had additionally kept up contact with an author who had expressed interest in writing Browne's life story.

"First, I would like to apologize for becoming testy near the end of our last meeting," Browne would write to Hess several weeks later. *"Normally, I'm able to keep these feelings in check . . . the always present physical pain had increased to a level that lessened my self-control."*

Browne immediately returned to the subject of being transferred from Canon City, and preferably Colorado altogether. *"I will need to be relocated to a safe (and comfortable) location until the final deal is concluded,"* he wrote. *"To put me in danger now will not strengthen the hand I am negotiating with. It will only anger me."*

"That was more like the old Robert I knew," says Charlie. "But I could see his point. Aside from killing a little girl, which had already made him a pariah in the prison, there was also the fact that if a book was actually written and his name became well-known, there would for sure be some guy on the cellblock only too anxious to kill a famous killer. I could appreciate the position Robert was in." In fact, Hess had reached a turning point almost without knowing it. Browne's continuing and sometimes vociferous complaints and demands obscured the fact that the two had reached an unspoken agreement that would carry them forward into the grim closing chapters of Browne's three-decade rampage. "It was still necessary for me to play the game," Charlie contends. "I made sure he had a little money and that the wheels were turning on his transfer and on the book project. But at the same time, it wasn't strictly tit-for-tat anymore. We'd come to an understanding, and I believe it had to do with the fact that he really *liked* me. I had been careful not to judge him and tried my best to improve his quality of life. He needed a friend, so I stepped into that role, and that encouraged him to tell me things he'd never told anyone else."

Through the waning months of 2004, Hess would visit Browne several more times, always wired now, as per the dictates of the Sheriff's Department, and in the company of Detective Jeff Nohr. But nothing seemed fundamentally to change the dynamic between the two men. "Robert was always polite when Nohr was around," Hess recounts, "but I wouldn't exactly call him forthcoming. It was more as if he had learned to trust me and, as long as I was in the room, that trust was intact."

With Rocio Sperry and the trio of Louisiana slayings well documented and corroborated as existing unsolved cases, Hess moved in on the remaining tangible clues Browne had provided over the course of their correspondence. The first was the Texas hamlet of Flatonia, which Browne had initially referred to in his taunting letter of early 2003. *"The year was approximately 1984 or 1985,"* he had written. *"A young woman was killed and her body was found near this town."* The name had come up

again on the cryptic single sheet of paper he had included in
his letter of October, with only the block-lettered words,
ETHER/ICE PICK.

"Robert already knew we had followed up some leads on
the Flatonia case," Charlie explains. "We had a tentative identification for a body, Melody Ann Bush, and a cause of death,
acetone poisoning. The time and place seemed right: her body
had been found beside a rural road in 1985, but there were no
ice-pick wounds or any punctures of any kind. So we couldn't
be totally sure, especially because of the advanced state of de-
composition that the corpse was in at the time it was discovered."

In an attempt to clear up the discrepancies between Robert's
recollections and the lonesome death of the twenty-one-year-
old dancer, Hess again broached the subject of Flatonia in a
conversation late in 2004.

Robert nodded, accustomed now to sliding easily into the
slipstream of events that had occurred so many years before.

"That was back when I was delivering silk flowers," he
began. "I'd stopped at a motel just off the highway which was
on my regular route. There was a bar in back of the place, called
the Deer or the Stag or something like that."

Charlie nodded. "The Stag Bar," he confirmed, recalling the
name from the Fayette County sheriff's report on the Bush
homicide which he had read. So far so good, the accounts
matched on this significant point. He also knew that based on
Finley's investigation, the bar had been along Browne's regular
delivery route. Texas authorities would later interview a witness who remembered him stopping by once or twice a month
over a half-year period and even passing out the artificial
blooms to patrons of the place.

"So," Charlie pressed, "if anyone could put you at the scene,
it would be the bartender at this place." This was crucial. An
essential police eyewitness to the events of that night had been
a female bartender, who remembered both the victim and the

man she had left with, whom she also described as "a regular."

The killer shrugged. "I guess. When I first came in, she was talking to this lady who ran the bar." More confirmation: Browne had matched the bartender's gender.

"What were they talking about?" asked Charlie.

"She was saying how she'd just had a fight with her husband and how he'd ditched her and gone up the road a couple of miles to some other joint," Robert related. "Since I was the only other one in the place, the bartender asked me if I would drive her out in my van to find her husband. She didn't want her in there."

"Can you describe the girl?" Charlie prompted.

"She was wearing jeans and some sort of blouse or T-shirt and was barefoot," Browne recounted. Again, the killer was echoing the testimony of the bartender. "At first I didn't want anything to do with her—she was drunk off her ass—but then I agreed to give her a ride." He paused, his dark eyes hardening. "Like I said before: it was an opportunity. I'd seen her type a million times before, a real low-life. And sure enough, we weren't five minutes down the road when she started groping at me and sticking her tongue in my ear. So I took her back to my motel room, next to the bar where I'd picked her up."

"Anyone see you?"

Browne heaved a sigh. "I have no idea," he replied, and Charlie made a mental note of the killer's growing impatience. He suspected he wouldn't have much longer to follow his line of questioning. "Anyway," Browne next volunteered, "by that time I already knew where this was going."

"And you had sex?" Charlie wanted to know.

Robert nodded, his gaze still flinty. "She was slobbering drunk, just acting like the whore she was. It was no problem. Afterwards she passed out. I carried some ether in the van, so I just soaked a cloth with it and stuffed it in her face."

"Ether," repeated Charlie. "Not acetone or anything like that?"

"No. Ether. I'd used it a couple of times before."

Hess wondered if Browne really knew the difference between acetone and ether or even the active ingredient he called
chloroform in the red ant killer that had been his previous fu-
migant of choice. For that matter, how sure was the Fayette
County coroner that Bush had been overcome by acetone?
"Okay," he nodded. "Ether. Did that do the job?"

"Well," Browne ventured, "it put her out. That's for sure.
Then I used an ice pick on her. The best I can remember, anyway."

The conditional clause was revealing. Perhaps Browne's
blooded-spattered tableaux had become confused, running into
one another, blending into a composite of all the victims he had
dispatched and all the ways he had done it. Charlie thought it
worth the risk to test his theory. "You know," he said, "the person we're thinking of, she didn't have any ice-pick wounds."

"Really?" Browne seemed unperturbed. "Must have been
somebody else, then," he shrugged.

"Do you remember what happened next?" Hess asked after a
moment.

"I left her on the bed, I think, got dressed and went down to
the bar until closing time. After that I had breakfast at a truck
stop with the lady bartender."

This was new, a fact that had not come out in the police report. Did the bartender have something to hide? "So later,"
Charlie carefully queried, "you know, when they found the
body, why do you think this bartender lady didn't come forward?"

Browne shrugged again. "She probably didn't put it together," he ventured. "I was nice to her. You know, the way I
can be."

"So after breakfast, you . . . wrapped it up?"

"Yeah," Browne acknowledged, "I went back and loaded her
into the van. It was early in the morning. There was no one
around. I drove north, I think, on a country road until I got to a

271

bridge or a culvert with tall grass everywhere. I dumped her off the railing."

Ten days after his dawn disposal, the corpse of Melody Ann Bush was finally discovered. "A lot of the pieces fit together," Hess would later affirm. "But not everything. As far as I was concerned, Robert Browne killed Melody Ann Bush. I chalked up the inconsistencies to faulty recall. But, of course, there was also a distinct possibility that he was making the whole thing up, that he'd pulled the story out of the local newspaper or got it through the grapevine in prison. Maybe he was claiming credit for a murder he didn't commit, trying to run up the total to show off or increase the chances of selling his book. I wouldn't put it past him. There were parts to this puzzle I knew we weren't ever going to fit together perfectly. Robert had his own reasons for whatever he did. In the end, most of the stuff he told me I believed. But there was some that he threw in purely for effect. I'm convinced of it, although I'm not sure that by then Robert really knew the difference. He'd been living inside his head for so long, the lines were starting to blur."

Whatever mix of truth and fantasy was coloring Browne's account, one fact was indisputable. "Bodies were piling up in the locations and condition he described. It was becoming increasingly possible that he actually *was* one of the most prolific serial killers in American history. You had to ask yourself how he knew about all those bodies and how it was that they were all unsolved cases.

"But even then we kept running into static from the higher-ups," Hess continues. "They wanted something definitive, like a grave that only he could lead us to. There was what you might call an abundance of caution on the part of the district attorney's office. Of course, you couldn't really blame them. They had to be convinced. That was part of their job."

It was with that in mind that Hess pressed Browne further during a meeting in early 2005. "I haven't any doubt about the things you've told me," he reassured the inmate, "but is there a single case you can think of that could prove beyond a shadow of a doubt that it had to be you?"

Browne laughed, retorting, "There's not enough information on this planet to prove anything beyond a shadow of a doubt. There's no such thing as absolute proof."

"Sure," replied Charlie, "but there are certain things that happened in some of these cases where the only person who could ever know was the one who did it. Even the cops—"

"—The cops don't know what happened in Sugar Land," Browne interrupted. "Apparently I'm the only one around here that knows what happened there. But that doesn't necessarily mean anyone can prove it."

"I'm trying to help you here, Robert," Hess insisted. "If I'm going to get you transferred, I need to tie you to one of these things definitively. That's the only thing that's going to convince them." He paused. "Let's try Sugar Land, shall we?"

Hess already had a substantial amount of information relating to a murder Browne had first made reference to back in April 2003 as "A body (in parts) . . . discovered off U.S. Highway 59 in the Southwest Houston area. You would think someone would remember that."

Someone did. After being provided with that geographic fix, Hess and the team began a systematic canvas of local law-enforcement agencies in the general area to which Browne had pointed them. Asking after unsolved cases involving dismembered bodies, they got a hit almost immediately in Sugar Land, a small, thriving city named for an antebellum sugar plantation, sprawled near the Gulf Coast near suburban Houston and Baytown. "I talked to a sergeant in the police department," Hess recalls. "He knew almost immediately what I was talking about."

One of the most shocking crimes in the history of the region, the 1984 homicide of a seventeen-year-old topless dancer named Nidia Mendoza would have been hard for anyone to forget.

"I met her in a strip club off Highway 59," Browne told Charlie, "but I couldn't tell you where, exactly." The name of the place was in fact the Dames Club, where Mendoza had worked since arriving from her native Panama a year earlier. "She was small and kind of Asian looking," he continued, and Hess couldn't help but note that for all of Browne's lack of a cohesive MO, Mendoza certainly fit the description of the kind of women who caught the killer's attention.

Her death was likewise only too familiar. "I waited around for her to get off her shift," Browne recalled, "and we went to this pretty nice hotel not far from the club. I remember the room had a kitchenette."

The amenity would prove convenient for Browne when, after they had sex and he strangled Mendoza with his bare hands, he found what he described as a "very dull butcher knife" in the drawer of the closet-sized kitchen. Carrying her petite body to the bathroom, as he would do more than a decade later with the corpse of Rocio Sperry, he placed Mendoza in the bathtub and began his grisly work.

"I cut off her head and her arms and legs," he told Hess before hesitating a moment and then adding, "you know, I might have left her arms. I took her down in pieces in my suitcase to the van. It took a couple of trips."

It was, again, a vital piece of incriminating information. Mendoza's body had in fact been found in the same dismembered parts he described: legs, head, and torso with the arms intact. It was impossible for Browne to have known that undisclosed piece of information.

Hess had seen the coroner's photos of Mendoza, or what was left of her. He knew too well the savagery Browne could unleash without provocation. And despite his renowned professional reserve, which had taught him over the years never to ask why, he still grappled with the simple promptings of curiosity.

"So," he asked, carefully choosing his words, "when an opportunity like that arose, did your antennas go up? I'm just trying to understand, if I can, what your line of thinking would be at a moment like that."

Browne considered the question. "I think a lot of it was just disgust with the person," he replied at length. "I found her very distasteful."

"I guess there was no plan, then?" Hess already knew the answer.

"I don't recall ever thinking about it ahead of time. You know, years could go by when nothing happened. You know the old adage about things coming in bunches? It seemed that opportunities would come along one after the other and then maybe not for a long time after that. I learned to take advantage of the chances I got. You never knew when you'd get another one."

CHAPTER TWENTY-FOUR

THE COWBOY LADY

As the deep winter of early 2005 brooded over the high passes of the Rockies and held fast in the flatlands, Hess and Browne continued their harrowing colloquy. Hunkered down in the stale air and harsh lights of Old Max, where Browne had been returned awaiting the outcome of his bid for a transfer to a more hospitable clime, they cast back further and further into the murderer's reminiscences, arriving at length at a place where the victims lost even their humanity, identified now only by those negligible circumstances of their deaths that Browne could recall.

All the while, prosecuting attorneys continued to mull over the implications of the case against the serial killer. As the response of several jurisdictions within the range of Browne's rambles had already demonstrated, thirty-year-old murders were considered water under the bridge. "Even in Colorado," Charlie contends, "there was a real wait-and-see attitude. People still remembered Heather Dawn Church, of course, but the feeling was that justice had been done."

Whether bringing additional charges against Robert was ever a high priority begs a morally complex legal question. The killer was behind bars for life with no possibility of parole. How important was what or how much he had done to get there? After all, there were other murderers still on the streets, as bad as or worse than Robert Browne. Shouldn't the emphasis by law enforcement be on catching them and not simply detailing the horrors of a sociopath already safely behind bars?

From that perspective there was a kind of equivalence to Browne's fate, as if the murder of Heather Dawn Church stood in for the murders of all his other victims. Whether that was an acceptable compromise was a matter of opinion. How important was it that the murdered be memorialized in the punishment of their murderer? Browne could only serve one lifetime, after all. Would adding centuries to his sentence help to heal the wounds he had inflicted?

"I think that's where we came in," Charlie muses. "Old cops like me and Lou and Scott working cold-case files here and there. We've taken on a responsibility to the victims and their families. It's another kind of justice we're trying to dispense: long-range, outside the system. It's a human consideration, like what we'd want if we were in their shoes."

During regular visits to Browne over the first half of 2005, Hess continued casting down into the grimmest reaches of Browne's brain, trying to find the bodies left unburied. It was a labor that went unappreciated by some.

Early on the two had discussed the single murder in Washington State, which was referred to on Browne's map and in his "trip letter" with its suggestive but maddening imprecise detail. He had written of a scenic overlook off an interstate with an extreme precipice over which he had apparently pushed a woman to her death. "We'd passed on that description to any county in Washington that might fit the criteria," Lou Smit recounts. "We eventually got a possible match from Grant County, right in the middle of the state. The sheriff there had an idea where the location might be and had had it searched, but nothing turned up except for some animal bones and a piece of leather sandal."

It was at that point that Hess pressed for more information on what might well have had the dubious distinction of being the killer's most random murder. Browne did his best to oblige.

"First of all," he said, "it wasn't a woman like I originally thought. I got it mixed up with another one. This was a guy. He pulled over next to me at this outlook, up in the mountains."

"Do you remember what you were looking at?" Hess asked.

"Scenery," Browne replied facetiously.

"Sure, but what direction?"

Browne thought about it. "Well," he said, mentally orienting himself, "I was heading west, so I was facing north."

"And this other guy pulled up."

"He said something about my Louisiana plates," Browne resumed. "See, I was driving this stolen pickup truck from back home. So I shot him." He patted his chest to one side, indicating a shoulder holster. "I was packing a .357 back then."

"And you threw him over the side . . ."

"Right. I got a couple of hundred bucks off him and then dragged him over this log railing."

As Hess subsequently mulled over the new information, he came to a possible explanation for why no body had been found earlier at the rocky bottom of the overlook, the only one in the region that met Browne's criteria. "When I checked the search report from that Washington sheriff, I realized they'd been looking on the wrong side of the road," he explains. "He was heading west, facing north. I had him facing south, my mistake."

Hess quickly placed a call to Ephrata, the Grant County seat. "I guess they took down the information," he recounts with no trace of recrimination, "but they never followed up. It would have been easy enough, but that's the way it goes. It was all so long ago." He pauses for a moment, squinting again at the question in the back of his mind. "I guess I never felt right about just being able to call that victim, whoever he was, 'the Scenic Overlook Guy.' I wish I knew his name. I wish I could tell somebody that I knew what happened to him; somebody who needed to know."

As Hess burrowed further, he would find more of the nameless. "Who was your first one?" he would ask Browne at an early February meeting.

"First one ever?" Browne replied, sparking to the memory

test. He thought for a moment. "That would be when I was seventeen, while I was stationed in Korea."

Charlie nodded. He was very familiar now with the shifting modulation in Browne's tone as he cast himself back. Mostly now, all he had to do was listen.

"I was in a bar in Yongsan, and this guy got jealous over a whore," Browne told him. "He came at me with a knife. I kicked him and we went down. His head was hung over the foot rail. I could have stopped when I put him down, but you don't let up once you get going. So I snapped his neck."

"Was it ever investigated? I mean, were you brought up on charges?

Browne seemed puzzled. "You'd think so, wouldn't you?" he said. "I was a GI, after all. But I don't remember a thing. Maybe it's on my record."

"What year are we talking about?" Charlie asked.

Browne looked at the ceiling. "God," he said, "1970?"

Hess would in fact check both Browne's military record and the record of army homicide cases in Korea at the time, but there was no trace of the incident the killer had related. The dead man would now be memorialized only as "the Soldier in Korea."

"There were others," Hess says. "A lot of others. People we couldn't name, who we'd never be able to name. In the 'trip letter' Robert had mentioned a lady he killed in a New Orleans Holiday Inn. That's what we called her: Holiday Inn Lady. She told him she was from South Philly. He'd picked her up in the French Quarter and took her out to his motel room. That's where he left her body. Not only did the New Orleans police have no record of a Jane Doe found in a Holiday Inn room in 1977, they couldn't even identify the hotel. We found out later by contacting the corporate headquarters that it had been torn down."

As winter thawed to an early spring, Hess's tally of anonymous victims continued to grow. "There was a woman he strangled here in Colorado Springs in 1994 or 1995," Hess recalls. "He'd picked her up at a bar called Cowboy's Night Club and remembered that she was wearing Western-style clothes. He kept her body in a bedroom of his trailer out on the Eastonville Road for two days while his wife was out of town. Then he wrapped her in a plastic tarp and dumped her somewhere in a ditch on the Gold Camp Road. He told me he made sure to keep the plastic, that maybe he could reuse it.

"When I showed a map of the area to Robert," Hess continues, "he gave us a general idea of where to look, not far from the Skagway Reservoir. We ended up finding some pieces of leather boot, but that's as close as we ever got to identifying the Cowboy Lady."

Even more heartbreakingly vague were the deaths of "the Couple on the Beach," whom Browne in 1986 had summarily dispatched using the same .357 Ruger with which he had killed the Scenic Overlook Guy.

He'd encountered them along a stretch of coastline he would describe in the "trip letter" as *a sandy beach . . . with lots of driftwood among boulders to the north side."* "They asked me if I wanted to smoke a joint," Browne told Charlie, "so I sat down and talked with them for a few minutes before I made my move. I went through their backpacks and then covered up their bodies with driftwood."

Tagging the locale as a few hundred miles north of San Francisco, Jeff Nohr contacted the Mendocino Country Sheriff's Office and was told only that if the two bodies had indeed been left on the beach, the tide would long ago have washed them out to sea.

In some cases, Browne could not even provide Hess with the way in which the killings were carried out, as if depriving the victims of even the dignity of the circumstances of their deaths. "Two Males in Mississippi" had been mentioned as being disposed of, according to the "trip letter," *very near the Alabama border . . . [in] a swampy area just north of the Inter-*

state." But despite Hess's unwearied prompting, Browne couldn't remember whether after shooting them, he had dismembered the two strangers who had triggered his retribution when "they started acting like bad guys."

"The Jackson County authorities said there had never been two male bodies found in the area Robert described, either whole or in parts," Hess recalls. "They made it clear that their records for that time were pretty sketchy and even clearer that they had no intention of investigating the case any further. All we could do was move on and hope that another puzzle piece might somehow fall in place eventually."

There were a lot of pieces falling as Hess continued his interviews into the middle months of 2005, but more often than not, they were only the fragments of stories long since lapsed from memory, even by the man who had assigned to himself the perquisites of absolute control over life and death. "You might think he'd have a better recall about the people he killed," Charlie speculates. "But it wasn't like that with Robert. Sometimes I got the impression that they were all just variations of the same murder played out over and over again."

There were, for example, "the Cajun Lady" and "the Hilltop Bar Lady," two more from his Louisiana grand total of seventeen. The first was known only by Browne's recollection of her distinct accent. Her strangled body was dumped into the Atchafalaya River. The second was a belated addition whom Browne recalled as predating the slayings of Wanda Faye Hudson and Faye Self: a newly married woman he had met in a Natchitoches bar called the Hilltop. Browne had been amazed, he told Hess, that the young wife was "already fucking around"—reason enough to strangle her and drop her body into the Red River, where it would be joined in time by that of Faye Self and, in all likelihood, others unknown and unnumbered.

Occasionally, the moniker assigned to the victim constituted virtually everything Hess and the team would ever know, gathered from the scraps and shards of Browne's random memory.

Case in point: "the Northern New Mexico Motorcyclist." *"I'm on an east-west highway . . . ,"* Browne had written in the "trip letter," going on to describe *"another scenic overlook"* with *"a tremendous rock face, grey in color. It can't be missed. Once again, there is a body over the precipice."*

Following up the lead proved one of the more frustrating and fruitless tasks of the whole investigation. "I called the New Mexico State Police," recalls Charlie, "and they told me there were three or four places that might fit that description, mostly along Highway 64. As far as bodies went, nothing turned up, although they found a motorcycle in one of the suspected locales. That was that. All we would ever know was that a motorcycle rider in Northern New Mexico never reached his destination. They later found his skull."

But not every victim was relegated to anonymous obscurity. Sometimes the team would get lucky, with just enough information to fill in a blank or match a name. "Mr. Hess visited Mr. Browne in prison and asked about the victim in Tulsa, Oklahoma," Jeff Nohr would later write in his official account of the investigation. Referring to the "trip letter," he quoted Browne's sinister invitation to *"go west to Tulsa, Oklahoma. Just southeast of there, along the south side of the Arkansas River is a flood plain. Lots of water grasses. There is also a male in the muck."*

"Mr. Browne said he drove to a large truck stop on the eastern edge of the city," Nohr continued in his redaction of Hess's interview with the inmate in late spring. "Mr. Browne said he was seated at a counter inside the restaurant when a white male sat next to him. Mr. Browne said he assumed the subject was homosexual. Mr. Browne said he allowed the subject to leave the restaurant with him. He said they drove to a park along the river. Mr. Browne said he does not recall the route they drove. Mr. Browne described the area as a swampy area.

"Mr. Browne said the subject was not very large. He said he thought he strangled the subject. He said the individual did not put up much of a fight. Mr. Hess asked Mr. Browne why he was in Tulsa, Oklahoma. Mr. Browne said this trip was one of his 'ramblings' where he would have just 'picked up and gone.' "

Nohr would also note that during a later interview, Browne would claim to have shot his Oklahoma victim—"You know, 'boom!' " The inconsistency would help authorities to make at least a tentative identification of the gay man at the truck stop. Report 1992-33419, which had been sent to Nohr by the Tulsa Police, described "an unsolved homicide which occurred 3/12/92 . . . a semi-nude male body discovered partially submerged in a creek in Mohawk Park. The victim was identified as Timothy Lee Warren, who was described as a homosexual who resided in Tulsa. The victim had been shot three times in the head with a .22 caliber weapon."

"We felt pretty sure we had a match," Charlie recalls, "although we'd never be able to prove it in a court of law."

Proof was likewise elusive in the next case he queried the killer about. *"How about Arkansas?"* Browne had asked Hess in his peripatetic trip letter of 2003. *"This is just across the Mississippi River from Memphis. . . . There is a marshy area a little southwest of there. That is where this lady was laid to rest."*

"You had to wonder why some of these people and their deaths stuck out in his mind while others just left vague impressions," speculates Charlie. "It all seemed so random, like picking up on some mundane detail of the day that had stayed with him."

Proving Hess's point, "the lady laid to rest" of which Browne had written was yet another in a long line of casual encounters that ended in sex, strangulation, and submersion in the nearest river. "But he remembered a lot about her," Hess added. "She was in her mid-twenties, he said, a light-complexioned black woman who was wearing what he called 'a short sweater dress.' He also had the details down on where he drove her that night after they'd met at a blues club in Memphis: down Interstate 40, across the Mississippi, down a two-lane road to a bridge, then another three or four miles to a waterfront."

It was this uncharacteristic depth of detail that allowed Hess and the team to make one last positive ID—at least as positive as the circumstances allowed. After they sent an inquiry to authorities in the Memphis area, a reply was received from a sergeant in the Arkansas State Police who had worked on a case in 1991 that fitted Browne's account. A decomposed body had been found that November floating in the St. Francis River, a light-complexioned black female in a "tube type dress." A subsequent autopsy ruled the cause of death to be "undetermined" and the manner of death "unknown."

Browne was no help in clearing up the matter. For all his focus on the particulars of this specific death, he could not remember whether or not he had strangled or shot his victim that night. Her name, Hess was later informed, was Lisa Lowe. She was the mother of four small children.

CHAPTER TWENTY-FIVE

THE PLEA

As the interviewing process continued at regular intervals throughout the summer of 2005, Hess could sense the fast-approaching point of diminished returns. The routine was grinding for both the interlocutor and his subject, given the rote recitation of otherwise random encounters, signified by shooting and strangulation and the splash of a body in dark running waters.

"I would have kept going indefinitely," Charlie avows, "as long as there was a chance of getting one more shred of information. But Robert was getting worn out, and his fatigue was rubbing off on me, too. Over all those hours I'd spent with him, I got to know him pretty well. I could gauge his moods, sense the way his thoughts and emotions ebbed and flowed, and trying to keep up with it all had a way of sapping your energy."

Compounding what was quickly becoming an impasse was the fact that Browne was growing increasingly impatient over his prospects for a transfer and increasingly dubious that the DOC's assurances would ever be fulfilled. His medical needs, such as they were, had been attended to, even while his literary ambition was slowly fading. His would-be collaborator moved on to other projects, and Hess, despite his best efforts, could find no feasible way around the Son of Sam laws. "It was one of those gray areas legally," Charlie explains, "a lot of conflicting state and federal regulations that ended up making it impossible to know if Robert or anyone he might designate could ever profit from the telling of his story."

The original Son of Sam law, passed in New York State in the late seventies, had been unanimously struck down by the U.S. Supreme Court in 1991 on First Amendment grounds. The 8-0 opinion found that the law was overinclusive and could have been used to prevent the publication of everything from *The Autobiography of Malcolm X* to Thoreau's *Civil Disobedience* to *The Confessions of Saint Augustine*. Similarly, Supreme Courts in Maryland, Nevada, and elsewhere invalidated their state Son of Sam laws on the same grounds, while many other states had simply stopped enforcing the statute altogether. There had been various challenges to these rulings, but none had been overturned. California and Texas, two states that could have had an impact on Browne's publishing ambitions, no longer recognized the Sam of Sam precedent, while Colorado still maintained a version of the law on its books. Colorado's legislature had even gone one step further, finding "a compelling interest in preventing any person who is convicted of a crime from profiting from the crime . . . including any assets obtained through the use of unique knowledge obtained during the commission of the crime." No one had a more unique knowledge of his thirty-year rampage than Browne himself—so much for his bid for immortality on the page.

He was not, however, about to give up on his demand for a more amenable incarceration, continually suggesting to Hess that more information would be forthcoming as soon as he was safely in his new surroundings. "It became an obsession with him," Charlie recalls. "He really wanted to get out of Colorado. He blamed the DOC there for everything, from the quality of the food to the fact they were reading his mail. He was convinced that the DOC was out to get him, and I became his only possible way to escape their clutches."

Eventually Hess, working closely with prison authorities, was able to elicit a tentative agreement for a transfer. "He wasn't going to a fire station or a minimum security work camp in Hawaii or Florida or wherever else he was fantasizing," Hess says with a smile. "The best I could do was Minnesota, which said it would take him in exchange for two of their own hardest cases."

Browne consoled himself with the dubious notion that while Minnesota hardly represented an improvement in climate, it was generally a more liberal—and therefore more tolerant—state than Colorado. But as summer wound down and the transfer seemed snarled in a hopeless bureaucratic tangle, Browne's irritation grew. As a consequence, the Apple Dumpling Gang was getting less and less useable information from the increasingly recalcitrant source.

"I tried suggesting that maybe we could make his stay more comfortable at Old Max if he continued to play along," Charlie recounts. "That didn't go over so good."

"What are they going to do?" sneered Browne when Hess offered the option in a late August interview. "Are they going to strip out the leaky duct work and glue sound dampening material on the walls? It's still going to be the same place. It's like putting lipstick on a pig."

"I'm doing the best I can here, Robert," Hess replied evenly.

Browne leaned across the table. "I'm sure you got the impression a while back," he said ominously. "I'm shutting down on any new information. My intention the whole time talking to you was to get certain conditions met. That's beginning to look less and less likely."

He leaned back, his arms folded across his chest, fixing Hess with a steely gaze. "I've been fed all kinds of bullshit on this whole deal," he continued. "Even before I ever pled guilty and ended up on this sentence. The public defender swore I'd get decent medical care and be in a position where I could be left alone. They told me that I'd get a job, something to occupy my time, so I could form some kind of life. I was not allowed any of that. Just total abuse from the very beginning." He stopped for a moment, struggling to contain his anger. "I'm not talking about your intentions," he resumed. "I'm talking about the DOC.

They'll say anything to do whatever. They're more con than the convicts."

"That was pure Robert," Charlie would later remark. "When he got going, you could really see it all come through: the rage, the contempt, the self-pity." He pauses, caught, it seems, between his friendship with the man and his disdain for Browne's consuming self-delusion. "Look," he admits at last, "maybe he *was* getting a raw deal from Colorado. They had promised him a transfer, and I was their messenger. I felt bad. I wanted to be able to deliver for him. It's important to keep your word, no matter who you're making it to."

After Robert's tirade, a long silence ensued before Hess answered, in as measured a tone as he could manage, "Okay, Robert. You've shut down. You're not giving us any new information. So, what can we expect?"

"You want more?" Browne asked in disbelief. "Don't expect anything more! You've already got a whole basket full of shit. Everything I've given you in the past should more than justify what I've asked for."

"I agree," Charlie replied. "But there are some people—people in a higher rank than I am—who believe you have more information to give."

"Are those the same people who started out for years saying I didn't have anything?" he spat back with withering scorn. "And now they believe I got more to give?" He shook his head in mock wonder. "My, my, my, how the world has changed."

The world had indeed changed. What Hess knew that Browne didn't was the fact that of all the states he had drawn on his murder map and named in his "trip letter," none were willing to move forward with an active prosecution.

"If you want to bring a criminal trial, expect to spend six figures," Hess asserts. "Who's willing to do that for someone named Cowboy Girl or Scenic Overlook Guy or the Couple on the Beach? The fact is, these weren't even really cases. They were little bits and pieces from Robert's rambles that kept drifting in and out of focus. We had to seriously ask ourselves: What were we in this for? Why were we knocking ourselves out for people whose existence we couldn't even prove?"

The relentless wrangling continued through the early months of a glorious Rocky Mountain autumn and reached a flashpoint when Charlie reminded the killer of their first face-to-face conversation together. "I'll tell you anything you want to know," Browne had said back then, even as Charlie was getting up to leave.

"Who says I haven't laid out everything I can remember?" Browne demanded when Hess repeated the killer's words—words that from this weary vantage, seemed to have been spoken a very long time ago. "I haven't said there's more or there's not more . . . one way or the other."

"You implied there was," Hess countered mildly.

"A lot of things have been implied." Browne scoffed, and then added cryptically, "There's more than I remember and that's more than enough."

Detective Nohr, who had been listening silently, chose this moment to interject. "This is coming from me, Robert," he began, "but I was wondering, you know, when all this is over, if we'd ever have the opportunity to sit down together and you could tell me . . . how things work with you."

"I could give you my philosophy," Browne replied, "my belief. I mean, you have two different people, you have two different points of view. But I can give you my opinion of what I am, and what created me and why. It's not that complicated."

"Well," said Nohr, adopting Hess's self-deprecating approach, "I'm a student. I like to learn. And you're the teacher."

"It's totally traumatic stress disorder," Browne announced with an air of profundity. A long silence followed. "You know, like in Vietnam," he continued, frowning at the puzzled look on Nohr's face. "I'm a sufferer of post-traumatic stress disorder. But not from Vietnam. From my childhood. I mean, read about it. I'm sure I haven't got any real depth on it but I'll bet you it would explain a lot. My basic understanding, it's minimal. But it seems to relate to me."

Two more months passed uneventfully, as Browne seemed slowly to deflate under the growing apprehension that nothing, moving forward, was ever going to change for him. And with that, it seemed as if the will to scheme and bargain, to demand and wheedle and charm was inexorably leeching away. Even should his cherished transfer one day come through, what was waiting for him at the other end? Only another cell behind another perimeter of razor-wired walls in the frozen fastness of the far North, forever removed from the busy world and its myriad opportunities.

"I'm tired," he told Hess one day in early November.

"Yeah, and I am too," Hess replied. "And I'm a lot older."

"This has been going on a long, long time," the killer continued, and once more Hess could hear the muffled burrowing in his voice, taking him down into the dark heart of his discontent. "I'm ready to say fuck it. You know, it's like greyhounds chasing a rabbit. Well, I've been chasing rabbits and I'm tired. This greyhound's going to lie down and rest. I'm frustrated, just fed up with the whole thing."

"Well," Charlie allowed, "I guess you could say that I'm frustrated, too, you know, that we didn't get to accomplish what we set out to do."

"I just want it to be over." Browne replied with a sigh. "I give and I give and it's never enough. What more can I do?"

It was an all-too-familiar lament, but something in Browne's tone caught Charlie's attention this time. "I had an idea in the back of my mind for a few weeks," he recounts. "I didn't quite know what it was until that moment. It was a last-ditch kind of thing, but from the way he was talking, what did I have to lose?"

"You could plead out," Charlie suggested, letting his words hang pregnant in the stale air for a moment. "Just the one case. Rocio Sperry, the Grand Am lady."

If Browne was angered, outraged, or even surprised by the

proposition, he didn't show it. "Why?" he asked instead. "What's that going to do for me?"

"Think about it," said Charlie, careful to keep his voice un-inflected. "They keep saying you haven't given us enough. And they're right, Robert. I don't think there's one of those cases that would stand up in court. Half the time you can't even remember exactly what you did or who you did it to. But Sperry's different. We've got you in the vicinity: the Kwik Stop. We've got the evidence: her TV in your trailer. There's the stuff you know about that situation, the things you told me, that no one else could know. It's the strongest case of all of them. If you plead guilty, just to the one, they'll know you're for real. They'll take you seriously. Listen to me. Do you want to get out of here? Someplace else . . . someplace better?"

"What do you think?" Browne replied. He was now all ears.

"Tell them what they want to hear," Hess replied. "Let them know you're not bullshitting, that you haven't been bullshitting all along. That's the way you can earn their respect. It'll put you in a position to make your demands heard. It'll give them a reason to listen."

"I could do that," Browne said, almost without hesitation.

For Hess, it was a moment of deeply conflicted victory. "I couldn't be sure that pleading out to Sperry was going to get him out of Old Max," Hess confesses. "I didn't know if it would make the slightest difference to the powers-that-be. All I really knew was that it would close that case and that maybe her friends and her family, her husband and her daughter, could finally move on.

"But at the same time," he continues, "I knew I wasn't being totally straight with Robert. I think we both realized that we'd come to the end of the road. Maybe it was a kind of relief for him to finally give it up and let it go. But I think I sold out our friendship to get the job done." He considered for a moment before adding, "That's one way of looking at it, anyway."

CHAPTER TWENTY-SIX

THE WAY HE DONE HER

"Hello, Charlie," Robert Browne wrote in one of his last letters to Hess, on June 6, 2006, four years and a month after their correspondence had begun: *"I am anxious to get this over with. If they do not want to do this my way, then it will not be done. If I am not on my way to Minnesota soon, then I will assume I was betrayed! By all involved!!!"*

As a final act of bravado, Browne's bluster had a listless quality to it. "He'd run out of options," Charlie asserts. "The truth was, he wasn't going anywhere without the DA's and the DOC's blessing. It was too late to threaten that he might pull out. He'd already agreed to the guilty plea. It was up to the system now, and we both knew what that could entail."

Yet even under his constrained circumstances, Browne managed to eke a few paltry concessions from the El Paso County District Attorney's Office in exchange for his promised plea, asking for concurrent life sentences and parole eligibility in forty years. It was not much to ask, considering that even if he was released after serving his time, he would be ninety-three years old.

"We also agreed not to seek the death penalty and not to object to a transfer," remarks Amy Mullaney in an interview with the authors. The county's assistant district attorney who served as the point person on the case, Mullaney remembers the caution with which prosecutors proceeded. "The first order of business was to get him adequate legal representation. We wanted to protect the longevity of the plea and not have him come back years later and claim to have been misrepresented in court. More importantly, we prepared ourselves to vigorously prosecute the murder of Rocio Sperry. If for any reason the deal with Mr. Browne unraveled, we were prepared to go to trial. After all, we were dealing with a man accused of multiple homicides, someone who said he was going to admit to first-degree murder with premeditation. We had to consider the possibility that he could change his mind at the last minute, after we had filed charges. We believed we had a good enough case to proceed regardless of what he might ultimately do."

With those meager dispensations in place, Browne made his appearance before the Fourth Judicial District Court on the bright and cloudless morning of July 27, 2006, to plead guilty to the death of Rocio Sperry nineteen years earlier. The entire proceeding, which included the filing of the first-degree murder charges, was over in less than two hours. Browne stood erect and emotionless before the bench when he asked to describe what he had done. "I caused the death of the individual" was his terse reply before being remanded to custody back to Old Max.

"I would like to point out," said his public defender, William Schoewe, going through the requisite motions, "that this case was finally solved only with the full cooperation of Mr. Browne. He came forward first. He came without prodding and without interrogation."

Despite the killer's insistence on no media coverage at his hearing, El Paso County Sheriff Terry Maketa promptly scheduled a news conference that attracted reporters from around the state and across the country. Nor did he stint on showcasing the most spectacular and sordid aspects of the four-year investigation spearheaded by the retired volunteers who would shortly become something of a media sensation themselves. After avowing that he believed Browne's claims, Maketa went on to announce that the Sheriff's Department had linked Browne to twenty murders nationwide, with claims supported by varying degrees of detail to another twenty-eight. With the addition of Heather Dawn Church, Browne had topped Gary Ridgway, the Green River Killer, by one, making him the most prolific serial murderer in American history. It was a claim Maketa seemed to accept at face value.

"Who knows?" Hess would later observe. "I always suspected that Robert was polishing his résumé, so to speak, especially when it came to all the mystic bullshit about the 'seven sacred virgins.' But there was so much buried in his head that you could never be sure."

Sheriff Maketa, on the other hand, had no apparent hesitation in proffering his own theories of Browne's means, methods, and motives, telling the crowded press conference that he suspected that at least a few of the victims might have been children.

"I think it would be reasonable if you look at the ages of some of the victims," he told reporters, pointing out that Browne frequently targeted young, small women. Sperry herself was fifteen years old and weighed a little over a hundred pounds.

"The younger the victims are, the less he's going to talk," Maketa continued. "He doesn't seem interested in talking about children. When detectives asked him, he completely shut down."

"That's true," Charlie concurs. "Whenever the conversation turned to the subject, he'd tell us it was 'off the table.' That was Robert's code for 'mind your own fucking business.' "

As to the efficacy and economy of bringing new charges against a man already serving a life sentence, Maketa borrowed a page from the playbook of the Apple Dumpling Gang. "This is unlike many cases where we're taking a threat off the streets," he explained. "This is an investigation that's really about bringing closure to family and friends."

Maketa was also careful to give full credit to the volunteer team, and in particular Charlie Hess, for breaking the case. "Charlie really opened a gateway to a lesson learned on this,"

he told reporters. "His demeanor and patience should be a reminder to all investigators, cold-case or even current homicide,
that sometimes you can't control everything. Sometimes you
need to let the suspect think that they have control."

Yet at the same time he admitted that the sentiments that
had for so long motivated the work and Hess, Smit, and Fischer
were not always shared by authorities in other jurisdictions,
most of whom had proven reluctant to prepare their own in-
dictments against Browne.

"We don't know anything specific enough to bring charges,"
an officer of the Arkansas State Police told *Colorado Springs
Gazette* investigative reporter Pam Zubeck in a subsequent
phone interview on the subject of Browne's possible involvement in Lisa Lowe's death. Texas authorities were even less
forthcoming. Flatonia police, Zubeck revealed, would not confirm that Browne was even a suspect in the murder of Melody
Ann Bush, while those in Sugar Land refused to provide any information at all. The distressing disinterest, however, did not
extend across the board. Zubeck also spoke to a Tulsa, Oklahoma, police detective who revealed that he had traveled to
Canon City a month earlier to interview Browne about the
death of Timothy Warren.

Maketa would also acknowledge that the true dimensions of
Browne's murderous career had yet to be fully measured. He announced the activation of two telephone hotlines set up specifically to take tips from citizens who might suspect Browne's
culpability in other unsolved murders. "We're setting them up
in anticipation of a lot of calls," he explained and he was not
disappointed. Within hours of announcing the numbers, the tip
lines had received over sixty calls, growing to hundreds, spaced
minutes apart, in the days that followed. Anxious inquiries
came from as far afield as Connecticut, Illinois, Kansas, New
York, North Carolina, Ohio, and Wyoming. A Shreveport,
Louisiana, teenager had been missing since the early eighties; a
twelve-year-old girl had been abducted in Arkansas a dozen

years ago; a woman had been murdered in Monroe County, Illinois, in 1977. A man wept as he described to the tip-line operator the disappearance of his sister in Baton Rouge twenty-one years before. Another sibling, this one of an Arizona woman, had disappeared from the Tucson Airport in 1973, her body found four months later in a shallow grave.

The doleful roll call continued unabated, and there was no shortage of possible victims. According to William Hagmaier of the International Association of Homicide Investigators, there are at any given time upward of forty thousand unidentified dead nationwide, the vast majority of them homicides. Referring to Robert Browne, Hagmaier told Pam Zubeck, "This is the kind of case that could prove extremely helpful. You have people missing and there are other places where you have corpses, and there could possibly be a lot of matches."

As calls came pouring in, reporters began to spread out, returning to the killer's hometown to fish for clues in the depths of Browne's personal history. His string of hapless spouses was duly tracked down. "When he was in his rages," claimed Rita Morgan, his third wife, from the front porch of her trailer down a dirt road in a dense pine forest, "it was always with someone he really cared about."

When those who'd actually had direct and often harrowing connections to Browne couldn't be located, a procession of neighbors, schoolmates, and local busybodies stepped forward only too eagerly. "He's devil-possessed," claimed one Coushatta resident, while another wanted the world to know that "he had a good mother and daddy." "You eat with him on Sunday," Coushatta Mayor Tray Murray sagely allowed. "You see him in a store. When something like this happens, it's disturbing." "He was kind of a loner," observed Johnny Norman, who had once been Browne's PE teacher, dusting off the hoariest of serial-killer clichés of them all. "He was a good student but he did have a little temper. In contact sports, if someone hit him hard, he'd blow up, want to fight."

In the processs of digging through the dirt and debris of Browne's gloomy past, journalists also inadvertently stumbled on simmering resentment over the way his hometown murder spree had been handled in the first place. "If he'd been stopped then," Faye Self's sister told Pam Zubeck, "there'd be a whole lot more people alive today." She went on to relate bitterly how, after Hudson had turned up missing, authorities "stood there and told me she just took off. She had an eleven-month-old baby. She wasn't going to just take off."

"I have learned more about her death from reporters from Colorado than I knew for twenty-three years," fumed Rusty Watson, the cousin of Wanda Faye Hudson, when contacted at his home in Mississippi. "I feel all along there has been a cover-up going on here."

"I wouldn't go that far," Charlie would caution after reading the accusation. "Let's just say I've learned never to underestimate the capacity of people not to see something they don't want to look at."

Among those with the most compelling reasons to turn away from the spectacle of Robert Browne's moment in the spotlight were the families of Heather Dawn Church and Rocio Sperry. Yet the killer's notoriety inevitably sucked them into the media vortex, demanding that they once again try to express in words the unutterable tragedy of their loss.

"He's nothing but a coward," Heather Dawn's father, Mike Church, told a reporter two days after Browne entered his guilty plea. "He's one sick, selfish, sadistic individual, and my concern is why he is saying all this now. What is he going to get out of this?" At the news that Browne sought a transfer to Minnesota, Church would bristle, "He just wants a change of scenery. He had no remorse, no regret. This is nothing to him. He's a predator. He's in the right place. I just want him to stay there."

"He took away my family, he took away my life," said Joseph Sperry, and of all the collateral damage inflicted by Browne, the alienation, addiction, and anguish suffered by the widowed husband of Rocio was indeed among the most heart-breaking. "The way my daddy raised me was to love and respect everybody," he continued, "but if someone tries to hurt your family, you do everything you can to defend them until you're dead. And what hurts the most is that I wasn't there. I couldn't do anything."

Sperry, who had been in court the day Browne admitted to "causing the death of the individual," seemed to hang precariously between relief and rage. Still in treatment for heroin addiction, he would tell the presiding judge, "Finally, it's over. After nineteen years, it's over. I knew some scumbag murdered my wife. I see that scumbag now."

Also on hand to witness the closing chapter of her mother's short, sad life was Amy Sperry, now a poised young woman who had only just begun the process of fully reconciling with her father after years of not being certain whether he might have played a part in Rocio's death. "He's going through a lot of pain," she told reporters on the subject of her father's raw emotions. "I want to move on," she added. "He wants to address everything. I cried when they told me they might have found who killed my mom. But it was more like happiness in a way. After so many years, anything is better than nothing."

As the dimensions of the story began to take shape, attention soon shifted to Charlie and the Apple Dumpling Gang. Extensive accounts of their exploits began appearing in both the mainstream media and law-enforcement journals, where they helped to bring awareness of the pioneering cold-case organizational and investigative procedures largely developed by Lou Smit. Hess's notoriety would eventually result in a cover story in the *New York Times Magazine* under the title of "The Confessor" and featuring a full-color picture of the veteran investigator. "Jo didn't like it," Charlie admits ruefully. "She said it made me look like a Russian mobster."

Hess is also a bit sheepish about both the notoriety he has gained and the pleasure he takes in it. "It's all basically bullshit," he says, "but I won't tell you it's not a little gratifying. We worked hard, we were dedicated . . . all those things our parents taught us. I suppose it's nice to be acknowledged for your merits, but I think it's even nicer to be acknowledged for just doing your job."

The strange relationship of Charlie Hess and Robert Browne has entered into the realms of law-enforcement legend. But it was, as it should have been, left to those who had survived the horrific depredations of Browne's cruelty and caprice to sum up best the human cost and the glimmer of hope that had somehow been salvaged.

"It just hurts too much to think about how he done her," wept Sybil Shaddox, the mother of Wanda Faye Hudson, who even after twenty-three years still kept a picture of her daughter in the nursing home where she languished.

Amy Sperry hurt, too. She said as much. But she also said something else, putting into simple words the possibility of healing and marking a place to start again.

"As for Robert Browne," she would tell reporters, "I would like to say may God be with his soul."

EPILOGUE

Robert Browne never did make it to Minnesota. After the high drama of his court appearance, he was returned to the contemptible familiarity of his Old Max cell where, it seemed, any bureaucrat who could facilitate his transfer had something else more pressing to attend to for the duration.

"That's not right," Charlie says with real regret. "A deal is a deal. Robert lived up to his part. We didn't, and as the one who was the most involved in putting the thing together in the first place, I have to take some responsibility. I bargained with Robert in good faith. But that good faith got lost somewhere in the shuffle.

"Robert was right in a way," he continues. "The system was out to screw him, maybe not intentionally, but just out of pure neglect. They just locked him up and threw away the key."

"You know," he says, still in a reflective mood, "maybe him staying here in Colorado was a part of his punishment all along. Old Max was hell to him, and he was ready to trade it for an unknown destination in Minnesota. But he didn't get out. In the end, he was back where he started. Maybe that's some kind of justification, maybe not."

Hess and Browne would continue to write sporadically to each other for a few more months until the letters from Old Max ceased entirely. "He probably didn't see the point, and I can't say I did either," Charlie reflects. "It wasn't like we had all that much to talk about anymore. It just kind of faded out. I don't know if he blames me for what happened, but I wouldn't blame him if he did."

"I'm anxious to make the move," Browne would write in one of his last letters. *"If it's going to be a while until my final move, I wouldn't mind a temporary move to someplace where I would be more readily available to you and others. Hope to hear from you soon to finalize the situation."*

"It's kind of pitiable in a way," Hess remarks on the pleading undertone of the letter. "He wanted to make himself 'available' to me. What happened to the swagger and bluster, all those threats, the way he thought he was better than all the rest of us? To tell you the truth, I kind of missed that. He was a worthy adversary."

As much as the Browne case proved a landmark in dogged police work, it also proved to be the last roundup for the Apple Dumpling Gang. Even while continuing to work at the margins of the JonBenet Ramsey case, Lou Smit, who had spent years caring for his ailing wife Barbara before her death in 2004, became romantically involved. "He just kind of pulled up stakes and left town," Charlie relates. "I think he was ready to live another part of his life, and I'm all for it. But if you want to get in touch with him, don't come to me. I have no idea where he took off for.

"Lou taught me so much," Charlie continues, conscious now of the necessity to pay tribute to the tireless dedication and intuitive brilliance of his partner and friend. "Then again, I taught him a few things, too. I think that's why we always had such respect for each other. We were never too old to learn something new. And that kept us young."

Scott Fischer likewise handed in his volunteer sheriff's badge, determined now, after dodging the prospect for so long, to embark on his official retirement. "A lot of our work was about burying ourselves in paper, excavating evidence from testimony, police reports, whatever," Charlie remembers. "Scott knew how to do that. He had an eye for detail. I guess it came from being a newspaperman, or maybe a photographer. But he also had a tremendous amount of confidence, in himself and in us. It was an energy that he gave us, and we used it to keep going, to keep believing that if we just didn't give up, we could break it."

As for Charlie Hess, he doesn't go by the tiny, cramped office of the Sheriff's Department cold-case room any more. The reason is, naturally, the absence of his partners, but it goes deeper than that. "Pretty soon after Robert's case broke, I started getting this feeling," he recounts. "Police departments are a lot like other bureaucratic environments, in many ways: lots of politics, petty jealousies, jockeying for position. The problem was, the three of us were never really exactly a part of the official structure. We reported to the powers-that-be and we did what they told us to do in the course of the investigation, like me wearing a wire whether I liked it or not. But we were also independent, operating somewhere outside their radar. That's how we got things to happen in the first place.

"After Robert," he continues, "and after all that attention and excitement, you could really feel the tension. Having us with our names in the paper kind of stole their thunder. I'm not saying they didn't appreciate what we did. I'm just saying they'd probably have appreciated it more if they'd done it themselves."

Matters came to a head in early 2007, after the Browne case, when the department asked Hess to sign a statement promising not to discuss with the press any future or ongoing cases to which he might be assigned. "I told them to go fuck themselves," Hess smiles. "In that way, I'd picked up a tip from Robert, who was always trying to sell his life story. Maybe my life story would be worth something, too. I felt like my integrity was being challenged."

These days Charlie and Jo live their quiet, close life together in a mobile-home park in a pleasant residential neighborhood just east of downtown Colorado Springs. It is perhaps a bit too quiet for the former FBI agent, polygraph operator, CIA operative, and intimate confidant of a mass murderer. "I got a guy up north," he says, "I'd rather not say where right now. He's serving a life term and has some interesting stories to tell. We're writing pretty regularly. You'll be hearing about it when I've got something to tell you."

Yet even if Charlie's latest foray into the familiar criminal darkness yields nothing, he seems to have come to terms with this slow trailing terminus of his years—grateful for the love of a good woman; flush with memories of a life well lived; hopeful that, when all is said and done, he did his best to leave his mark.

It is a mark that to his mind has much to do with his motives. "It's great to be able to solve cold cases and bring closure to the families of all those victims," he allows. "But when I think about it, there are other, more personal reasons for doing what I did. I used to feel a lot of guilt about not being able to stay sober when my parents were still alive. There was a lot of shame that I had disappointed them so deeply by my drinking. I hold on to the hope that somewhere, somehow, they're able to see that I've accomplished something worthwhile after thirty years of sobriety. It helps to lift that burden from my shoulders.

"I also wanted my wife, Jo, to be proud of me. When I get together with my FBI and CIA buddies and we talk about the old days, I sometimes see a look in her eyes as if she feels like an outsider in that part of my life. The Browne case was something she could share in and be a part of."

In 2006, Hess would receive a Medal of Merit from the El Paso County Sheriff's Department, recognizing his extraordinary contributions to the community. "Jo wears that medal as a necklace on a gold chain," he reveals. "To me that makes everything worth the effort."

And while Hess basks in the glow of his twilight years, down the steel corridors of Old Max, a cold wind blows from the high peaks of the Rockies, chilling the marrow in the bones of Robert Charles Browne.

ACKNOWLEDGMENTS

Former El Paso County Sheriff John Anderson, El Paso County Sheriff Terry Maketa, El Paso County Sheriff's Office Chief Joe Breister and Commander Brad Shannon, Lieutenant Ken Hitte, partners Scott Fischer and Lou Smit, Detective Jeff Nohr, Colorado Springs Police Department, Colorado State Department of Corrections, *Colorado Springs Gazette*'s Pam Zubeck, El Paso County Assistant District Attorney Amy Mullaney, Sugar Land Texas investigators, Texas Rangers, Arkansas State Police, Memphis Sheriff's Department, Washington State Attorney General's Office, Northern California County Sheriffs, New Mexico State Police, and Louisiana State law-enforcement officials.

Davin Seay would like to thank Pam Zubeck for introducing him to Charlie and for her sterling reportage, Lou Smit and Scott Fischer for the ice-tea and good company, Larry and Melissa Jones for their hospitality, and, of course, Charlie Hess for so generously sharing his life and his spirit. He also dedicates his work to Jon Miank, in appreciation of his courage and honesty. And Diane, as always, a blessing.

INDEX

Abeyta, Christopher, 14
acetone, 221, 229, 249, 269, 270–71
Agency for International Development, 82
Air Force Academy, 33–34
Alabama:
  in Browne's letter, 227, 228
  on Browne's map, 178–79
Alexander, Willie, 15, 34
Alice's Wagon Wheel, 263
Almond Brothers Lumber, 68
America's Most Wanted, 34
Anderson, John, 99, 229
  Church case reopened by, 44–45
  on JonBenet Ramsey case, 108
  news conference of, 161–62
  in sheriff campaign, 40–42, 92, 93, 94
  Smit promoted by, 42, 43, 45–46
Apple Dumpling Gang, 117–18, 123, 162, 185, 297
  on Browne case, 172–73, 181, 201, 207, 217, 220–21, 230, 232, 236, 247–48, 253, 259, 289, 301
  end of, 304
  Hudson murder investigated by, 259
  Self murder investigated by, 259
  see also Fischer, Scott; Hess, Charlie; Smit, Lou

Arkansas:
  on Browne's map, 178
  in "trip letter," 227, 284
Arkansas State Police, 285, 298
Army, U.S., 219
  Browne in, 82–84, 124–25, 136, 158, 186, 188, 193
Aryan Brotherhhood, 139
Atmel, 4
Attorney, U.S., 88
Auel, Jean M., 203, 220, 221, 226
Autobiography of Malcolm X, 288
Automated Fingerprint Identification System (AFIS), 16, 47–48, 50

Backster, Cleve, 85
Bahia de los Angeles, 88–89
Bamberg, Old Man, 149
Bambi, 55
B&C Wood, 68
Barbara Walters, 108
Barclay, Carrie, 126, 127, 129
Bartels, David, 12
Baton Rouge, Ill., 299
Beckner, Mark, 103, 108
Bistineau, 68
Black Forest, Colo., 3–4, 14, 15, 33, 39, 47, 49, 70, 126, 130, 145, 154, 162, 166
Black Lake, 68
Black Power, 27
Border Patrol, 88

INDEX

Boulder, Colo., 101–10, 112
Brashear, Gwen, 51–52
Breister, Joe, 180, 185–86
Brigham Young University, 6–7
Browne, Alex, 70, 131
Browne, Beulah, 70
Browne, Diane Barclay, 51, 53,
    55, 61, 125–26, 134, 140,
    152–53, 172
  divorce desired by, 132
  Pastors and, 154–56
  police interview of, 126–31,
    132–33, 151
Browne, Donald, 67, 69, 132, 158
Browne, Mary, 125
Browne, Raymond, 67
Browne, Rebecca, 131, 132–34
Browne, Robert, 299
Browne, Robert Charles, xi, xii,
    50, 52–53
  appeals of, 168, 172
  Apple Dumpling Gang on,
    172–73, 181, 201, 207, 217,
    220–21, 230, 232, 236,
    247–48, 253, 259, 289, 301
  Arkansas murder of, 284–85,
    298
  in army, 124–25, 136, 158
  Breister's letter to, 185–86
  Bush murder committed by,
    221, 229, 249, 269–72, 298
  Cajun Lady murdered by, 282
  childhood abuse of, 70–71,
    197, 257–58, 291
  childhood of, 68, 70–71, 197
  Church murder account of,
    164–65, 166–67, 217
  Church murder arrest of, 55,
    126
  Couple on the Beach murder
    of, 281, 290
  in court for Church case,
    161–64

  Cowboy Girl murdered by,
    281, 290
  as cryptic, 174–75, 190, 200,
    205, 216, 217, 228, 233,
    268–69
  death penalty and, 161, 163,
    166, 185–86, 295
  depression of, 66, 132
  description of, 51, 59–60
  desire to write book, 209, 210,
    211, 215, 218, 272, 287–88
  in Diane's interview, 126–31
  domestic abuse by, 150, 151,
    152
  drugs taken by, 66, 141–42,
    143–45, 148, 152, 261
  Faye Self murder and, 157,
    158, 164, 165, 179, 260,
    263–64, 282
  fingerprints, 52, 61–62,
    63–64, 124, 126
  Finley and Hodges's prison
    visit to, 164
  Finley's letters to, 173, 177,
    181
  Finley's visit to, 236
  first murder of, 280
  in Fremont, 258–59
  Grand Am (Sperry) murder
    committed by, 240–43,
    245, 246, 247, 253, 259,
    265, 292–93, 296, 300–301
  guilty plea in Church case,
    163–64, 166–68
  Hays murder in, 265
  health of, 195, 230, 231–34,
    236, 237, 238, 248, 249,
    250, 257, 258, 259, 267,
    287, 289
  Hilltop Bar Lady murdered
    by, 282
  on homicide motivation,
    195–96

hotlines set up regarding,
298–99
hypothetical questions posed
by, 185, 186, 191, 194
invention of, 209–10, 215
Jon Miank and, 135–36,
137–38, 140, 141–45,
147–48, 196
letter to Finley by, 175–77,
178–79, 185, 190, 206, 233
Louisianians on, 149–53, 157
map of, 178–79, 185, 191,
206, 228, 260, 278
marriages of, 66, 125–31, 149,
150, 151, 152–53, 210, 299
medical issues of, 66
Mendoza murdered by,
273–75
Mississippi murders of, 227,
281–82
molestation accusation
against, 153–54
money desired by, 239, 248
Northern New Mexico Motorcyclist murdered by, 283
number of murders attributed
to, 177, 178, 296–97
Pastors and, 154–56, 161
poems of, 174–75, 190, 217,
233, 234
police interrogation of, 60–67,
125–26
previous arrests of, 51, 64–65,
137
prison diet of, 195, 231, 237
prison number of, 184, 190
prison routine of, 165–66,
201, 216
psychiatric evaluation of,
164–65
psychotropic drugs taken by,
250
reading by, 65, 202–3, 204–5,
220, 221, 226, 230
Rebecca Browne on, 132–34
Ronald Browne on, 131–32
search of property of, 53–54,
55–58
sex life of, 63, 130, 132–33,
142, 151
sex of victims of, 229, 258
siblings of, 52, 67, 70, 71, 149
Stephanie Bustin sexually as-
saulted by, 142, 148,
153–54, 161
stipend of, 239
temper of, 142–43, 150, 151,
152, 299
transfer desired by, 248–49,
251, 258, 259, 267–68, 273,
288–89, 290, 292, 293, 295,
303–4
Tulsa murder of, 283–84
in Vietnam, 125, 152, 188,
193
Wanda Faye Hudson murder
and, 157, 158–59, 164, 165,
179, 260, 264, 282, 302
Washington (Scenic Overlook
Guy) murder of, 227, 228,
278–79, 290
"Whom it May Concern" letters of, 119, 172–75
see also Hess, Charlie,
Browne's relationship with
Browne, Ronald, Jr., 67, 125,
131–32, 158, 159
Browne, Ronald, Sr., 69
Browne, Ruby, 67
Browne, Thomas, 125, 126, 127,
136, 210, 215
Browne, Wera, 67
Browne, Will, 67
Bundy, Ted, 27, 178, 189
Bureau of Alcohol, Tobacco, and
Firearms, 118

Burgess, Don, 37
Bush, Melody Ann, 221, 229, 249, 269–72, 298
Bustin, Aaron, 139, 144
Bustin, Stephanie, 139, 142, 148, 153–54, 161

Caddyshack, 56
Cajun Lady, 282
California, 51, 178, 227–28, 234
    Son of Sam laws in, 288
Cannon Slew, La., 152
Canon City, Colo., 123, 147, 184, 201, 236, 237, 258, 298
capital punishment, *see* death penalty
Capone, Al, 79
Carnes, Julie, 112
Carney, Tom, 50, 51
Center for Missing and Exploited Children, 14
Central Intelligence Agency (CIA), 78, 83, 85, 184, 186, 188, 305, 306
Cheers, 26
Child Development I, A Systematic Empirical Theory, 56
ChildSafe, 33
Church, Diane, 4–5, 152–53
    with bereaved parents, 35
    in court, 163
    and discovery of Heather's body, 35, 36, 37
    in divorce, 4–5, 7–8, 11, 13, 33, 38
    and investigation, 11, 12, 14, 16
    on night of Heather's murder, 5–6, 7, 8, 9, 10–11
    on police work, 39–40
    Smit and, 54
    wishful thinking of, 38–39
Church, Gunner, 4, 5, 8, 37

Church, Heather Dawn, 4, 67
    description of, 10, 14
    father's abuse of, 12
    memory of, 172
    on night of murder, 5–9
    rumors on, 15, 33–34, 39, 46
    search for, 8–9, 10, 11–12, 13, 14–15, 16
Church, Heather Dawn, murder of, 40, 41, 60, 61, 62, 123, 126, 136, 154, 157, 179, 229, 242, 259, 277, 278, 297, 300
    Anderson's reopening of investigation into, 44–46
    Browne's account of, 164–65, 166–67, 217
    court case of, 161–64
    discovery of body in, 35–38, 65, 147–48
    fingerprints and, 16, 45, 49–50, 51–52, 61–62, 63–64, 124, 126
    pajamas discovered in, 36, 49, 128–29, 167
    Smit's investigation of, 43, 44, 45–47, 49–50, 54, 100
    time of, 166–67
    see also Browne, Robert Charles
Church, Kristoff, 4, 5, 8, 37
Church, Michael, 4–5, 40, 44
    abusive behavior of, 12
    alibi of, 13–14
    in court, 163
    and discovery of Heather's body, 35, 36, 37
    dismissed as suspect, 46
    in divorce, 4–5, 7–8, 11, 13, 33
    and investigation, 12, 13–14
    on night of Heather's murder, 10

on police work, 39
Smit and, 54
Church, Sage, 5, 6, 7, 8–9, 37
Cicero, Ill., 79
Civil Disobedience (Thoreau),
 288
Civil War, 69
Clan of the Cave Bear (Auel),
 203
Claspell, William, 55, 57
Clovis, N.M., 115
CNN, 101
Cochran, Molly, 202–3
cold cases, 234
 Fischer's study of, 116–19,
  179–81, 185, 201, 278, 298
 Hess's study of, 94–95,
  113–15, 116–19, 179–81,
  185, 187, 201, 278, 298,
  301
 Smit's study of, 113–15,
  116–19, 179–81, 185, 201,
  278, 298, 301
Cold War, 80
Cole's Directory, 253
Collins, Mike, 12
Colorado, 228, 289
 on Browne's map, 178–79,
  191, 206
 death penalty in, 162–63, 166,
  167
 Son of Sam laws in, 288
Colorado Crime Information
 Center, 50–51
Colorado Department of Corrections (DOC), 164, 199, 210,
 211, 220, 221, 236–37, 249,
 267, 295
 Finley at, 179, 185
Colorado Department of Rev-
 enue, 51
Colorado Springs, Colo., 13, 15,
 19, 25, 51, 53, 65, 75, 77,
 87, 89, 98, 106, 125, 136,
 139, 227, 231
 Grand Am in, 200
 Sperrys in, 245
Colorado Springs Gazette, 34,
 116, 298
Colorado Springs Police Depart-
 ment, 17, 32, 33, 40, 50, 60,
 99
Colorado Springs Sheriff's De-
 partment, 180
Colorado State Penitentiary, 172,
 184, 237, 258
Colorado Supreme Court, 186
Communion (Streiber), 9
Condren, John, 15
*Confessions of Saint Augustine,
 The,* 288
"Confessor, The," 301
Connecticut, 298
Conway, Tim, 117
Cooper, Adam, 76–77, 90
Corbett, Michael, 27–29, 30–31
Cosby, Gene, 77–78
Couple on the Beach, 281, 290
Coushatta, La., 50, 52, 53, 67–69,
 70, 124–25, 136, 150, 157,
 164, 197, 263, 299
Coushatta Depot, 68
Cowboy Girl, 281, 290
Cowboy's Night Club, 281
Cream Cup, 68
Criminal Investigation Institute,
 40
Curry, N.M., 115
Custodian of Voting Machines,
 69

Dames Club, 274
Davis, Red, 40
Davis, Tom, 55, 56, 57
"dead man's shoes," 32, 97
Dead Poets Society, 56

death penalty:
  in Browne arrest, 161, 163,
    166, 167, 295
  Browne's curiosity about,
    185–86
  in Colorado, 162–63, 166,
    167
DeGraffe, Thomas, 76–77, 90
Democratic National Committee,
  233
Denver, Colo., 201, 246
*Diane and Robert Browne Wed-
  ding*, 55
Dilts, Daniel, 60
Dinosaur Depot, 123
District Attorney's Office, 259
Dixie (bloodhound), 11, 12
Donnell, Doreen, 130
Donnell, Simon, 130
*Dragon Legacy, The: The Secret
  History of an Ancient
  Bloodline* (von Draken-
  berg), 204–5
Drakenberg, Nicholas de Vere
  von, 205
Drug Enforcement Agency, 36
Dunn, Larry, 28–29
Dupree Gravel Pit, 149

Earth Children (Auel), 203
Ebert, Colo., 51
El Paso, Tex., 81
El Paso County, Colo., 15, 36, 42,
  43, 51, 55, 70, 87, 229, 295
El Paso County Sheriff's Depart-
  ment, 40, 92–93, 97, 113,
  155, 186, 206, 259, 268,
  296, 305, 306
*Emotions Impacted by Job
  Change*, 55
Estep, Park, 98
ether, 249, 269, 270–71

Falcon Middle School, 10, 38
Farry, Ed, 166, 167
Fayette, Tex., 220, 269–72
Federal Bureau of Investigation
    (FBI), 118
  Fischer and, 115
  in Heather Church investiga-
    tion, 14, 47
  Hess in, 78, 80–81, 82, 83, 84,
    88, 184, 186, 305, 306
Federal Defenders, 84–85
fingerprints, 47–48
  in Heather Church case, 16,
    45, 49–50, 51–52, 61–62,
    63–64, 124, 126
Finley, Mark, 11, 12–13, 15, 50,
    51, 54–55, 60, 92, 124, 126,
    165, 191
  Browne interrogated by,
    60–67
  Browne's letters read by, 173,
    175–77, 178–79, 185, 190,
    206, 233
  Browne visited in prison by,
    164
  letters to Browne by, 173, 177,
    181
  Louisiana investigation of,
    148, 150–51, 153, 156–59,
    197, 259, 262, 269
  visit to Browne, 236
Fischer, Scott, 17, 115–16, 304–5
  on Browne case, 181, 198,
    205, 230
  cold cases studied by, 116–19,
    179–81, 185, 201, 278, 298,
    301
  methods of, 117, 298
  see also Apple Dumpling
    Gang
Flatonia, Tex., 219–20, 222, 227,
    229, 249, 268–69, 298

Ford Motor Company, 191, 193
Fort Carson, 14, 28, 29, 240, 245
Fort Polk, 124–25
Fort Wayne, Ind., 79
Fountain, Colo., 137
Fourth Judicial District Court,
    296
Fowler, Hendrix "Mutt," 69
Fowler, Jerry, 69
Fowler family, 69
Fox Run Regional Park, 34
Frady, Rick, 221, 230, 232, 253
Frasier, 26
Fremont, 258–59
Friends of Heather Dawn Church
    Foundation, 15, 35, 36

Garden of the Gods, 147
Garland's Kitchen Store, 149
Gatti, Claudia, 10
GI Bill, 79
Gilmore, Gary, 186
Glenn, Freddie, 28, 29, 30–31
Gonzales, Lou, 110
Gordon, Jim, 233
Grammer, Karen Alicia, 25–27,
    29–31
Grammer, Kelsey, 26
Grand Am, 246, 252
    in Browne's letters to Hess,
        200, 216, 217, 218, 219
    in Browne's letter to Finley,
        176
    in Hess's visit to Browne,
        240–43
    investigation of, 201, 205,
        221, 230, 231, 232, 253
Grand Am lady (Rocio Sperry),
    240–43, 245–47, 248, 253,
    259, 265, 268, 274, 292–93,
    296, 300–301
Grand Bayou, 68

Grandmaster (Murphy and
    Cochran), 202–3
Grant County, Wash., 278
Great Depression, 21, 79
Greenlee, Bob, 101, 102
Green River Killer (Gary Ridg-
    way), 177–78, 297
Green River Task Force, 178

Hagmaier, William, 299
Hamburg, Germany, 125, 136
Harding, John Wesley, 42
Hatch, Richard, 50, 51, 54, 55, 58
Hays, Katherine Jean, 265
Heim, Chuck, 28, 30
Hemingway, Ernest, 65
Herbel, Brenda, 151–52, 153
Hess, Charlie, 17, 300
    childhood of, 79, 299
    in CIA, 78, 83, 85, 184, 186,
        188, 305, 306
    cold case files studied by,
        94–95, 113–15, 116–19,
        179–81, 185, 187, 201, 278,
        298, 301
    drinking of, 81, 86, 87, 88,
        183, 184, 306
    fatalism of, 183, 184
    in FBI, 78, 80–81, 82, 83, 84,
        88, 184, 186, 305, 306
    first marriage of, 81–82, 85–86
    heart attacks of, 86, 93, 183,
        198, 200
    hip problems of, 181, 183,
        198, 200, 202, 216–17, 226,
        230
    on human goodness, 118, 196
    JonBenet Ramsey case investi-
        gated by, 111–13
    Maketa on, 297–98
    Medal of Merit received by,
        306

Hess, Charlie (*Continued*)
 methods of, 114–15, 117, 225,
  298
 in Mexico, 81, 88–89, 111,
  257
 in *New York Times Magazine,*
  301
 polygraph studied by, 84–85,
  88, 92, 184, 186, 305
 retirement of, 305–6
 son-in-law's murder and, 75,
  89, 91, 94, 183, 189
 in Vietnam, 82–84, 186, 188,
  193
 volunteer police work offered
  by, 92–93
 see also Apple Dumpling
  Gang
Hess, Charlie, Browne's relationship with, 302
 active principle in, 202, 204
 Arkansas murder discussed
  in, 284–85
 Browne as "simple country
  boy" in, 203, 218
 Browne's Christmas card in,
  208
 Browne's Derkesthai signature
  in, 204–5
 Browne's descriptions of murders in "trip letter,"
  227–30, 231, 278, 281–82,
  283, 284, 290
 Browne's refusal of visit, 188,
  205–6, 236
 Browne's stir-craziness in,
  199, 248
 Browne's writing style in,
  187–88, 190, 199–200
 Bush murder in, 229, 249,
  269–72
 Cajun Lady murder discussed
  in, 282

Charlie's desire to buy gift for
  Browne, 202–3
Charlie's proposed visits, 199,
  205–6, 223, 231, 236
Couple on the Beach murder
  discussed in, 281
face-to-face meetings in,
  237–43, 247, 249–52,
  257–58, 259–65, 268–75,
  277–85, 288–93
fish picture in, 194–95
friendship in, xii—xiv, 194,
  208
Grand Am in, 200, 205, 216,
  217, 218, 219, 292–93
Hays murder in, 265
Hess on failure to transfer
  Browne, 303
Hess's birthday card for
  Browne in, 202, 207
Hess's empathy in, 226
Hess's flattery in, 188–89, 205
Hess's photo in, 194–95
Hess's writing style in, 187
Hilltop Bar Lady murder discussed in, 282
Hudson murder and, 260–63
Korean murder discussed in,
  280
letters from Browne to Hess,
  188, 190–91, 195–98,
  199–200, 202, 203–5,
  206–7, 208, 209, 210,
  215–16, 218, 219, 226–28,
  230, 232, 248–49, 295,
  303–4
letters from Hess to Browne,
  184–85, 186–87, 188–90,
  193–94, 198, 199, 202,
  205–6, 208, 211, 217–18,
  221–22, 230–32, 233–34,
  235, 267, 268–69, 303
Mendoza murder in, 273–75

Mississippi murders discussed in, 227, 281–82
Northern New Mexico Motorcylist murder discussed in, 283
Self murder and, 260, 263–64
trust in, 202, 233, 268
Tulsa murder discussed in, 283–84
Vietnam in, 188, 193
Washington (Scenic Overlook Guy) murder discussed in, 227, 228, 278–79
wire worn by Hess, 259, 268
Hess, Christine, 79
Hess, Jo, 87, 88, 89, 92, 226, 230, 236, 249, 252, 301, 305, 306
Hetterick, Terry, 125, 149, 152
Higgs (Wanda Hudson's boyfriend), 262
High Priestess, 191
in Browne's letters, 175, 190
investigation of, 202
Highway 10, 220
Highway 59, 222, 273
Highway 64, 283
Hilltop Bar Lady, 282
Hodges, Michele, 53, 54, 60, 124, 126, 131
Browne interrogated by, 60–67, 125
Browne visited in prison by, 164
Candice Vought's friendship with, 92
Diane Browne interviewed by, 132
with Jon Miank, 147
Louisiana investigation of, 148, 153, 197
Hoffman, Darney, 103
Holiday Inn, 227, 280

Hong Kong, 99
Hoover, J. Edgar, 80, 81, 82
Houston, Tex., 81, 227
HPS 1992 President Club Commemorative, 55–56
Huckaby, Buddy, 149
Hudson, Wanda Faye, 157, 158–59, 164, 165, 176, 179, 259, 260–63, 264, 282, 300, 302
Hunt Corrections Center, 51
Hunter, Alexander, 102, 103, 105
Huynh, Tuyet, 125, 152–53, 210

Illinois, 298
International Association of Homicide Investigators, 299
Interstate 10, 227
Interstate 40, 284
Interstate 94, 227, 229
IRS, 88
IT, 210, 215

Jim Crow, 68
Johnson, Heidi, 13–14
Jones, John, 55, 57

Kamen, Dean, 210, 215
Kastner, Larry, 180
Keppel, Robert, 178
Kessler, Donald, 60
King County, Wash., 178
Knotts, Don, 117
Koby, Tom, 102, 104
Korea, 125, 158, 280

Lady and the Tramp, 55
Lake Charles, La., 209
Larry King, 108
Last Video: Foreign Slut, 57
Lawrence, Susan, 164–65
Leibhardt Mills, 68

Long, Huey, 68
Louisiana, 64, 234, 268, 282
   Browne investigated in, 148,
      150–51, 153, 156–59, 181,
      197
   on Browne's map, 178–79,
      206
   Hess's visit to, 209
Louisiana State Police, 51, 69
Lowe, Lisa, 285, 298
Lucas, Henry, 189

McGarry (technician), 16
McLuen, Cynthia, 98
McMorran, Ric, 55
Maketa, Terry, 229–30, 296–98
Mangham, William, 76–77, 90
Manitou Springs, Colo., 136
Marino, Jo, 88
Martin, Larry, 148, 158
Martinez, Gilbert, 55, 153, 162,
      163, 167, 168
Maryland, 288
Matthews, Gloria, 34–35
Matthews, Jim, 34–35
Matthews, Jonelle, 35
Memorial Park, 15
Memphis, Tenn., 284–85
Mendocino, Calif., 281
Mendoza, Nidia, 273–75
Mexico, 81, 82, 88–89, 111, 257
Miami, Fla., 241
Miank, Jon, 125, 135–45,
      147–48, 172, 196
Miank, Marcia Ann Bustin, 53,
      125, 136, 139–40, 141, 144,
      161
Miller, Eileen, 35
Miller, Michael, 35
Milligan, Les, 10
Minnesota, 236, 289, 295
Mississippi, 227, 228
Mistretta, William, 11, 14

Mohawk Park, 284
Monroe County, Ill., 299
Morgan, Rita, 150, 151, 158–59,
      262, 299
Mormons, 4, 6, 15, 37, 130
Mullaney, Amy, 295–96
Munger, James, 97
Murphy, Warren, 202–3
Murray, Tray, 299
Murray Boulevard, 241, 246,
      247, 248, 249

Natchitoches, La., 282
Natchitoches Meat Pie factory,
      68
National Criminal Information
      Center, 50
NBC, 108
Nevada, 288
New Mexico, 228, 234, 283
   on Browne's map, 178–79
New Mexico State Police, 115,
      283
New Orleans, La., 227, 229, 241,
      280
New Orleans Saints, 209
New York, 298
New York, N.Y., 82
New York Times Magazine, 301
NFL, 257
Nohr, Jeff:
   California murder investi-
      gated by, 281
   on Sperry/Grand Am murder,
      230, 232, 253
   Tulsa murder discussed by,
      283–84
   on visits to Hess, 259, 268,
      291
Norman, Johnny, 299
North American Aerospace De-
      fense Command, 123
North Carolina, 298

INDEX

Northern New Mexico Motorcyclist, 283

Ohio, 298
Oklahoma, on Browne's map,
178
Old Heidelberg, 17, 18, 41, 111,
117, 119
Old Max, 277, 289, 293, 296,
303, 306
101 Dalmations, 55
Oregon, 178
Owens, Bill, 108

Pacific Coast Highway, 227
Paglia, Camille, 101
Parents of Murdered Children,
90
Pastor, Angela, 154–56, 161, 172
Pastor, Ron, 154–56, 161, 172
Pentecostal church, 178
Perkins, Warren, 52
Peterson Air Force Base, 14–15
Petry, Carl, 100
Phantom Creek, 65
Philippines, 79
Pietras, Diane, 9
Pike's Peak, 3, 241, 247, 248,
249, 253
polygraphs:
    in Church case, 37, 39
    Hess's study of, 84–85, 88, 92,
    184, 186, 305
    of Ridgway, 178
Post Office, U.S., 118
Presley, Stan, 13
Profitt, Winfred, 29
Puerto Rico, 82

Rampart Range, 3, 35–36, 38, 49,
128, 147–48, 167
Ramsey, John, 101, 103–6, 107,
109

Ramsey, JonBenet, 101–10,
111–13, 304
Ramsey, Patsy, 101, 103–6, 107,
109
Rand, Larry, 147
REA Road, 140
Red Lobster, 25, 27, 29
Red River, 282
Red River High School, 68
Red River Parish, La., 68,
156–59, 174, 197, 259
Reichert, Dave, 178
Reisman, David, 126–31, 156
Rhodes, James, 98
Rhodes, Larry, 52–53, 157
Ridgway, Gary Leon, 177–78,
297
Riverside Apartments, 157, 260,
263
Roy, Arthur, 168
Royal Gorge Scenic Railroad,
123
Russell, Robert, 27, 31, 108

St. Francis River, 285
San Antonio, Tex., 81, 152
San Diego, Calif., 81, 82, 84, 85,
86
San Diego Police Department, 88
Sanitation Department, 217, 243
satanic cults, 15, 34, 46
Saturday Night Fever, 56
Scenic Overlook Guy, 279, 281,
290
Schalk, Jan, 9
Schoewe, William, 296
Scott, Judy, 36–37
Scott, Willy, 15
Sears and Roebuck, 79
Seattle, Wash., 177
Self, Faye, 157, 158, 164, 165,
176, 179, 259, 260, 263–64,
282, 300

319

seven virgins, 191
  in Browne's letters, 175, 190,
    233, 297
Shaddox, Sybil, 302
Shannon, Brad, 78, 93–94, 113,
  115, 116, 129, 180
Sheck, Barry, 102
Shelters of Stone, The (Auel),
  203, 220
Sherman, Brad, 87
Shreveport, La., 298
Sibley, La., 53
Sierra, Jorge, 161–62
Simpson, O. J., 102
Skagway Reservoir, 281
Smit, Barbara, 21, 23, 99, 100,
  104, 106, 111, 304
Smit, Lou, 92, 230
  awards of, 43
  on Browne case, 181, 198,
    220, 253
  children of, 99
  on Church case, 43, 44,
    45–47, 49–50, 54, 100, 124,
    147, 148, 165, 166
  cold cases studied by, 113–15,
    116–19, 179–81, 185, 201,
    278, 298, 301
  on fingerprints, 48–50
  on Grammer case, 25–27,
    30–31
  gut feelings trusted by, 18
  JonBenet Ramsey case investi-
    gated by, 101, 102–10,
    111–13, 204
  methods of, 17–20, 30–31,
    97–100, 113–15, 117, 298
  in Navy, 21
  police force joined by, 22–23
  promoted to head of investi-
    gations, 42, 43
  religious feelings of, 20–21,
    23, 31, 183

as sergeant, 25
  see also Apple Dumpling
    Gang
Son of Sam laws, 287–88
Spencer, Dave, 98–99
Sperry, Amie, 245, 247, 301,
  302
Sperry, Joseph, 245–47, 253,
  300–301
Sperry, Rocio Chila Delpilar
  (Grand Am lady), 240–43,
  245–47, 248, 253, 259, 265,
  268, 274, 296, 300–301
Stag Bar, 269
Stapleton Airport, 246
Star Cuts: Angel Kelly No. 17,
  57, 58
State Department, U.S., 82
Stewart, Martha, 68
Stiewart, Del, 36
Stokes, Gene, 24
Streiber, Whitley, 9
Sugar Land, Tex., 273–75, 298
Supreme Court, U.S.:
  capital punishment struck
    down by, 31
  Son of Sam law struck down
    by, 288
Suthers, John, 39, 109, 162, 166

Tacoma, Wash., 177
Teller County, 43
Texas:
  on Browne's map, 178–79
  Son of Sam laws in, 288
Thomas, Steve, 106
Thoreau, Henry David, 288
Thornbirds, 56
Today, 108
Today Show, 110
Toledo Bend, 68
Toole, Ottis, 98, 189
Toth, Richard, 90

"trip letter," 227–30, 231, 278,
   281–82, 283, 284, 290
Tulsa, Okla., 227, 283–84, 298
Tuscon Airport, 299
20/20, 108
Two Males in Mississippi, 227,
   281–82

Uncle Albert's Chicken Shack, 264
Union Pacific Railroad, 220
Utah, 186

Van Lone, Daniel, 28–29, 30
Vann, John Paul, 83
Victim's Assistance, 90
Vietnam, 125, 152
Vietnam War, 82–84, 152, 186,
   188, 193, 291
Viewpoint, 253
Vineland, N.J., 41
Vought, Candice Hess, 76–78,
   79, 89–92, 93, 94, 111
Vought, Don, 76

Vought, Steven, 75–78, 87, 89,
   91, 92, 94, 183, 189
Vought, Steven, Jr., 76, 90–91, 92

Warren, Timothy Lee, 284, 298
Washington, 227, 228, 234,
   278–79
Watson, Rusty, 300
Watson, Winslow, 28, 29
White, Amber, 9
Wilson, Denise, 5
Wilson, Diane, *see* Church,
   Diane
Wisconsin, 209
Wisconsin State University, 79
Wyoming, 298

Yongsan, Korea, 280

Zebulon Pike Detention Center,
   77
Zook, Dan, 167
Zubeck, Pam, 298, 299, 300